LUIS DE CARVAJAL

Luis de Carvajal

THE ORIGINS OF NUEVO REINO DE LEÓN

Samuel Temkin

SUNSTONE
PRESS

SANTA FE

Figure 11.1 is reproduced by permission of the Archivo General de la Nación, Mexico City.

Figure 1.4 is reproduced by permission of the Arquivo Nacional Torre de Tombo, Lisbon.

Figure 11.3 is reproduced by permission of the Bancroft Library, Uniersity of California, Berkeley.

Figure 4.2 is reproduced by permission of the Benson Latin American Collection. The General Libraries, The University of Texas at Austin.

Figure 4.1 is reproduced by permission of the Library of Congrss, Washington.

Figures 3.2, 3.3, 4.3, 4.4, 5.1, 5.3, 6.1, 7.2, 9.1, 10.2, and 10.3 are reproduced by permission of the Ministerio de Cultura, Archivo General de Indias, Seville.

Sunstone books may be purchased for educational, business, or sales promotional use. For information please write: Special Markets Department, Sunstone Press, P.O. Box 2321, Santa Fe, New Mexico 87504-2321.

This book is printed on acid free paper.

Library of Congress Cataloging-in-Publication Data

Temkin, Samuel, 1936-
Luis de Carvajal : the origins of Nuevo Reino de León / by Samuel Temkin.
  p. cm.
Includes bibliographical references and index.
ISBN 978-0-86534-829-5 (hardcover : alk. paper)
1. Carvajal, Luis de, 1567?-1596. 2. Inquisition--Mexico--History--16th century.
3. Jews--Mexico--History--16th century. 4. Jews--Mexico--Biography.
5. Nuevo León (Mexico : State)--History--16th century. I. Title.
F1231.C32T46 2011
972'.004924--dc23
                              2011020389

Published in

WWW.SUNSTONEPRESS.COM
SUNSTONE PRESS / POST OFFICE BOX 2321 / SANTA FE, NM 87504-2321 /USA
(505) 988-4418 / ORDERS ONLY (800) 243-5644 / FAX (505) 988-1025

To the memory of my brother

Contents

Figures, Maps, and Tables

FIGURES

Maps

Tables

Chronology for Luis de Carvajal

1537	Born in Mogadouro, Portugal.
1545	Carvajal's family moves to Spain.
1551	Carvajal is sent to Cape Verde.
1559	Appointed Treasurer in Cape Verde and Guinea.
1564	Leaves Cape Verde; marries Guiomar Núñez in Seville.
1567	Goes to New Spain as *Almirante* of a merchant fleet from the Canary Islands.
1568	Named *Alcalde Ordinario* in Tampico.
	John Hawkins abandons many men north of Tampico; most are taken prisoner by Carvajal. October 8-15.
	Martín Enríquez de Almanza is installed as viceroy of New Spain. November 5.
1572	Viceroy Enríquez appoints Carvajal as a captain and commissions him to discover a road from Pánuco to Mazapil and to punish certain Indians north of Tampico.
1573	Carvajal discovers the valley of Extremadura.
1574	Travels to Spain; returns the following year.
1576	Carvajal is commissioned by the viceroy to pacify an Indian rebellion in Xalpa and to build a fort there.
1578	Carvajal's *Información de Oficio* about his merits and services is presented before the Audiencia de México.; Carvajal travels to Spain.
1579	Philip II awards the Nuevo Reino de León to Carvajal and names him its first Governor and Captain General. May 31.
1580	Carvajal leaves Spain with his colonizers on June 10 and arrives in Tampico on August 24.

Lorenzo Suárez de Mendoza is installed as viceroy of New Spain. October 8. Carvajal presents his credentials. October 10–14

1581   Pacification of rebellion in Tamapache. January.

Carvajal goes to the north of his territory. October 25.

Foundation of Cueva de León. December 10.

1582   The Audiencia de México rules an early jurisdictional dispute in favor of Carvajal. January. 18

Foundation of León. April 17.

1583   Carvajal returns to Tampico.

Foundation of San Luis..

Carvajal attempts to take over several towns in the province of Pánuco. June.

Viceroy Lorenzo Suárez dies. June 19..

Beginning of the Salazar-Carvajal pleito in the Audiencia de México. July 4. First ruling in Carvajal's favor. October 25.

1584   Archbishop-Inquisitor Pedro Moya de Contreras is installed as viceroy of New Spain. September 25.

1585   End of Salazar-Carvajal pleito. The Audiencia issues a Royal *Ejecutoria*, giving Carvajal all contested places. June 7.

Foundation of Almadén.

1585   Álvaro Manrique de Zúñiga, is installed as viceroy of New Spain. October 18.

1586   Carvajal returns to the province of Pánuco.

Viceroy Manrique orders that Carvajal soldiers leave Nuevo Reino de León, and orders him to go to Mexico City. September 4.

Viceroy Manrique annuls the Ejecutoria. Valles and other towns in the province of Panuco are returned to Francisco Guerrero. September 4.

San Luis and Léon are destroyed by rebelling Indians. October–December.

1587   Carvajal leaves Mexico City without permission from the viceroy. January. Visits ruins of San Luis. Goes to Guadalajara.

The Audiencia of Nueva Galicia sends Carvajal to pursue English corsair Thomas Cavendish. September.

The Audiencia de Nueva Galicia receives Carvajal's *Información de Oficio*. September-November.

	Captain Juan de Zayas takes Carvajal prisoner in Guadalajara. The Audiencia releases him.
1588	Carvajal leaves Guadalajara and goes to Almadén.
1589	Captain Alonso López takes Carvajal prisoner in Almadén and takes him to México City. January (?).
	Carvajal is transferred to the Inquisition. April 14
	Viceroy Manrique is deposed by the king..
1590	Luis de Velasco II is installed as viceroy. January 25.
	Carvajal is sentenced by the Inquisition. February 13. Abjures his sins in the *Auto-da-fe* of February 24..
1591	Carvajal dies in the jail of the Crown. February 13.

Portuguese and Spanish Names and Terms

The book contains, or refers to, names and terms in Portuguese and Spanish that were in use in the sixteenth century. Some of these items are still in use today, albeit with different meanings, or have well-known translations into English. Because of this, some conventions had to be adopted. Thus, with regard to names of existing places that appear in the narrative, the convention used here is as follows: Familiar names of places are given in English, thus New Spain, instead of *Nueva España*. Less familiar names are not translated. Thus, *Tras-os-Montes* instead of Over-the-Hills. A similar convention is used for the titles of Crown officials, for example, viceroy, and governor. But *alcalde, fiscal, oidor, Sargento-Mor* and so on are left in the original language since most of them do not have exact English equivalents. The same is true of document-names such as *auto, capitulación, and cédula*. These terms are either explained when they first appear or in the Glossary.

A further clarification is necessary with regard to places whose names are now spelled differently. For the sake of consistency, I refer to them using their sixteenth century spellings. For example, *Xalpa* and *Guejutla* instead of Jalpan and Huejutla. This is particularly important in those instances where similar names are now used to denote very different entities. Thus, Carvajal's territory is here referred to by its full name—Nuevo Reino de León—to differentiate it from the modern Mexican state named Nuevo León. While this state is historically connected to that territory, the two entities have very little else in common. The same comments apply to New Spain which some authors refer to as Mexico, the name of the modern country that evolved from that Spanish colony. For a similar reason, I use the name *Nuevo México* to denote the Spanish province that in the sixteenth century was located well to the northwest of New Spain, but whose limits were never specified.

By and large I have left the names of most of the individuals appearing in the narrative in their original form. The most notable exception is the use of Philip II instead of Felipe or Filipe II to denote the sixteenth century king.

On the other hand, the names of some other individuals who appear in the original documents in both Spanish and Portuguese have required a different approach to avoid confusion. In such cases, I have used the Spanish name in the narrative but have left it in Portuguese in quotations and citations.

Acknowledgments

The writing of this book would not have been possible without the help of the personnel in the Spanish and Portuguese archives, particularly in the Archivo General de Indias, in Seville, and in the Arquivo Nacional Torre de Tombo, in Lisbon. Guillermo Pastor Núñez, Director of the Section of Information of the Archivo General de Indias, in Seville, provided me with some documents pertaining to Carvajal's people and introduced me to Asmaa Bouhrass whose help in finding several important documents in that archive and in the Archivo Histórico de Protocolos de Sevilla was essential. In Lisbon, I benefited from the help of Odete Martins, Coordinator of the Reference Department in the Arquivo Nacional Torre the Tombo, and of Marta Pascoa, who helped me locate and translate some important documents from the Portuguese Inquisition. I am especially grateful to Iva Cabral, Director of Documentation and Parliamentary Information of the National Assembly of the Republic of Cabo Verde for her help in locating important documents.

I am also grateful to many friends who over the years were willing to listen to my stories about Carvajal. Their questions helped me focus on several important points. In this regard, it gives me pleasure to acknowledge the invaluable help of Elizabeth S. Pease whose comments and observations are incorporated throughout the book, and whose continued encouragement made the completion of this work possible.

Introduction

Nuevo León had been discovered and pacified by Luis de Carvajal,
its first governor, personage little known in the history of Mexico,
who, however, because of his conquests and foundations . . . deserves
that some news about him be given.

Vicente Riva Palacio, 1880.[1]

More than four hundred years ago, Philip II awarded a Portuguese man
named Luis de Carvajal a new entity in the Spanish New World called Nuevo
Reino de León and appointed him as its governor. This entity was to become
part of New Spain and was to include a vast, but essentially unexplored territory. The appointment carried many rights and privileges and was to last two
lives—his and that of a successor chosen by him. Nearly ten years later, he
was arrested by orders of the Spanish viceroy, brought in chains to Mexico
City, and put in jail without a formal charge. From there, he was taken to the
Inquisition, where, after a long trial, he was found guilty of allowing his relatives to practice Judaism and of covering up for them. Finally, on February
13, 1590 he was sentenced to a six year exile from the New World. However,
before the sentence was carried out he was sent back to the Crown's jail, where
he died a year later. Thus ended the life of a remarkable man whose activities
in New Spain spanned more than twenty years.

Long after his death, the story of Luis de Carvajal become known when
the records of his Inquisition trial as well as those of his sister and of several
of her children were found in the Mexican Archives. These records showed
that he and his sister were descendents of Jewish families that had converted
to Christianity only a few generations earlier, and that his sister and most of
her children were burnt at the stake as heretics. Although the inquisitors were
not able to show that Carvajal was also a heretic, the inquisitors suspected he
also practiced Judaism. That suspicion has been shared by some authors who
started writing about him and his family in the 1930s. Some of their writings

give considerable attention to the religious aspects of his life, but leave aside the most important component: his remarkable contributions as an explorer, conqueror, and colonizer of large territories in the New World.

As described below, this component has since then received some attention by historians, but to date no serious, full-length biography of Carvajal has been published. This is all the most surprising since his nephew, Luis Rodríguez de Carvajal, El Mozo, has been the subject of several works, including an excellent biography by Martin A. Cohen.[2] It is probably no exaggeration to state that the life of El Mozo has overshadowed that of his uncle. Of course, the two lives intersected for a brief time in New Spain; after all, Carvajal had named his nephew as his successor as the governor of Nuevo Reino de León. But El Mozo's life was centered around the religion of his ancestors. There is no doubt that his life as a Jewish mystic was remarkable. However, it had little to do with the creation, discovery, conquest, and colonization of the enormous territory awarded to his uncle.

Of course, the religious life of the Carvajal family, including that of the governor himself, is important and is touched on in this work. But the book's main concerns are his non-religious activities. It is here that our knowledge about him is most incomplete. True, Carvajal's self-defense in his Inquisition trial contains some autobiographical material that he, writing in one of the secret jails of the Inquisition, considered relevant to his trial. On the few folios available to him he described what he had done in the 22 years that had passed since his arrival in New Spain. Although sketchy that description included a series of services that he said he had performed on behalf of the Crown. This part of his auto-defense become known three hundred years later when the distinguished Mexican author Vicente Riva Palacio published it. As the epigraph at the head of this Introduction indicates, Riva Palacio credited Carvajal with some important feats and stated that Carvajal's activities should be better known.

More recent historians have not generally shared Riva Palacio's view of Carvajal. In fact after the record of the Inquisition trial of the governor was published in 1932, several writers questioned the veracity of Carvajal's auto-defense, particularly regarding the basis upon which Philip II awarded him that new entity in New Spain. Although Carvajal did not state that the award was made because of his merits and services, that conclusion is implied in his auto-defense. However, as the following examples show, some influential Mexican authors questioned the reasons behind the award:

Vito Alessio Robles: "How could Carvajal obtain that royal decree, so magnanimous in privileges and yet without the requirements established by law? Did Jewish gold . . . intervene in an able and corrupting manner?"[3]

Mariano Cuevas: "How could it be that a man devoid of merits, who had not spilled even a drop of blood in the Americas, and without the efforts of a conqueror was given such a large dominion?" How was it possible to hide from the advisors of King Philip II that the Carvajals were renowned Jews . . .[4]

Primo Feliciano Velázquez: "Knowing, as we know, that before 1580 Carvajal did not . . . do anything significant in the service of the king we find it amazing that [Viceroy] D. Martín Enríquez favored him so strongly."[5]

Of course, other scholars have expressed different views. For example, writing at about the same time as these authors and relying on the same documents available to them, Leslie Byrd Simpson stated that Luis de Carvajal was: "the most enlightened and humane of the conquistadors. His conquest of Nuevo León was the most successful ever undertaken in New Spain . . ."[6]

However, more recent writers have adopted the views of Robles, Cuevas, and Velázques. Notable among them is Eugenio del Hoyo who stated that: "With his [Carvajal's] extraordinary ability to lie, and with his great imagination, he was able to convince the viceroy of his many merits and services."[7] To support his contention that Carvajal lied, and forgetting that lack of evidence is not evidence of lacking, Hoyo cited one of Carvajal's claims stating that: "Here everything is a lie. We have carefully studied the records . . . and have not found even the smallest notice of what he says."[8]

The reader will probably agree that Hoyo's views of Carvajal, as well as those by Cuevas, Robles, and Velázquez, are biased against Carvajal. While it is not difficult to read between the lines to understand the basis for that bias, it is possible that the supposed lack of contemporary material supporting Carvajal's claims may have contributed to those views.

As it turns out, many previously unknown documents related to Carvajal that were written during his lifetime exist in the Spanish and Portuguese archives. These documents, found during the course of this work, confirm every one of the claims Carvajal made in his self-defense and permit us to answer, without resorting to speculation, many important questions about him. They show, for example, that Carvajal's rise to power was not the result of a bribe to the Spanish Crown but was due to his many abilities, to his willingness to serve the Spanish Crown, and to the meritorious services he performed on its behalf. The documents also show that his downfall was the result of a scheme based on charges that his enemies fabricated for the purpose of recovering certain lands that had been adjudicated to him after a long-lasting legal fight held in the Audiencia de México. Those fabrications portrayed Carvajal as an Indian abuser and slave trader; they have been repeated so often that they have become the accepted truth and have bestowed on him the label of slaver, a label which is used, or implied, in several recent works.[9]

The recently-found contemporary documentation has also permitted us to examine Carvajal's life in more detail than was possible before. That examination conveys an image of Carvajal that can be summarized using the same words as used by Leslie Simpson. That view, expressed in this work, differs significantly from those of most other authors. Because of this drastic difference we include in the narrative a fair amount of primary-source material about Carvajal's activities and about the views that his contemporaries held of him.

Of course, the fact that this archival documentation is contemporary to the events described in them does not mean that all of the statements found in it are truthful or unbiased. Quite the contrary, some documents show a clear tendency to distort the facts. Nevertheless a careful reading of all the documents makes it possible to detect most of those distortions. To that effect, hearsay testimony has been avoided as have the sworn affidavits by witnesses who stood to benefit from their testimony. Also, the places where those affidavits were presented are important in assessing their credibility. For example, although the testimonies presented before the Audiencia of México and Nueva Galicia are not free of bias, they are far more reliable than those presented before minor officers in small towns and villages.

As indicated in the Table of Contents, the book follows Carvajal's time line. With the exception of the first chapter, which represents a rather rough sketch of his first thirty years, the book deals with the last twenty four years of his life. That period is divided into two nearly equal parts: the first starting with his arrival in New Spain in 1567 and ending in 1579, when he was appointed Governor of Nuevo Reino de León, and the second beginning with that royal appointment and ending with his death in 1591. Most of this last period was spent trying to meet his obligations to the Crown to discover, pacify and settle the territory granted to him, a territory that until then had not been conquered by the Spaniards. Although his efforts were hampered by the actions of an overzealous prosecutor and an egomaniacal viceroy, his contributions to the growth of New Spain and to the development of northeast Mexico were remarkable.

I

In the Old World

From an early age he was with a gentleman of the court of Castile, where he learned the language as well as good habits.

Alonso de León, 1649.[1]

Nearly ten years after Philip II named him governor of Nuevo Reino de León, Luis de Carvajal was brought before the Inquisition in Mexico City to be questioned about the heretical activities of one of his nieces. During his arraignment he first gave his name, title, birthplace, age and genealogy. He was then asked about his religion and that of his ancestors, and was told to give an account of his life. Carvajal's responses were clear but brief, particularly about what he did before he settled in the New World. This chapter considers what is now known about him and his activities prior to 1567, when he left the Old World to settle in New Spain.

1. ORIGINS

On 14 April of 1589, at his arraignment before the Inquisition, Governor Luis de Carvajal said that he was born in Mogadouro, a Portuguese town in "the *Reino y Raya* de Portugal near Zamora and Benavente."[2] La Raya was the region adjacent to the Portuguese-Spanish border, shown in Map 1. The map's inset shows the northeast corner of that border and includes the places named by Carvajal or by his ancestors. Of special importance to this section are Mogadouro, in Portugal, and Benavente, in Spain. Later sections touch upon Cape Verde and the Canary Islands, also shown in the map.

Mogadouro's history dates back to the times when the Moors controlled the Iberian peninsula. By the first third of the sixteenth century, it had become an important "dry port" of entry into Portugal.[3] It also was a center for the production of silk, most of which was exported to Spain. Benavente, in the old Spanish Kingdom of León, goes back to Roman times, when it was known as *Intercacia*.[4] It become the center of the Condado de Benavente in 1398, when King Enrique III of Castile named João Afonso Pimentel, a Portuguese noble-

Map 1. The Portuguese-Spanish world where Luis de Carvajal spent the first thirty years of his life.

man, as its first count. The sixth Conde de Benavente was Antonio Alfonso Pimentel (1530–1575), a friend of Philip II. In all likelihood it was this man to whom Alonso de León referred in the epigraph at the beginning of this chapter.

The next item in Carvajal's declaration was his age, which he said was fifty, "*poco mas o menos*" [a little more or less]. This ambiguity in fixing dates, prevalent in most of the contemporary documents referred to in this work, is of no consequence to the narrative as a whole. It is nevertheless useful to determine the year of his birth as close as the primary sources permit. As described later, these indicate that Carvajal was born in 1537. The next item in his declaration was his genealogy. Although Carvajal named the members of his immediate family and said that his ancestors were Old Christians, earlier Portuguese documents provide considerable more reliable and complete information. As discussed later these documents show that contrary to what he said, his ancestors were of Jewish descent and had become Christian only two or three generations earlier. To simplify the discussion Carvajal's paternal and maternal ancestral families are considered separately.

Vázquez-Carvajal

According to Carvajal, his paternal grandparents were Gutierre Vázquez de la Cueva and Francisca de Carvajal. He also said that Gutierre was born around Bermillo del Sayago, near Zamora in Spain, but had moved to Portugal. Carvajal did not state the reasons for the move, nor did he say when it took place.

Considerably older information is now available about Carvajal's paternal grandmother and her family, some of which has been used to construct the family tree presented in figure 1.1. This shows four generations, marked with Roman numerals I–IV, of the Carvajal family, starting with her parents. For example, grandmother Francisca de Carvajal appears as a member of generation II. In this context it should be added that while the names of some of Carvajal's ancestors were given by him in Spanish, the older documents give them in Portuguese. The text here uses the Spanish version if the names were given by Carvajal, while the family tree shows those names in Portuguese if they are appear in the Portuguese documents, or in Spanish if they do not. Thus, for example, the name of Carvajal's paternal grandfather appears in both text and family tree as Gutierre Vázquez, whereas that of paternal uncle Melchor Vázquez appears in the family tree as Belchior Vaz (generation III).

The older information shows that grandmother Francisca de Carvajal was born around 1485 and that her parents were Álvaro de Carvajal and Catarina

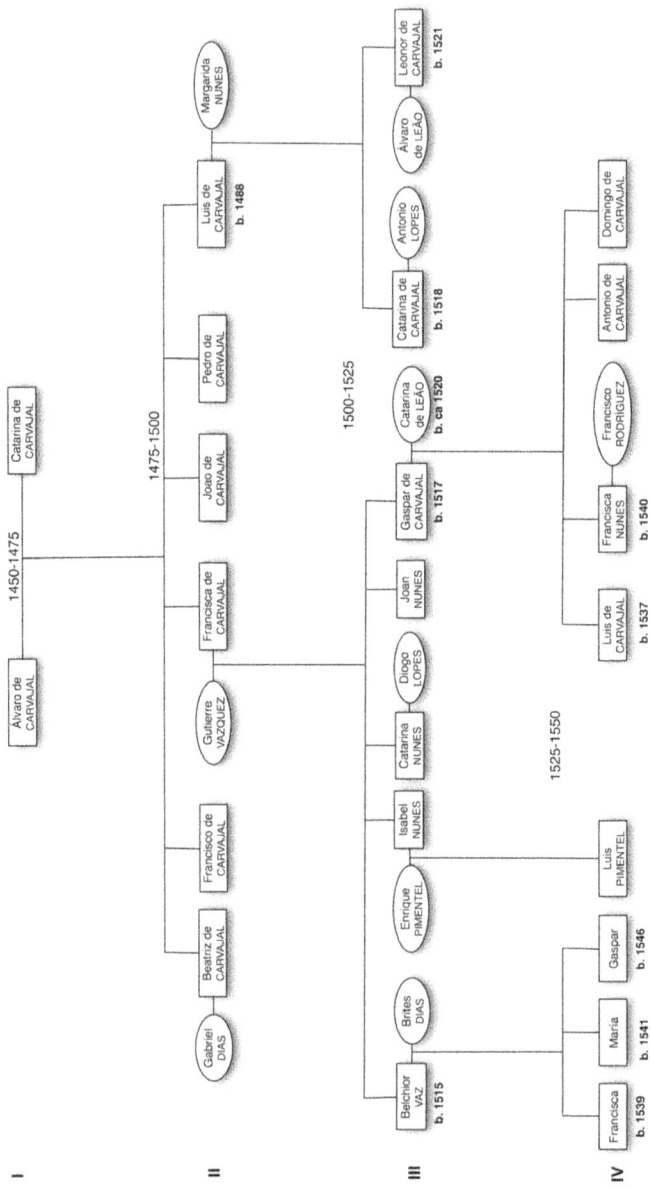

Fig. 1.1. The Carvajal Family, 1450–1550.

de Carvajal (generation I). Francisca had a sister and four brothers, all sur-named Carvajal. None of her siblings were mentioned by Carvajal and, with the exception of his great-uncle Luis de Carvajal (generation II), not much is known about them, other that they returned to Spain before 1546.

The immediate family of great uncle Luis illustrates the connections be-tween the Carvajal family with others such as the León, Núñez, and López families. For example, Luis was married to Margarida Nunes, or Núñez, a native of Mogadouro. This marriage shows that a connection between the Carvajal family and a Mogadouro family whose surname was Núñez existed in generation II. Connections with the León and López families are shown by the marriages of Luis daughters, Leonor and Catarina de Carvajal (gen-eration III). Thus, Leonor was married to an Antonio López, and Catarina was married to Álvaro de León (generation III), a maternal uncle of Carvajal. However, a connection between the Núñez and León families seems to have occurred at in an earlier generation for one sister of Margarida was married to a Cristóbal de León, with whom she lived in Benavente in 1558.[5]

The sons of Gutierre Vázquez and Francisca de Carvajal were Melchor Vázquez, Joan Núñez, and Gaspar de Carvajal, the latter being Carvajal's father.[6] Incidentally, in Carvajal's deposition Joan Núñez appears as Juan de Carvajal, Although the surnames of Gutierre's sons seem arbitrary, they ap-pear to follow some naming traditions that are described later. Gutierre and Francisca also had two daughters, Isabel and Catarina Núñez, but only Isabel was mentioned by Carvajal.

Although Carvajal said very little about his paternal ancestors, a contem-porary record shows that uncle Melchor was born in Fermoselle around 1515, and that the family moved to Mogadouro in Portugal when he was "a very small boy" [*muyto pequenho*].[7]

As for Gaspar de Carvajal his surname seems to indicate that he was born in Portugal, very likely in Mogadouro, where in due time he married Catarina de León, one of the daughters of Antonio de León.[8] Apparently the León fam-ily had been living there for some time, though as their name indicates, they originated in the province of León, in Spain. This point and others related to it are discussed later on.

Carvajal also said that he had two brothers and one sister, all younger than he. The brothers were Antonio, a "man of arms" in the southern part of New Spain, where he died. Domingo, the youngest, was a Jesuit monk in Medina del Campo, who died "around 1562 or 1563." Their sister was Francisca Núñez, who appears in the records of the Spanish Inquisition in New Spain

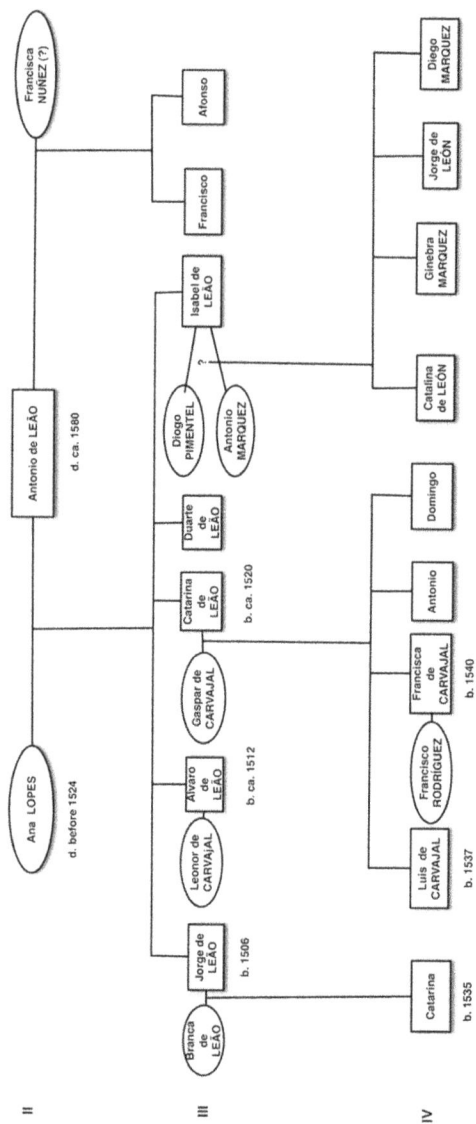

Fig. 1.2. The Family of Antonio de León.

Francisca NUÑEZ (?)

Antonio de LEÃO
d. ca. 1580

Ana LOPES
d. before 1524

Francisco

Afonso

Isabel de LEÃO

Diogo PIMENTEL

Antonio MARQUEZ

?

Catalina de LEÓN

Ginebra MARQUEZ

Jorge de LEÓN

Diego MARQUEZ

Duarte de LEÃO

Catarina de LEÃO
b. ca. 1520

Gaspar de CARVAJAL

Alvaro de LEÃO
b. ca. 1512

Leonor de CARVAJAL

Jorge de LEÃO
b. 1506

Branca de LEÃO

Luis de CARVAJAL
b. 1537

Francisco RODRÍGUEZ

Francisca de CARVAJAL
b. 1540

Antonio

Domingo

Catarina
b. 1535

II

III

IV

as Francisca de Carvajal.[9] In 1589 she told the inquisitors that she was about fifty years old, "or even less", and that she was born in Benavente.[10] However, in 1595, during her second Inquisition trial, she said she was fifty five years old, which suggests that she was born in 1540.[11]

The family of Antonio de León

Considerable more information is known about Carvajal's maternal family, some of which stems from what he said before the inquisitors in 1589. In his arraignment in Mexico City he said that his maternal grandparents were Antonio de León and Francisca Núñez and that his uncles were Francisco Jorge de Andrade, Jorge de León de Andrade, Antonio de León, Duarte de León, and Álvaro de León. Later on he added aunt Isabel de León. However, while evidence that these individuals were, in fact, the sons and daughters of Antonio de León, no evidence has surfaced that confirms that Francisca Núñez was Carvajal's maternal grandmother. In fact, older records show that before 1525 Antonio's wife was Ana Lopes, a native of Mogadouro.

Antonio de León originated in the Spanish province of León, most likely in Benavente, for according to Carvajal it was that there that he was buried. Also, fifteenth century documents state that in 1448 an Antonio de León helped free the third Conde de Benavente, and went with him to Mogadouro, where they took refuge for a few months.[12] It is likely that this stay resulted in some lasting connections that may explain the move of the family of Carvajal's maternal grandfather from Benavente to Mogadouro. In any event, several documents show that he lived in Mogadouro. One such record is Carvajal's declaration that Antonio de León was a burgher [*vecino*] of Mogadouro. This means that he was not born there and that he was a man of substance, for otherwise he would not be referred to as a vecino.[13] Indeed, other contemporary documents show that a Castilian man by the name of Antonio de Leão, or León, was one of the most important merchants there during the 1520s and 1530s.[14] There is no doubt that this man was Carvajal's maternal grandfather. The records also show that he was born in Spain around 1480 and that he and some other members of his family moved to Mogadouro before 1500. The route followed by them probably took them through Alcañizas, a town southwest of Benavente.

After entering Portugal they passed through Miranda where another León family had been living for some time. It is possible that a familial connection existed between these two families. In any event, Antonio went to Mogadouro where he become a merchant. His business involved the trade of goods with Spanish merchants. Particularly important were embroidered silk garments that were made in Benavente, Zamora, and other locations in León, using Mogadouro's silk.

Figure 1.2 shows Carvajal's maternal family tree, starting with Antonio de León (generation II relative to that of the Carvajal family). As before, the names of all individuals are shown in the figure as they appear in the Portuguese records. Antonio married at least two times, the first with Ana Lopes. Another wife was, presumably, Francisca Núñez. He had seven sons and daughters, all of whom were born in Mogadouro and carried his surname, as indicated below. The mother of those born before 1525 was Ana Lopes, who had died before that year.[15] This indicates that she was the mother of Jorge, Álvaro, and probably Catarina (or Catalina), Carvajal's mother. It is also possible that Ana was also the mother of Duarte and of Isabel. However, she could not be the mother of Francisco and of Afonso, for in 1544 Francisco was a young man and Afonso was a small boy.[16]

In any event, most of the sons and daughters of Antonio de León played important roles in Carvajal's life, as is demonstrated by his mentioning each of their names and occupations before the Inquisition. The following entries present what Carvajal and the older documents show about each of them.

Fig. 1.3. Houses in Mogadouro's Old Quarter. (Photograph by the author.)

Jorge de León. Carvajal gave the name of this uncle as Jorge de León de Andrade, and said that he had lived in Cortiços, between Mirandela and Mogadouro.[17] Although the older documents also cite Cortiços as his residence, the second surname, Andrade, does not appear in them. Jorge was born in Mogadouro in 1509, was married to Branca de Leão at an unknown date and, by 1545, had a daughter named Catarina.[18] Like other members of the family he returned to Spain, for Carvajal's nephew, Luis Rodríguez de Carvajal—referred to here as El Mozo—stated that Jorge was the owner of the butcher shops [*carnicerias*] in Valladolid.[19] This statement is confirmed by earlier Spanish documents.[20] It should also be mentioned that a 1581 document shows that a certain Jorge de León de Andrade was then a close associate of Carvajal in New Spain.[21] If this man was Carvajal's uncle, it would mean that at least two of his maternal uncles, Francisco and Jorge, went there.

Álvaro de León. According to Carvajal, this man lived and died in Medina del Campo, in Spain, but a contemporary document shows that in 1544 Álvaro lived in Cortiços.[22] He was five or six years younger than Jorge and was married to Leonor de Carvajal, the sister of Catarina de Carvajal. Álvaro's mother, like Jorge's, was Ana Lopes, not Francisca Núñez.

Catarina de León. This was Carvajal's mother. As pointed out earlier, the exact year of her birth is not known but assuming that she was about 17 when her oldest child was born, she probably was born around 1520, married Gaspar de Carvajal around 1535 and become a widow around 1547, not quite thirty years old.

Isabel de León. The name of this maternal aunt is missing from Carvajal's initial arraignment before the Inquisition, although he added it two days later, saying he had forgotten her. Her birth year is also unknown. According to her brothers Jorge and Álvaro, she was first married to Diego Pimentel. Apparently Diego died when Isabel was young for she later married Antonio Márquez.[23] In fact, the names of Isabel's sons and daughters who later accompanied Carvajal to the New World indicate that the father of some of them was surnamed Márquez.

Duarte de León. According to both Álvaro and Jorge de León, Duarte was still single in 1544, which probably meant that he was younger than both of them. In his trial Carvajal stated that Duarte was a Crown contractor in Guinea. This is confirmed by contemporary documents that show that he had gone there before 1545. However, by 1552 he was living in Lisbon, for that year he received a *Carta de Perdão*, or Letter of Pardon, issued by king João III.[24] In that letter, Duarte, identified as a merchant who lived in Lisbon, was pardoned for bringing silk garments into Portugal. Obviously, Duarte had become an important merchant, for otherwise the king would not have pardoned him. A few years later Duarte was appointed Crown Contractor in Cape Verde, where he was in partnership with Antonio Gonçalves de Gusmão, a business relation that extended from before 1566 to June of 1574.[25] It is likely that as Crown contractors Duarte and his partner were engaged in the slave trade. These records substantiate what Carvajal stated in his trial. Not substantiated but quite interesting is a statement made in 1596 by El Mozo in the Inquisition. Under the threat of torture, he said that one of the brothers of his maternal grandmother, was a man "whose name is Duarte de León, who is in Lisbon, very wealthy, whose son-in-law is D. Rodrigo de Castro."[26] A similar statement was made by his mother. However, it is not possible to verify that information because, at that time, there lived in Lisbon several distinguished men by that name.[27]

Francisco Jorge de Andrade. This seems to have been the name adopted later in life by maternal uncle Francisco, who in 1544 was studying in Salamanca. According to Carvajal, Francisco had been a *factor*, or agent, and captain of the military forces of the Portuguese Crown in Guinea, after which he had gone to New Spain, where he was an Augustinian friar under the name of Francisco de Andrade. So far as the first part of this statement is concerned, there is evidence that Francisco had, indeed, spent some years in Rio S. Domingos (in present day Bissau-Guinea), and that he represented Duarte de León's interests there. That evidence stems from a record of the Portuguese Inquisition in Lisbon, where it was claimed that a number of New Christians who lived in Rio S. Domingos had met in the house of a Francisco Jorge, factór of Duarte de Leão, to perform some heretical celebrations.[28]

Francisco's name change to Francisco de Andrade is very interesting because other records show that a person by that name occupied various Crown positions in Cape Verde in 1580, including that of *Sargento-Mor*, or senior military leader, and that in 1582 the same person wrote, in Portuguese, a report to the king describing Cape Verde and Guinea.[29] Whether this man was Carvajal's uncle is not known, but several facts seem to support the idea that he was. One was that he was in Cape Verde at the same time as Carvajal's uncle; second, he was the military leader there; and finally he, like Carvajal's uncle, was educated in Spain, a fact that is made evident by his use of Hispanicisms in that report.[30]

Afonso de León. Carvajal stated that this maternal uncle was killed by Frenchmen, possibly corsairs, when he was traveling from the New World to Spain. It is possible that he had been in New Spain before Carvajal went there, but no evidence has surfaced that support this possibility.

The foregoing shows that at least three members of Carvajal's ancestral family in Portugal had gone to the New World; that some others had moved to Spain, some of whom were returning to it after a long absence; and that some others remained in Portugal. The reasons for these movements are an important component to this narrative and will be considered after a brief review of the historical forces that produced them.

2. HISTORICAL BACKGROUND

The back and forth change of country of residence of the Carvajal family raises additional questions which are important in the context of the Iberian Jews and their emigration to the New World. While a detailed description of the forces that produced those changes are beyond the scope of this book, it is necessary to examine the reasons behind the border crossings of the Carvajal family. In general, those crossings were normal for those living in La Raya. There, commerce across the border was common; also common was to find families separated by the border.[31]

However, the crossings that concern this work were of a very different kind as they involved relocations of entire families, that is, relocations that required a considerable effort. Consequently, these movements must have been caused by forces that acted only on one segment of the population. Individuals belonging to it shared something in common: They were either practicing Jews, or crypto-Jews, that is, Jews who had converted to Christianity but had continued to practice Judaism under cover.

The Spanish Inquisition and the expulsion of Jews from Spain in 1492 played very significant roles in driving entire families to Portugal. However, the movement of Spanish Jews to Portugal had started earlier owing to previous religious persecutions, particularly that of 1391, which had its beginnings in Seville.[32] Those persecutions induced many Jews to move to areas in the east of the Iberian peninsula, particularly to León and Galicia.[33] Later on, as the Inquisition gained strength in Spain, many of the them moved to Portugal.[34]

Of course, Portugal had a Jewish population from much earlier times. This meant that some of the Jews entering that country were able to join Jewish communities that already existed there, adopting their language and traditions, while maintaining whatever connections they could with their place of origin, perhaps thinking that one day they, or their descendants, would go back, as many did years after their expulsion from Spain.[35]

The fate of the Jews who converted to Christianity in Spain is well known. A fraction of them were accused, justly or unjustly, of continuing to practice

Judaism, accusations that helped establish the Spanish Inquisition, first in Seville in 1481, and subsequently in other Spanish cities. But the largest influx of Jews into Portugal occurred in 1492, when King Fernando and Queen Isabel ordered their expulsion from Spain. Although the numbers of those expelled is not known with any degree of certainty, it is estimated that at least 100,000 Jews left Spain, of which approximately one-half entered Portugal through pre-assigned ports after paying a fee of two cruzados per person.[36] This influx resulted in a significant swelling of the Jewish population there, which some authors estimate to have been about 3-6% of the total.[37] A significant component of that influx originated in the old kingdom of León. Because of its vicinity to the Portuguese province of Tras-os-Montes, many Jews who had been living in such places as Zamora, León, Medina del Campo, and Benavente made that province their home upon entering Portugal.

Although the permission to stay was to be limited to six months, most Jews ignored that limitation. However, their ability to practice their religion was significantly curtailed a few years later when Fernando and Isabel would not consent the marriage of their daughter, Isabel, to King Manuel I of Portugal unless he rid his kingdom of all "heretics", that is Jews and Muslims.[38] To comply, Manuel first ordered the forced mass conversion of all Jews, and in 1496 he ordered the expulsion of those who had not been converted. These actions officially ended Judaism there, but left the country with a very large number of New Christians, many of whom, remaining Jewish at heart, continued to practice the religion of their ancestors.

However, in 1536 João III agreed to establish the Portuguese Inquisition.[39] For that purpose Inquisition tribunals were established in Lisbon, Évora, and Coimbra. This meant that relatively isolated areas like Tras-os-Montes were not, except for isolated incursions, initially affected by inquisitorial activities, although as the years passed those activities increased noticeably everywhere. The arrests of crypto-Jews continued until 1546, when Pope Paul IV issued a general pardon which released a large number of crypto-Jews from the Inquisition jails. However, since the pardon was accompanied with stricter penalties for those who might relapse, many Portuguese crypto-Jews whose ancestors were Spanish, returned to Spain, thinking they would be safer there.

This return of Spanish-Jewish families to their homeland got an additional boost when Spain annexed Portugal in 1580. This made it possible for many Portuguese New Christians to go to the Spanish New World. An indication that the total number of such emigrants was large is provided by the large number of Portuguese individuals tried by the Inquisition in the Spanish

Colonies. For example, between 1590 and 1650, about 270 individuals were accused of following the law of Moses in New Spain.[40] Most of these were born in Portugal, and many of those claiming to be Spanish had a Portuguese ancestry.

3. Family Movements

Consider now the reasons behind the exodus from Spain of Carvajal's ancestors. Although both branches of his family moved to Portugal, more information is available about the Carvajal family. The first point that should be addressed pertains to the time of their move. As described before, Carvajal's father was born in Portugal, while uncle Melchor was born in Spain. Thus, Gutierre Vázquez and Francisca de Carvajal moved to Portugal after 1515, when Melchor was born.[41] The date suggests that the reason for the move might have been related to the activities of the Spanish Inquisition. Indeed, the trials held by the Portuguese Inquisition in the mid 1540s show that to have been the case. One of these trials relates to Luis de Carvajal (generation II), one of the brothers of Carvajal's paternal grandmother Francisca.[42] This man was born in 1488 in Fermoselle. His parents were Álvaro and Catarina de Carvajal, names they adopted at the time of their conversion to Christianity. Their conversion probably took place in 1492, for Luis said that he had been Jewish but that he was made Christian at the time when his parents converted, when he was very small. However, the conversion was not sincere; the family continued to practice Judaism, albeit under cover. Eventually, the Spanish Inquisition in Valladolid learned about those practices and arrested Luis' sister, Francisca. While the records of her trial have not been located, her sentence must have been light for she did not have to serve it in jail. However, no matter how light the sentence might have been, Francisca refused to serve it for, according to her brother Luis, "she came to live in Mogadouro with her husband because she did not want to serve the sentence given to her." It is therefore indisputable that the Carvajal family practiced Judaism undercover in Spain and moved to Portugal in order to escape the Spanish Inquisition. It is also clear that she intended to continue her religious practices there.

Although evidence that the León family practiced Judaism in Spain has not surfaced, subsequent activities of some of its members show that they also practiced Judaism under cover in Spain. Their conversion to Christianity had taken place much earlier, possibly during the persecutions of 1391, for as mentioned earlier, it appears that an ancestor of Antonio de León carried a Christian names already by 1448. It also appears that the family's move to

Portugal was caused by the anti-Jewish riots that took place in Benavente during the decade before the expulsion.[43]

The Portuguese Inquisition

As stated before, the Portuguese Inquisition was officially installed in 1536. At first its activities were limited to the areas around Lisbon, Coimbra, and Évora.[44] Later on its powerful arm would move into Tras-os-Montes, affecting the lives of many of the New Christians who lived there, including the families of Antonio de León and of Gutierre Vázquez. On October of 1544, Jorge de León, one of the sons of Antonio, was brought to the Inquisition jail in Évora.[45] A month later his brother Álvaro was also arrested.[46] It is also possible that their father, Antonio de León, was also a target of the Inquisition but seems to have escaped it. It is not difficult to imagine his reaction, or indeed that of the many crypto-Jews who lived in the area surrounding Mogadouro. Sensing the danger, Antonio de León must have decided to go to Spain and take with him those members of his family who were still free. This included his daughter Catarina de León, her husband Gaspar de Carvajal and their children, Luis, then eight years old, and his younger siblings Francisca and Domingo.

Some members of the Carvajal family also left Portugal at that time, for example Francisca de Carvajal and three of her brothers. Other members stayed behind, probably thinking that they would not be caught. This sense of security was reinforced by Pope Paul IV's general pardon to New Christians who had reverted to their previous religion. However, a few years later the Inquisition renewed its anti-heretical activities and arrested some of those members of the family who had remained in Portugal. Among them were Carvajal's uncle Melchor Vázquez, great uncle Luis de Carvajal, and his daughter, Carvajal's first cousin, Catarina de Carvajal.

Family names

Before proceeding we consider the surnames taken by Jews at the time of their conversion. That information can be useful when attempting to determine the origin of some of the people who appear in the narrative, particularly those who years later followed Carvajal to the New World after being named governor of Nuevo Reino de León.

At the time of their conversion, Jews had to adopt Christian names. Some took the names of famous families or the names of those sponsoring their conversion. Others adopted names with religious connotations, such as *de la Cruz*, probably to try to convince Old-Christians that their conversion was sincere. Also common was the association with 'new' locations, for example *Barrio Nuevo*. But the most common surname taken by *conversos* was toponymic. For example, a Jew living in a given place might simply add the name of that place to his adopted (or forced[47]) Christian first name, prefixed by the preposition *de*. The naming system worked reasonably well, but failed when two or more individuals had the same given and family names. This multiplicity of names required the addition of a suitable identifier, often another surname. An example of this is provided by Carvajal himself. His surname, as he signed it in the Spanish world, was Luis de Carvajal. But in the royal documents appointing him as the governor, the coda *de la Cueva* was added to differentiate him from others who had the same name.[48]

The move to Portugal involved yet another complication, namely, the different naming traditions of Spain and Portugal. In the Spanish tradition, the given name of a person is followed by the surname of his/her father, and then, by that of the mother. In the Portuguese tradition the surname order is reversed, so that the father's surname appears last.[49] Not all Spanish families adopted the Portuguese tradition upon entering Portugal, for example the León family. On the other hand, the Vázquez-Carvajal obviously did. Thus, Melchor, born in Fermoselle, carried his father's surname, albeit as Vaz, whereas Gaspar, born in Portugal, carried his mother's surname. However, some of the Spanish families that had adopted the Portuguese naming tradition, would later return to Spain and change their surname order to adopt to the Spanish tradition. Carvajal's name may provide an example. Having been born in Portugal, his first surname was probably Leão.[50] But after the move to Spain it become Carvajal, a name that reflected the Spanish tradition. To complicate matters, some individuals changed their surnames in an apparently arbitrary manner, as demonstrated by the names of Carvajal's sister and of her children. Such changes make it nearly impossible to trace, with any degree of certainty, the origins of a particular family name, even after only a few generations.

4. EARLY YEARS

Although Carvajal spent the first thirty years of his life in the Old World, not much is known about him or his activities during that period, particularly about his early childhood. Most of what is known stems from his Inquisition trial which took place when he was over fifty years of age. It is unlikely that he remembered every event from his early childhood or that he understood the reasons for some of them. In any case, in his trial he told the inquisitors that he lived the first years of his life in Mogadouro, where he attended school, and that at the age of eight his father took him to Spain.

Although his ancestors practiced Judaism under cover, Carvajal was too young to be informed of the religion of his parents; such information in the hands of a young child would have been very dangerous to the family. This means that he was raised as a Christian and that he must have been confirmed as such at the age of seven. By that time he had started school, probably in the local church. There he learned to read and write and continued to be indoctrinated in the Catholic doctrine. Obviously that education was in Portuguese. And given that his parents were both born in Portugal, that language must have been his first.

Carvajal's birthplace was in the Tras-os-Montes region of Portugal. This was also the birthplace of Magellan. Nearby was Belmonte, the birthplace of Pedro Álvarez de Cabral, the discoverer of Brazil. It is likely that young Carvajal's imagination was influenced by their stories, for throughout his mature life he showed a desire to discover new places. Closer to home, the business activities of his maternal grandfather must have also influenced him.

In any event, at the age of eight Carvajal was taken to Spain. Ostensibly, the purpose of the journey was to seek a place where he could get a better education than then available in Mogadouro. However, as mentioned in the previous sections, the reason for the move was to run away from the Portuguese Inquisition. Nevertheless, Carvajal said that he and his father initially went to Sahagun, where the Abbot was a distant relative [*deudo*], but, apparently, it a more suitable place was found in Benavente, for in his self-defense Carvajal stated that he was there when his father died.[51]

In fact, Carvajal spent some years in Benavente. After all, his maternal grandfather was probably born there and had some business associates who could help the family relocate to that city. Also, the León family had some connections with the counts of Benavente going back to the fifteen century. As discussed below, such connections proved useful to find a place for the young boy. However, Carvajal chose not to mention Benavente during his arraignment before the inquisitors. Nevertheless those years seem to have made a permanent change in his life, for long before his arraignment before the Inquisition, he claimed to be a "*natural de Benavente*," that is, that he was born there. Apparently the claim was never questioned by Crown officers which means that his speech and manners did not betray a non-Spanish upbringing.

One possible explanation for the origin of his speech and manners is the statement by Alonso de León, presented in the epigraph at the head of this chapter, that Carvajal learned the Spanish language and manners in the house of a member of the Spanish court, which was probably a reference to the Count of Benavente. As it turns out, a Spanish document—written well before Alonso de León was born—shows that the statement was correct. The document refers to Miguel Núñez, Carvajal's father-in-law, who in 1571 went to the *Casa de la Contratación,* or House of Trade, in Seville to seek permission to trade in the Indies. Apparently, that permission had been denied because the judges thought he was Portuguese.[52] To counter this he argued that although his parents took him to Lisbon when he was small, he was actually born in Castile. And to support his case he added that "one of his daughters married Luis de Carvajal, a Castilian, *criado* of the Conde de Benavente."[53] In current use, the word criado means servant, but in the sixteenth century being a criado of a person often meant having been raised in the house of that person.[54] Thus, as Alonso de León stated, Carvajal had a gentleman's upbringing in the house of an important Spanish nobleman.

It is likely that young Carvajal, like some young sons of Spanish noblemen living in the Count's castle, served him as a page while receiving some education, learning how to speak Spanish properly, and getting a solid Christian indoctrination. Also important is the fact that during the years that he lived there, many members of the Spanish nobility were guests of the count. One of them was Prince Philip, later Philip II, whose home was in nearby Valladolid. The interaction with members of the Spanish nobility must have helped young Carvajal develop a well-polished personality, as well as an ability to feel at ease in the presence of important people.

The question remains, however, as to what reasons did Carvajal have for not mentioning having spent some years in the house of the Count of Benavente. There are several possible reasons that may explain that omission. One was that he knew that mentioning Benavente would induce the inquisitors to request an inquiry about the count's family. Another possibility is that the count in whose house Carvajal lived as a child had died in the 1570s. More likely, however, is that what Carvajal mentioned during his arraignment was, as requested by the inquisitors, a short account of his life. Evidence for this is the brevity with which he described other events of his life.

Carvajal seems to have left Benavente in 1551, six years after arriving as a child of eight. Those years were very influential in forming his character, habits, and in giving him a solid Spanish façade. Thus, in spite of his Portuguese origin, Carvajal could easily pass as a Spanish *hidalgo,* a fact that must have been very helpful later on, when he asked the king for an award.

Cape Verde Islands

Having reached the then mature age of fourteen Carvajal was ready to face the world. His education in the Count's house had prepared him for a better occupation than that of a soldier or a monk—occupations chosen by his younger brothers. But to do anything else he needed guidance and support. However, his father had died when he was ten years old and his mother could not help him in any way. On his father's side there were two uncles, Melchor and Juan. The whereabouts of Juan were not known and Melchor was probably still in the jail of the Portuguese Inquisition. Fortunately, things were different with the León family. Not only was their location known but uncles Jorge and Duarte were engaged in profitable businesses. Although it could be that Carvajal was given the choice of working in the butcher shops of Jorge, or in one of Duarte's enterprises, it is more likely that the family made that decision for him. Thus, in 1551 uncle Duarte came to Benavente to take Carvajal To Lisbon. Although he was engaged in businesses in that city, the plan was to send the young man to Cape Verde, where he could acquire some skills that might prove useful later in life.

Carvajal's stay in Lisbon lasted only three months. There he probably met Miguel Núñez, his future father-in-law, who was living there at the time, although he had spent considerable time in Santo Domingo, apparently engaged in the slave trade.[55] As mentioned before, this was one of the activities of Duarte de León. It is also possible that Miguel Núñez was related to Carvajal's family, in which case there was an additional reason for the meeting.[56] In any case, young Luis was sent to Cape Verde islands, where he spent the next thirteen years of his life.

The Cape Verde Archipelago was discovered in the 1480s by a Genoese merchant and navigator.[57] Although it was uninhabited at the time of it discovery, by the middle of the sixteenth century it had a fairly well developed trade, particularly slaves from Guinea as well as cotton and other products from the mainland and from other islands of the archipelago. Santiago, the largest of the Cape Verde islands, served both as the center of trade and as the seat of government. That seat was in the city port of Ribeira Grande, known today as Cidade Velha. In his 1582 report to the king, cited in note 29, Francisco de Andrade stated that Ribeira Grande had then 508 burghers who together owned more than 5000 slaves. This indicates that the main business in that city was the slave trade: Ribeira Grande was the port through which Guinea slaves were sent to Portugal, Brazil, Spain and to the Spanish New World. Although it was the Portuguese who led in that trade, the English, the French and the Spaniards also profited from it. An example of an English corsair fleet going to Cape Verde to capture and enslave Africans in Guinea for the purpose of selling them in the Spanish colonies is presented in Chapter 3.

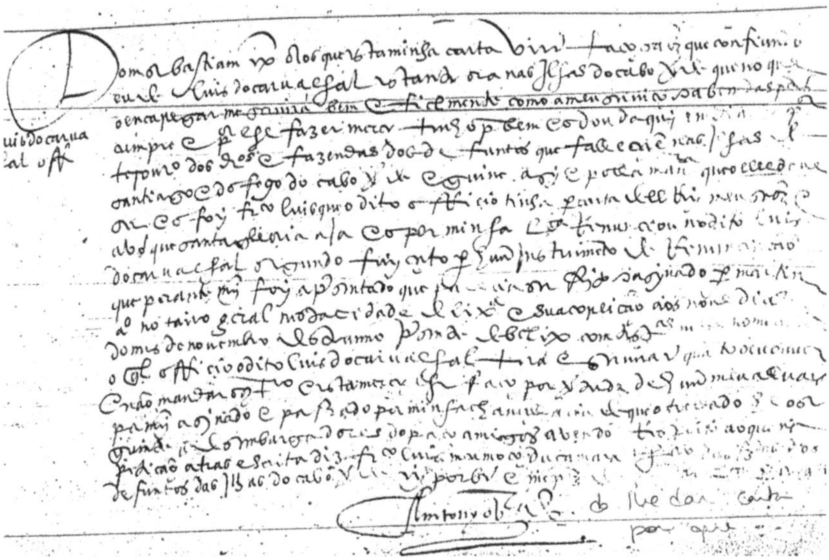

Fig. 1.4. Carvajal's appointment as treasurer in Cape Verde and Guinea.

As discussed earlier, Duarte de León was a Crown contractor in Cape Verde, meaning that he could participate in the whatever trade existed between Portugal and Guinea. His agent in S. Domingos, a Portuguese settlement in Guinea, now a city in Guinea-Bissau, was his brother Francisco, who seems to have become the highest military leader there under the name of Francisco de Andrade. It is therefore likely that young Carvajal was initially under Francisco's supervision.

During the early part of his thirteen years in Cape Verde Carvajal probably learned accounting and other business skills from uncle Duarte. It is also possible that he received some military training from uncle Francisco. However, in 1589 Carvajal only mentioned that he had been "treasurer and accountant for the king of Portugal."[58] A recently-found document confirms what Carvajal said. That document, shown in figure 1.4, is a royal decree appointing Luis de Carvalhal as the "treasurer of the rights [*direitos*] and assets of those who died in the islands of Santiago and Fogo, of Cape Verde, and in Guinea."[59]

The appointment makes it evident that his years in Spain had not erased his knowledge of Portuguese, an ability that must have helped him get that royal position. And the fact that he could also function well in Spanish must have been useful to Spanish businessmen in their trading activities in Cape Verde, and to Portuguese businessmen trading in the Spanish world. Although hard evidence has not surfaced, it is likely that Carvajal traveled with the traders to the New World. A particularly important destination was the Spanish island of Hispaniola. Perhaps not coincidentally, Miguel Núñez was then living in Santo Domingo, either as a businessman serving, as he said, the needs of the traders or, as Carvajal said, as the Portuguese Crown representative in that trade. Finally, given that Carvajal later become a master of a merchant ship, it is clear that he learned something about ships and seafaring from the masters of those ships in which he traveled while he lived in Cape Verde.

Carvajal stay in Cape Verde ended in late 1563, for that year he was given a license so that he "could go to the court to negotiate his business for a period of two years."[60] Thus, it is likely that he left Ribeira Grande in early 1564. This date is important because it provides the needed information to construct a chronology for him. Thus, since he spent thirteen years there, it follows that he left Benavente no later than 1551. Further, since he was born in 1537, it follows that he was about fourteen years old when he left that city.

At the time of his departure from Cape Verde he was twenty seven years old and was probably thinking it was time to get married and to try his fortune elsewhere. And so, he went to Lisbon, supposedly to try to obtain a more rewarding position from the Crown than the one he had held in Ribeira Grande. However, it seems that he had something else in mind, for after a short stay in Lisbon he went to Seville.

This raises the question as to why, having been in the Portuguese world for such a long time, did he want to leave it. After all, uncle Duarte lived in Lisbon and could easily help him negotiate a better position. A possible answer is that Seville was then the center of the commercial trade between the Spanish New World and Spain, and so he might have thought that because of his Spanish upbringing, his opportunities would be better there than in Lisbon.

A more likely explanation is that Miguel Núñez, being active in the Portuguese slave trade, had met Carvajal earlier, either in Cape Verde or in Santo Domingo, or, as mentioned before, in Lisbon during Carvajal's earlier stay there. It is possible that Núñez had told Carvajal about the business opportunities in Seville and about his two unmarried daughters. It is not known whether this conversation took place, but contemporary documents show that only a few months after leaving Cape Verde, Carvajal went to Seville where he married Guiomar Núñez, the oldest daughter of Miguel Núñez and

Blanca Rodríguez.[61] Incidentally, the name of the other daughter was Isabel Núñez, the same as Carvajal's paternal aunt and the same as Miguel Núñez's mother.[62] While this does not prove a blood relationship between Carvajal and Guiomar, it does provide some support for that possibility.

After his wedding, Carvajal resided in Seville for about two years, which he spent as a merchant in the wheat trade, probably in partnership with his father-in-law. This was an important business in the sixteenth century and Carvajal's experience in maritime travel was useful because the enterprise required the transportation of wheat by water. Although lucrative, the business was somewhat unreliable because wheat production in any one area was not consistent from one year to the next. Also, bad weather, or unscrupulous activities among the sailors, could result in losing the cargo.[63] Apparently something went wrong one day, for in his arraignment before the inquisitors Carvajal said that he lost some of his capital in a wheat contract, implying that it was that loss that made him decide to try something different.

This was unlikely. Later events show that his assets were not small. Rather, having established himself as a talented and capable man and having learned about the many opportunities in the New World, a plan was designed to extend the family business to the Spanish colonies where his upbringing in the castle of a Spanish Grandee would prove useful. It is at this point that the narrative switches to the New World, starting with his first known voyage to New Spain, considered next.

To New Spain

*The first time that I entered this New Spain . . . I came as the Almirante of a
fleet that was formed . . . in the island of La Palma by means of a royal cédula
but without salary.*

Luis de Carvajal, 1589.[1]

A little more than three years after leaving Cape Verde, Carvajal made
another significant change in his life. Whether he had suffered a financial
setback or not, he wanted to find a more rewarding activity than trading in
wheat. To him, an ambitious man of thirty, the New World offered many
opportunities and no place there offered more than New Spain. This chapter
considers his first known voyage to that Spanish colony as well as his initial
activities there, including one as the leading Crown officer in Tampico.

1. THE FIRST VOYAGE TO NEW SPAIN

Before going to New Spain in 1567, Carvajal had been engaged in the wheat
business with his father in law. This involved buying wheat where cultivated,
transporting it to places where it was needed, and selling it there. This he did
for about two years, but a bad contract made him look for a different activity.
That is what he told the inquisitors. More likely, having heard the fables about
the lands on the other side of the *Mar Océano*, as the Atlantic was then called,
he must have thought of trying his fortune there. It is also likely that Duarte de
León, his maternal uncle, and Miguel Núñez, his father-in-law, endorsed the
idea and probably provided some money to help their young relative achieve
his goal. The only question was how to proceed. Of course, Carvajal was well
acquainted with the commercial traffic between Seville and the New World,
and knew that in order to participate in it he would have to get a permit from
the Crown through the House of Trade. He also knew that those who wished
to take merchandise to the Spanish colonies in their own ships would have to
join one of the official fleets that each year departed from Seville. However, he

had lived in that city only a short time and could not get the required permits. The same was true of Miguel Núñez, who had tried to get one in 1571 but was initially turned down.[2]

Of course, there were other ways to achieve his goals. On his voyages between Cape Verde and Lisbon Carvajal must have made port many times in one of the Canary Islands (see Map 1 on page 2) and was therefore aware that merchant ships from those islands could either join the Seville fleet, or could form their own fleets provided they be accompanied by two armed ships, both commanded by Crown-appointed officers. These two ships were the *Capitana*—or flagship— leading the fleet, and the *Almiranta*, in the rear-guard, protecting it. In this respect, the Canary Island's fleets did not differ from those from Seville, except that the Crown did not provide either of the two required ships.

Although the Crown had allowed Canary Island merchants to send their goods directly to the Spanish colonies, it had also imposed many restrictions on the traffic. Particularly important was the long-standing order that Jews, Moors and New Christians should not be allowed to go to the New World.[3] Other orders dictated that no foreigner—particularly Portuguese—should be allowed to go there.[4] However, the orders had proved to be ineffective. This induced the king to appoint judges in those islands whose role was to insure that the regulations were followed. These judges also had the final say on whether a fleet would be allowed to depart and, if it were, had the responsibility of naming its General and its *Almirante*.

The first person to be appointed as *Juez Oficial* in the Canary Islands was Francisco de Vera. The appointing cédula states that he should reside in La Palma "so that from there he attends the dispatch of the ships that from those islands would be sent to our Indies. . . . And that those ships should only be registered in La Palma."[5] The choice of La Palma was dictated by its western position within the archipelago. That location, being closer to the New World than most of the other islands, made it the best suited point of departure for the longest part of the voyage. Although the appointment order was signed in January of 1564, Vera did not arrive in La Palma until March or April of that year. His service ended when his replacement, Gaspar Maldonado, arrived in the second half of May of 1567. In any event the inspection system was in place by 1567, when Carvajal left La Palma for the New World.

Strictly speaking Carvajal could not go to the New World because he was Portuguese. However, that origin was not apparent because his demeanor was that of a Spanish nobleman. On the other hand, he did not have a certificate of *limpieza de sangre*, that is, proof that his ancestors had been Christian for at least three generations, or, simply stated, that he was not a New Christian. This could have been a serious impediment in Seville, where the officers of the House of Trade would have demanded that certificate, but not in the Canary islands, where the review system was lax. Knowing this, Carvajal proceeded with his plans. What he wanted to do was to settle in a place in the New World that offered riches. New Spain seemed to be the best choice. It apparently had an unlimited amount of silver, was closer to the Canaries than Perú, also famous for its silver, and was next to large territories that had not yet been conquered or even explored. It is possible that another factor for selecting New Spain was that he knew some people there, including his brother Antonio, his maternal uncles Francisco de Andrade and Jorge de León de Andrade, and his nephew Gaspar de Carvajal.

The next step was to decide how to get there. Carvajal could, of course, travel as a passenger in one of the ships leaving La Palma, but he either owned a ship or could buy one that could be used to take merchandise and passengers to the New World. However, a better way was available to him. As stated in the previous chapter, he was also versed in seafaring and in military matters. These abilities were useful to those merchants in the Canary Islands who were in need of qualified individuals to serve as officers in their fleets, particularly if they could provide their own ship. And so, it appears that Carvajal was recruited to serve as the Almirante of a Canary Island fleet.

Some of the events that followed were described briefly by Carvajal during his Inquisition trial in 1589 and earlier and in more detail by several eye-witnesses whose affidavits appear in a 1578 document that surfaced only recently. The formal title of the document is given in the notes. For simplicity it is referred here as the *Méritos de Carvajal.*[6] From this document it appears that Carvajal went to Seville where he purchased a *Galeaza.*[7] This was a fairly large type of ship which in the second half of the sixteenth century was mainly used as a warship because it could be equipped with heavy artillery.

Having purchased and armed his ship to make it suitable to serve as the fleet's Almiranta, Carvajal loaded it with some merchandise—mostly wine— and went to La Palma where he took some passengers. The date of departure to the New World can be estimated from other records. One was the affidavit of the fleet's scribe who said that the fleet had ten or more ships under the command of General Rodrigo de Loranca, and that it "was dispatched by Pedro de Estopiñán, lieutenant of Francisco de Vera, Juez Oficial appointed by H.M."[8] Another document shows that Vera had left La Palma by mid May of 1567 leaving Pedro de Estopiñán in charge, thus confirming what the fleet's scribe said years later.⁹ Finally, as stated earlier, Gaspar Maldonado had arrived in La Palma late May. Thus, the fleet must have left La Palma soon afterward.

The route followed by Carvajal's fleet was the same as that used by the Seville fleet after it passed by La Palma, ten to fifteen days after leaving Spain. From La Palma the fleet would begin the longest, non-interrupted part of the voyage across the Atlantic. Thirty to thirty five days later it would, if everything went well, reach *La Deseada*, one of the islands east of Puerto Rico. At that point the ships going to *Tierra Firme* (South America) would separate from those going to New Spain. These would head for the island Hispaniola, often making port at Ocoa, near Santo Domingo, on the southern part of the island. That portion of the trip would last about ten days. The final destination would be San Juan de Ulúa, in New Spain, which would be reached some twenty days later. Thus, a typical, one-way voyage from Seville to San Juan de Ulúa would take about two and a half months. If the duration of Carvajal's fleet was typical, it probably arrived in New Spain late July or early August of 1567. As hinted in the epigraph at the head of this chapter, this was not the first time Carvajal had traveled to New Spain.

On this occasion, Carvajal's fleet made a stop in Santo Domingo where it took water and other supplies. It also took in more passengers. Among them were the governor of Jamaica and an important man named D. Pedro de Arellano.¹⁰ Also boarding Carvajal's galeaza as a passenger was Manuel de Morales, a Portuguese physician, who, years later, was burnt in effigy at an *Auto-da-fe* in Mexico City.

Continuing the voyage, the fleet went to Jamaica, but as they approached it, they saw, ahead of them, three ships that did not seem to be Spanish. Fearing that they might belong to pirates, the fleet's general, and the captains of the other ships went to the Almiranta to discuss with Carvajal what the next step should be.¹¹ The normal action would have been to ascertain who owned those ships, and to board them in case there were foreign. However, because the galeaza was too large to follow them into the port, Carvajal and half of the men in the fleet went after them using small boats, but by the time they caught up with them, the ships were anchored. Noticing that they were indeed foreign, Carvajal and his men boarded them, only to find that they had been abandoned. As it turned out the ships belonged to French corsairs who were trading, illegally, in the Spanish world. In their rush to escape they left behind their merchandise, mostly leather goods. The governor of Jamaica, who had accompanied Carvajal in his pursuit of the corsairs, told him that he would find and prosecute them, and that the goods they were carrying should be left with him because Jamaica was his jurisdiction, to which Carvajal consented. In his self-defense, Carvajal stated that he surrendered the pirates' ships, which only meant that his pursuit forced the pirates to abandon their ships. Of course, he had no way of knowing that the ships had been abandoned, a fact that he felt gave some merit to his actions.

After releasing the corsair's ships and their contents to the governor, Carvajal and his people returned to their ships and continued their voyage. A few days later the fleet arrived in their final destination, the island-port of San Juan de Ulúa, across the city of Veracruz in the mainland.[12] There, Carvajal had his wine caskets unloaded and sent to Mexico City and Zacatecas, where they were sold by his agents. It is not known who these agents were, but it is likely that they told him about the many opportunities that existed in New Spain. At that time the most profitable business there was silver, and Zacatecas was then the most important silver center in New Spain. However, that city was located on the frontier of the yet unconquered region, which the Spaniards referred to as *Tierra Adentro*. Carvajal must have heard a great deal about the ferocious Indians who lived there. More interesting must have been the stories about some mysterious lands, somewhere to the north, lands that, supposedly, had gold.

Those stories must have been irresistible to a man of Carvajal's nature. No other activity could possibly be more enticing to him than the discovery of lands that supposedly had precious metals and Indians to extract them. This was the dream of every European adventurer arriving in the New World in the sixteenth century and Carvajal was no exception. However, contrary to most of them, Carvajal had at his disposal a fair amount of money to support his attempts to fulfill his dreams.

As stated before it would seem reasonable to speculate that Carvajal had a plan of action in New Spain. Subsequent events show that he had kept all the weapons from his ship, but it is not known what he decided to do with the ship itself. However, that decision was essentially irrelevant to the course of events that took place in the following twenty two years.

2. New Spain in 1567

In 1519 a Spanish armada consisting of eleven ships and 540 men under the command of Hernán Cortés arrived at the shores of a land in the New World that was unknown to them. After landing they were received by emissaries of Moctezuma II, commonly known as Montezuma, the emperor of a large

Fig. 2.1. Ortelius map of New Spain.

nation that many years later was to be called the Aztecs. The Aztec Empire had its seat in the great City of Tenochtitlán, some 300 miles away and thousands of feet above the landing site, named Villa Rica de la Vera Cruz by the Spaniards. From that city the Aztecs dominated a vast area that included several other Indian nations. As subjects these nations paid tribute to their lords, a tribute that included a number of young men to be sacrificed in the great temple in Tenochtitlán.

In spite of their far superior weapons, the Spaniards could not, because of their small number, defeat the Aztecs. Nevertheless, they managed to achieve that goal two years later thanks to the help of the Tlaxcaltecs, an independent Indian nation that had been an enemy of the Aztecs.[13] This feat enabled the Spaniards to become the new landlords of most of the lands that had formed the Aztec Empire. Those lands become known as New Spain. Tenochtitlán was adopted by the Spaniards as their own seat of power, although they renamed it as (City of) México because its Indian inhabitants called themselves the Meshica (or Mexica, using the sixteenth century Spanish pronunciation of the letter x). Soon after the conquest the Spaniards began to attempt to extend their dominions, with incursions into areas of the Aztec Empire that were part of it but on a semi-autonomous basis. An idea of the physical setting at the time Carvajal arrived in New Spain can be gathered from a map ascribed to Ortelius and referred to as the *Hispaniae Novae Map*, a reduced copy of which is shown in figure 2.1. While the map is dated 1579, it was drawn on the basis of information gathered years earlier. Also, the ability of explorers and navigators to pinpoint the location of a place was quite limited. Thus, while latitudes could be determined fairly accurately, an accurate method measurement of longitude was not yet available.

The map shows three different land areas, two of which display a large number of named places, and a third, nearly empty, mostly covered by the map's title. As stated above, the Spanish conquest left the Spaniards in possession of most of the territory that had been under the control of the Aztecs, as well as in a good position to conquer adjacent lands. These additional conquests included the Pánuco region to the northeast of México City, and the Petén area to the southeast.[14] A few years later Nuño de Guzmán conquered the Tarascan empire to the west, and named it Nueva Galicia.[15] Much later, in 1554, Diego the Ibarra conquered lands to the northwest, which become known as Nueva Viscaya.[16]

The lands initially conquered by Cortés appear in the original map in green, and are shown by the dark grey area in figure 2.1. Slightly to south of the two dark spots in that area is Mexico City, whose name appears there simply as México. Nueva Galicia was the populated land to the west and northwest, and Nueva Vizcaya occupied the sparsely populated lands to the north and west of present day Zacatecas, which appears in the map's top-center as Çacatecas. Finally, the *empty* area to the north and northeast of the dark grey area—mostly covered by the map's title—remained unexplored and in possession of the Chichimeca. This was the name given by the Aztecs, and then by the Spaniards, to a number of primitive, semi-nomadic tribes who had been able to resist subjugation.

By the time Carvajal arrived, the area south of the Chichimeca region was considered to be pacified, that is, under Spanish control. However, even there some of the conquered Indians continued to rebel in their attempt to regain their freedom from Spanish subjugation. The reasons for these uprisings are easy to understand. After the conquest, the Spanish put in use the *Encomienda* and *Repartimiento* systems, whereby the Indians in conquered regions would be distributed among the Spanish conquerors and forced to work in their mines, fields, and houses.[17] Although those systems were ostensibly set up to help indoctrinate the Indians, they actually exploited them. In addition, near slavery was practiced everywhere in New Spain from the earliest times after the conquest. In this practice, the service of those Indians accused with even minor charges, real or false, would be sold for a number of years.[18]

Except for the accidental travels of a few Europeans, such as those of Álvar Núñez Cabeza de Vaca in 1528–1536, the Chichimeca territory had remained unexplored.[19] Further to the northwest there were advanced native nations that had been the focus of several formal expeditions, for example, the 1540–42 expeditions of Father Niza and Juan Vázquez Coronado to the legendary lands of Cibola and Quivira.[20] Other expeditions took place later, particularly to Nuevo México, but these occurred after Carvajal's arrival in New Spain.

Governance

Although the Spanish possessions were divided into several provinces, there was a central government, headed by a viceroy who was appointed by the king. The viceroy also presided over the *Real Audiencia de México*, the highest court in the land, and was in charge of all military activities in New Spain.

The Audiencia was a very important ingredient in the governance of New Spain as it ruled on all matters of law and could be overruled only by the king. Officially, it consisted of a president and four to six *oidores*, or judges. While the viceroy formally presided over that body, he could not vote on judicial matters, unless he was a *letrado*, that is, unless he had studied law. During

Carvajal's years in New Spain, no viceroy had such an education, although Luis de Velasco II, viceroy of New Spain from 1590 to 1595 and from 1607 to 1611, seems to have studied for a while in Salamanca.

The Audiencia de México was installed in Mexico City in 1527. Later on, in 1548, another Audiencia was created in Nueva Galicia, first in Compostela but later moved to Guadalajara. Although the Audiencia de Nueva Galicia was initially subservient to that in Mexico City, it become an independent body in the early 1570s, a fact that created considerable friction between the viceroy and the Crown officers in Nueva Galicia. As discussed in later chapters, both audiencias played important roles in Carvajal's life.

Under the viceroy there were the governors of the various kingdoms that had been formally established. At the time of Carvajal's arrival in New Spain, there were two of these: Nueva Galicia and Nueva Vizcaya. Although the governors formally served under the viceroy, they ruled with a great deal of independence. At the local level there were a variety of officers, the most important of which were *alcalde mayor* and *alcalde ordinario*. The first of these was reserved for officers in charge of large areas or of towns having a sizable population. These and other minor offices were sold by the Crown.

While the viceroy served at the pleasure of the king and nearly always asked him to decide most important matters, in reality he did what he wished. Time and distance were on his side. If the king decided something else, the viceroy could always cover up his mistakes. Also, if any complaints about him managed to reach Spain, the king would seldom react, and if he did, a long time would pass before his reaction would be known in New Spain. Sometimes, however, the news arriving in Spain from the New World would be sufficiently worrisome that the king would appoint a *visitador*, or independent examiner, with special powers to review the actions of the viceroy, or those of some other high-level officer. Sometimes these *visitas*, also called *residencias*, would result in some suspensions. Of course, normal visitas would also take place after important officers had completed their terms of appointment, but these visitas were not intended to be punitive.

Fig. 2.2. Viceroy Gastón de Peralta.

Political conditions

The above remarks give a rough idea about New Spain when Carvajal first arrived there, but do not address its political conditions in any way. As it turns out, New Spain was then in upheaval because of the supposed incompetence of Viceroy Gastón de Peralta, Marqués de Falces, who had been suspended, and because of a conspiracy among some of the most powerful individuals then living in Mexico City. That conspiracy had its beginnings in the early 1560s and apparently had to do with the desire by some to break away from Spain. One of its leaders was D. Martin Cortés, the legitimate son of Hernán Cortés. When the conspiracy was discovered, a notice was sent to the king, who on 16 June 1567 appointed two *visitadores*: Alonso Muñóz, and Luis Carrillo, to investigate its roots.[21] While the actions of these individuals had a strong impact on the colony, this is not the place to describe them in detail. Suffice it to say that by 1567 several leading citizens had been executed and others, such as D. Martín, had been tortured, sowing terror among the European inhabitants of Mexico City. However, complaints of these events had reached the king, who late that year appointed two other visitadores, Luis de Villanueva and Vasco de Puga, ordering them to go to New Spain to stop the atrocities. The crises ended after Villanueva and Puga arrived in Mexico City on 13 April 1568 and presented Muñóz and Carrillo the king's order, which discharged them of their duties.

It is not known whether these troubling conditions were of any significance outside Mexico City. Also, although Gastón de Peralta had appealed his suspension, the king had already named another viceroy. This was Martín Enríquez, who arrived in New Spain in 1568 and who is said to have been one of the best viceroys that served in New Spain.[22] As discussed in later chapters Enríquez played a most important role in the ascendancy of Carvajal.

3. Settling in Tampico

As stated earlier, Carvajal had apparently planned to remain in New Spain to seek his fortune. It is likely that he had planned a business venture there; after all, he had been engaged in trading for a good part of his life. Thus, after selling his wine, he and Capt. Sebastián Rodríguez bought a cattle ranch from Lope de Sosa.[23] While raising cattle was a profitable business in New Spain at the time, it was not the occupation Carvajal had in mind.

A hint about his plans is offered by the fact that the hacienda he purchased was not far from Tampico, then a small village located on the northern frontier of New Spain. Beyond that frontier were the feared Chichimeca who controlled the lands coveted by the Spaniards. It was in these lands that Carvajal established a solid reputation as an effective Crown officer. The services he performed there in the first year after his arrival will be examined later on. However, because that province plays a very important role in his life, it is useful to first describe its conditions when he arrived in 1567.

Pánuco and the Chichimeca frontier

The province of Pánuco had been initially conquered by Cortés himself, but it was not until later that Nuño de Guzmán began to settle and explore its northern region.[24] By the time Carvajal arrived, the largest towns in the region were San Luis de Tampico; San Esteban del Puerto, later known simply as Pánuco, located some seven leagues from the coast; and Santiago de los Valles, the oldest town in the province, further west. Near Tampico the province was limited on the north by the river Pánuco. West and south of Valles the province was bordered by the Sierra Madre Oriental, a high and massive mountain range separating the it from the high Mexican Plateau. To the north of the Pánuco river there were no physical barriers impeding the Spanish expansion of their territories. However, that region belonged to the Chichimeca. Although the Spaniards had attempted to settle the immediate area north of that river prior to 1567, the attempts had failed.

The region that concerns this chapter included territories on both sides of the Pánuco river, as well as lands to the west of Tampico. That area was known as the Guasteca, or Huasteca. Its extent can be appreciated from another map by Ortelius which is shown in figure 2.3. Although the names of the places in it are difficult to read, the map can be used to guide the discussion that follows. The map, made around 1580, shows many small settlements whose population is represented by the size of the church icons and by their number of bell towers. For example, Valles appears in the map as S. Iago Vallum. Its icon shows two bell towers, whereas Tampico, appearing in the map as Tampice, has none.

To the south of Tampico, Pánuco, and Valles, the area was well on its way to be under complete control of the Spaniards, except for the mountainous regions to the south, where Indian rebellions continued to occur. But to north and northwest lived the Chichimeca, who continued to attack the Spanish settlers living close to the frontier. These attacks hampered the growth of those settlements because they involved significant loss of life and property. According to contemporary records, more than 400 Spaniards had been killed before 1567 north of Tampico alone. To the west, the region included some settlements and towns, but the Indians living in them, who had previously

Fig. 2.3. Ortelius map of the Guasteca made around 1580.

been conquered and baptized, continued to rebel against the Spaniards, as it will be seen later in more detail. An idea about the conditions that prevailed there may be gathered from several documents written around the time of Carvajal's arrival in New Spain. The first is a letter from Fray Pedro de San Luis who stated that he had entered the Chichimeca territory several times and that:

> The fourth time I entered from a town named Tames. . . . And since this town was next to the Chichimeca, these have perverted them and destroyed their crops in such a manner that all of our work would be for nil if these are not punished or exiled from there, because they not only have destroyed all in the Guasteca and all in Pánuco, but also in the road to Zacatecas . . . where they kill and rob many people and make many damages.[25]

Very clearly, the close proximity of the "pacified lands" to the Chichimeca territory made life quite difficult to the Spanish settler living in the frontier. Although not comparable, European settlers in the American Southwest probably experienced similar difficulties three hundred years later.

Returning to 1567, European life in the frontier near Tampico and Pánuco was also hampered by economic issues. These are discussed in a petition to the king made a few months before Carvajal's arrival. The petition, initiated by the leading officers of those two villages, asked that large ships coming directly from Spain be allowed to anchor in their ports. Apparently, the request had been denied.[26] Because of that denial, they said, the people living in the region had started to leave it. Juan Lorenzo, one of the witnesses presented by those officers added that "arriving the ships form Castile to said ports, the population would increase, and those who reside there would greatly profit."[27]

These were good arguments, but what mattered most to the Crown were the revenues it would receive and the conversion of the Indians. Knowing this another witness, stated that:

> If the king were to allow ships from Spain to come directly to Tampico, the Chichimeca . . . would be fearful and would come to peace and become Christian, all of which would benefit the royal treasury. . . . But that if the king did not favor the province, it would be abandoned, and without Spaniards the infidel Chichimeca would enter it easily, taking it and forcing the converted Indians to return to their pagan rites.[28]

These statements clearly show that the province where Carvajal first settled was not yet stable and that two things hampered progress: One was the neighboring Chichimeca who sporadically attacked pacified towns, endangering the lives of the Spaniards and of the Indians who already were "in the service of H.M." Another was that the price of Spanish goods brought from Spain to Tampico and Pánuco was excessive. The reason for such high prices is not difficult to understand. By royal decree, goods from Spain could enter New Spain only through Veracruz and would then be sent to Mexico City from where they would be distributed to other places in the colony.

A different issue was related to the silver from the mines in Nueva Galicia and Nueva Vizcaya, which had to be transported to Veracruz via Mexico City. Not only was this a long distance, but also, the road from Zacatecas to Mexico City was not secure. The problem had become more acute when new silver mines were discovered in Mazapil, a village situated north of Zacatecas. The Pánuco settlers had, for a long time, hoped that the silver traffic would take place through their province. This, however, required that several problems had to be solved first. One was the large-ship issue referred to above. Another was that powerful interests in both Mexico City and Veracruz did not want to lose their share of that traffic. But the most difficult obstacle was the *Sierra Madre Oriental,* a high mountain chain that impeded the communications between Zacatecas and Tampico. Although some believed that a passage existed that would facilitate its crossing is, no serious attempt had so far been made to find it. Furthermore, if one could be found, it would have to be through Chichimeca land. Thus, the idea had been set aside by 1567.

As for the Chichimeca, the problem was that the Spaniards had not yet been able to vanquish them, nor would they be able to entirely do so for another 200 years. Thus, in a report written in 1748, an observer noted that "pagan Indians who had not been conquered lived in the border of ... Nuevo México, Nueva Vizcaya, Nuevo Reino de León, Coahuila, and Tejas."[29]

In spite of these problems, the region continued to attracted new European settlers who wanted to expand it. However, only few of them were sufficiently wealthy or militarily inclined to undertake that task. One of these was Carvajal, although, initially, he seemed interested in raising cattle.

4. ALCALDE ORDINARIO

Although the exact location of Carvajal's hacienda is not known, it must have been near Tampico because it was there that he built a house in 1567. By 1568 he had become Tampico's highest magistrate. The appointment was reported by Juan Lorenzo, then official scribe of Tampico, who said that:

> When said Luis de Carvajal was received as a burgher, this witness was the scribe for the council and wrote the corresponding document. And because he was an important person, he was named alcalde the following year.[30]

The reference to Carvajal being an important person simply meant that he was a wealthy man. As such he was able to outbid others in purchasing that office, a fact that caused some resentment among older residents of Tampico. For example, Diego Ramírez, one of the founders of Tampico said, sarcastically, that he had seen Carvajal use the charge of alcalde ordinario *regal* (emphasis added).[31] Although Lorenzo did not state the date of the appointment, events discussed later show that Carvajal had that position during 1568.

From the beginning Carvajal displayed a concern in the affairs of the town, and "would help in the service of God and H.M., and in the attacks that the Chichimeca made, and that he would come with his arms to what was needed to fight them and that he would give arms to others so that they could come in the defense of the town."[32] The statement shows that Carvajal must have had a small arsenal, most likely obtained from the ship he commanded on his voyage from the Canary Islands.

To the rescue

One of the first services that Carvajal performed as alcalde ordinario was the rescue of Dr. Luis de Villanueva, a past oidor of the Audiencia. The incident was reported to the king by Viceroy Enríquez years after it occurred:

> Attempting to arrive to this New Spain, the ship of Dr. Villanueva foundered on the coast and in *Tierra de Guerra* of Chichimeca, who every day threw arrows at them. And having walked many leagues by foot without having anything to eat, they arrived in the village of Tampico.[33]

The inclusion of that incident in a letter from viceroy to the king makes it clear that the event was deemed important. It is also noted that Enríquez did not mention Carvajal in his letter, which is not surprising. The issue at hand was Villanueva, not Carvajal.[34]

The rescue of Villanueva is described in another document that states, in part, that:

> Having received notice that in a ship in which Dr. Villanueva ... had foundered in the Río de Palmas, Tierra de Guerra, Capt. Luis de Carvajal went to help them with people, food, horses and arms.[35]

Backing this claim was Dr. Villanueva himself, who said that:

> When this witness was coming [to New Spain] ... the ship in which he came foundered in the coast of La Florida, in Tierra de Guerra. And together with him thirty three men on foot ... and he saw how said Luis de Carvajal, with people, came to the encounter to succor him, and brought horses and supplies. And that without the succor and the provisions ... it would have been impos-

sible to arrive alive to land of peace because for eleven days they had only eaten herbs, and that the water they had drank was from near the sea . . . and they were very fatigued.[36]

Of course, getting food was important to Villanueva, but the fact that the rescue took place in Tierra de Guerra made it meritorious in the eyes of other Crown officers. For example, Alonso Ortiz de Zúñiga, the alcalde mayor of the province, stated that Carvajal had "performed a great service in the rescue of very lucid people, among them a person of importance and class." Apparently Ortiz was so impressed with Carvajal that he appointed him as lieutenant of alcalde mayor to make the necessary inquiries and reports.

It remains to determine the date when the rescue took place. Of course, it occurred in 1568, when Carvajal was alcalde ordinario in Tampico. A more precise time is fixed by Juan de Urribarri, who said that "He knows that having gotten lost in the Río de Palmas the ship in which came Dr. Villanueva . . . which happened *before* (emphasis added) the Englishmen came."[37]

Fig. 2.4. Dr. Luis de Villanueva. (From the *Codex Mendoza*.)

The Englishmen referred to by Urribarri were a large number of people who were abandoned by John Hawkins north of Tampico in October of 1568. Thus, the rescue mission took place between January and October of 1568. This range is narrowed by other sources that deal with the arrival in Mexico city of Luis de Villanueva and Vasco de Puga on 13 April 1568, carrying letters from the king ordering Alonso Muñoz and Luis Carrillo to return immediately to Spain. Given the atrocities that these individuals had been inflicting on prominent inhabitants of the colony, one can only wonder what would have happened if Villanueva had not been rescued by Carvajal.

The next important event in Carvajal's life is related to the people that were abandoned on the shores of New Spain by John Hawkins. This event played a most important role in the ascendancy of Carvajal and is described in the next chapter.

3

The Pirates of John Hawkins

When I was alcalde ordinario in Tampico, there came one hundred Englishmen, of those that escaped with John Hawkins, and against the opinion of all the burghers, who of fear wanted to leave… I with twenty men went to them and surrendered them.
Luis de Carvajal, October 1589.[1]

In September of 1568 an English fleet under the command of John Hawkins arrived in San Juan de Ulúa, the gateway to New Spain. Hawkins, later knighted by Queen Elizabeth I, was regarded by the Spaniards as an illicit trader and contrabandist whose activities differed little from those of a pirate. His arrival resulted in one of the earliest maritime battles between England and Spain, a battle that ended with the near destruction of Hawkins' fleet and affected the relations between the two nations for years to come. These events are relevant to this work because Hawkins was forced to abandon many of his men north of Tampico. Although the main focus of this chapter refers to the encounter between the men left ashore and Carvajal, it is useful to present first a brief description of Hawkins' voyage, as it helps put the encounter in context.

I. The Third Voyage of John Hawkins

The voyage begun on 2 October 1567, when Hawkins' fleet left England on its way to Cape Verde.[2] The fleet consisted of six ships: two of which, the *Jesus of Lubeck*, the flagship, and the *Minion*, the Almiranta, to use the Spanish term for the better-armed ship, were said to belong to the English Crown. The other ships were the *Angel*, the *Swallow*, the *William and John*, and the *Judith*, commanded by Francis Drake, also knighted later by Elizabeth I. Before sailing plans were made to meet in Tenerife, one of the Canary Islands, but seven days after departure, the fleet encountered a storm that dispersed it. On the 11th the weather changed allowing them to proceed. However, only some ships, including the *Jesus*, in which Hawkins traveled, made it to Tenerife. The remaining ships in the fleet had gone to La Gomera, forcing him to leave Tenerife in order to join them, although, according to his narrative the reason for leaving was that he suspected an attack by the Spaniards.[3] The Spanish account of Hawkins' departure is somewhat different. The governor of the Canary Islands at that time was Eugenio de Salazar, a distinguished jurist and writer who years later played a very important role in the downfall of Carvajal.[4] In a letter he wrote to the king he stated that what he did soon after he arrived in Tenerife "was to send away from the port of Santa Cruz in the island of Tenerife, much against his wishes, John Hawkins famous English corsair who was anchored in the port with an armada of the Queen of England that had four large ships."[5]

In any event, on November 4, Hawkins' fleet left La Gomera and went toward the coast of Guinea, arriving there on the 18th of the same month. Their purpose was to "obtain some Negroes." Hawkins experienced considerable difficulties in achieving his goal, but by the time his fleet left Guinea early February of 1568, he and his men had "obtained between four and five hundred Negroes." These he hoped to sell in the Spanish New World, where they were in high demand. Now, selling slaves there required a royal permit, which they did not have. Nevertheless, Hawkins managed, as he put it, "to do a reasonable trade" with the Spaniards. One place where he was able to do as he wanted was in Río de la Hacha, a port in present-day Colombia. After arriving there, he sent a letter to Miguel de Castellanos, the Crown treasurer in that port, "asking him to permit his burghers to do business with him and to buy his Negroes," but according to both Hawkins and Robert Barrett, the master of the *Minion*, Castellanos denied the request. Seeing that he was not permitted to do business, "Hawkins landed about three hundred men . . . and took the town and ordered certain old houses to be burned."[6]

As it turns out, Miguel de Castellanos reported the events to his king, stating in part that

> John Hawkins, English corsair, arrived off the port of this city. . . . As soon as he arrived . . . he sent me a letter in which he offered me great gifts if I permitted him to trade; and if I would not, he made great threats. I answered him . . . that I would by no means yield a single point. . . . In view of my determination . . . he landed his forces . . .[7]

Things were different in Cartagena. There the Spanish officials, having heard what had happened in Río de la Hacha, had prepared a strong defense and were able to prevent the landing. Hawkins version of what happened was that they could do no business with the Spaniards because "the governor was so strait . . . and because . . . we thought not good either to adventure any landing or to detract further time, but in peace departed thence the 24th of July hoping to have escaped the time of their storms." Nevertheless, the fleet was caught in "an extreme storm" on the 12th of August which badly damaged the *Jesus*.

2. SAN JUAN DE ULÚA

After the storm passed, Hawkins sought refuge along the coast of La Florida, that is, north of Tampico, where "we found no place nor haven to our ships." But while looking for a safe port they boarded and took a Spanish ship owned by a wine merchant who advised him that the only port that could accommodate large ships was San Juan de Ulúa. On the way there, Hawkins took two other vessels which belonged to a prominent burgher of Mexico City.[8] Finally, according to all accounts, the fleet docked in the island-port of San Juan de Ulúa. The date was 16 September 1568.

As it turns out, the Spaniards had been expecting the Spanish fleet for some days and, on seeing so many ships arriving, they sent a boat to greet them, thinking it was that fleet. Realizing their error, they become alarmed, although according to Hawkins, they felt much more relaxed when they were told he only wanted "to repair his ships and to buy victuals."

The Spanish accounts of Hawkins' arrival confirm the initial confusion. For example, Antonio Delgadillo, captain of the port, stated that on sighting the English ships, "which vessels this deponent supposed to be the fleet from Spain," and that after realizing his mistake "he attempted to make use of his artillery and of the people of the port, for defense, but not a man stood by excepting eight persons."[9] Seeing this, Hawkins took the fortified port and evicted the Spaniards left in it, actions that produced havoc in Veracruz, the mainland city across from San Juan de Ulúa. Later, he sent a letter to the authorities in Mexico City in which he requested that he be permitted to repair his flagship and to buy food.

Fig. 3.1. Viceroy Martín Enríquez.

The very next day, 17 September 1568, the Spanish fleet, consisting of thirteen ships appeared on the horizon. The fleet was under the command of General Francisco de Luján and Almirante Juan de Ubilla. Traveling in it was the new viceroy of New Spain, D. Martín Enríquez. After being informed that the ships anchored in the port belonged to English corsairs, Enríquez sent a note to Hawkins telling him that they would enter the port in peace. On the 20th, after some back and forth negotiations, the Spanish ships anchored next to Hawkins'.

Things remained peaceful for a day or two, but on the 23rd, apparently having decided to attack Hawkins' ships, the Spaniards started to move equipment and personnel. Noticing unusual activities near his ships, Hawkins sent Robert Barrett to inquire about those activities, but Barrett was taken prisoner.

The precise sequence of events that took place afterwards are unclear. However, the records show that Ubilla gave the signal to attack ahead of the pre-arranged time. The crew of the *Jesus*, upon hearing the signal—the sound of a trumpet—took it to mean that the Spaniards were about to attack and fired the first shots, thus starting the battle.[10]

In the end Hawkins' fleet was nearly destroyed. Of the eight ships it had on arrival, only two, the *Minion* and the *Judith*, managed to escape. The *Judith* was "a small barque of fifty tons . . . which barque the same night forsook us in great misery" wrote Hawkins about his own escape in the *Minion*. However, in addition to its own men, the *Minion* now carried many others from those ships that were lost. Worse yet, it had little water and food. Realizing this, Hawkins decided to leave ashore one-half of the men on board, which he did on 8 October of 1568. Their exact number is unknown; Hawkins stated it was one hundred, perhaps rounding up a more exact figure. He also said he went ashore with his men to say good bye to each and to bless them, giving them some advice. He then re-embarked and headed for England, where he arrived on 25 January 1569, a few days after Drake.

The men left behind

The best-known accounts of what happened to those left ashore are those of Miles Phillips and Job Hortop, two of Hawkins' men.[11] Although both narratives convey the difficulties they encountered, they were written well after the events took place. A much earlier account was given by Anthony Goddard, the man chosen as captain by those abandoned on the shores of New Spain. Unfortunately, his account is short and, with one exception to be discussed later, gives almost no information about the encounter with Carvajal. Regarding the *Minion* and its people, Goddard stated that:

> He was in the flagship as a soldier of John Hawkins the day of the battle in San Juan de Ulúa, and that after he and other 200 men, boys, and wounded, run away from the port in a ship called the *Minion*. . . . And that he and about 90 others had gone ashore because Hawkins left them there because of the lack

of food and that afterwards . . . the Indians showed them the way to where the Spaniards were, to which all went and arrived at a town named Tampico, and that all in agreement, including himself, surrendered to the Spaniards . . .[12]

According to Hawkins, the landing took place at 23.5 degrees north, that is on the Tropic of Cancer. If true, this means that the men were left about 90 miles north of present-day Tampico, in Chichimeca territory. On land, they did find fresh water, which some drank in excess, making them weaker. Things got much worse the next day when they were attacked by Indians, who killed eight of them. Having no weapons to defend themselves, they surrendered quickly, after which the Indians took from them whatever they liked, leaving some "stark naked." But then, taking pity on them, the Indians "pointed us with their hands which way we should go to come to a town of the Spaniards, which, as we afterwards perceived, was not past ten leagues from thence, using these words: 'Tampeco, tampeco, Christiano, tampeco, Christiano.' "[13]

According to Phillips the landing party divided itself into two equal groups: one going north and the other south. Three members of the first group made it back to England, but most of them returned to the southbound group.[14] Together they traveled in the direction of Tampico while "being stricken by the Indians, which stood behind trees and bushes, in secret places, and so killed our men as they passed." This went on for about a week, by which time Phillips' reckoning shows that their number was 78.[15] Finally, weakened by starvation, they came to "a great river . . . and presently, after we heard an harquebuse shot off, which did greatly encourage us, for thereby we knew that we were near to some Christians. . . . And so we came to the north side of the river of Pánuco . . ." [16]

The shot they heard came from Spaniards who were on the south bank of that river. It meant, of course, that they had been sighted. However, the encounter was not encouraging:

> One of the Spaniards took an Indian boat, called a *canoa*, and so came over . . . and, having taken a view of us, did presently row over back again to the Spaniards, who without any delay made out about the number of twenty horseman . . . and being come to that side of the river where we were, they saddled their horses . . . with their lances charged, they came very fiercely running at us. Our captain, Anthony Goddard . . . did persuade us to submit and yield ourselves to them, for being . . . without weapon, we could not make any resistance. . . . And when we were all come to the town, the governor there showed himself very severe unto us, and threatened to hang us all; and then he demanded what money we had, which in truth was very little . . . but from Anthony Goddard the governor took a chain of gold . . . and from others a small story of money.

Hortop's account was slightly different:

> At our coming to the river of Pánuco two Spanish horsemen came over onto us
> in a Canowe: they asked us how long we had bene in the wildernesse, and where
> our general was. . . . They returned to their governor, who sent them with five
> Canowes to bring us all over, which done, they set us in aray, where a hundred
> horsemen with their lances came forceably upon us, but did not hurt us.

It should be noted that while the narratives by Phillips and Hortop agree
with one another in certain details, they differ in some others, particularly in
the number of Spaniards that attacked them.

Although Phillips did not remember the name of the governor who took
them prisoner, it is clear that the governor had caused a strong impression on
him. As the reader has anticipated, the governor's name was Luis de Carvajal.
Here is what Anthony Goddard said one year after the encounter:

> And they came to a town called Tampico after having surrendered to the
> Spaniards. And being there, an alcalde ordinario named Luis de Carvajal took
> from him a black velvet purse that had two gold chains, a gold image of our
> Lady, some gold earrings, a scabbard of fine pearls, a medallion that said '*mater
> de memento*', and six ducats. . . . And that he also took 34 pesos and a golden ring
> with an emerald stone that this deponent liked very much. And that this alcalde
> also ordered this deponent to tell the others to give him all gold and silver and
> all other valuables they had, and that otherwise he would hang all of them. And
> out of fear they gave him up to 400 ducats.[17]

The narratives of Phillips and Hortop also describe the events that took
place after they were sent to Mexico City, but say nothing about the reaction
of the Spaniards to their arrival to the port of Tampico. That reaction is
considered next.

3. THE SPANIARDS IN TAMPICO

Soon after the battle in San Juan de Ulúa, the Audiencia ordered the officers
in other towns and ports to be on the lookout for pirates. Not knowing who was
in charge in Tampico, they sent a letter to Diego Ramírez ordering him "that he
should . . . give order to all ports he could reach, from Havana and other parts,
[so that] they should know that the pirate John Hawkins had been in the port
and had left it, running away."[18] Although the order had not been sent to him,
Carvajal was the highest magistrate in Tampico and therefore assumed the
responsibility for defending the port. As explained later, this resulted in some
heated arguments between the two men that, according to the alcalde mayor
of the province of Pánuco, were resolved thanks to Carvajal's "good attitude."[19]

Of course, there were reasons to be alarmed: While the English fleet had been reduced to two ships, the Spaniards knew that Hawkins escaped in the Almiranta, that is, in a well-armed ship. Not knowing his intentions the Spaniards' concern was legitimate. Also, his previous visits to other ports in the Spanish New World were known and had produced considerable fear among the Spaniards living there, most of whom had apparently run away when he arrived. Thus, the day after the arrival of the Spanish fleet in San Juan de Ulúa, Luis Zegri, alcalde mayor of Veracruz, wrote that: "Because of the alarm caused by the Englishmen's entrance into the port ... there is nothing to eat nor anyone at hand ... to procure it."[20]

On 8 October of 1568, the very day Goddard and his companions were put ashore, Carvajal started to document the events in Tampico "so that the president and oidores of the Audiencia de Mexico would know what had happened."[21] He then ordered that the men living in Tampico should get ready to defend the town in case of an attack. And to make sure they would heed his order he added that the fine for not obeying it would be 20 gold pesos.

Fig. 3.2. Carvajal's signature in 1568.
Note spelling of surname (Caravajal).
(*Courtesy Ministerio de Cultura.
Archivo General de Indias.*)

The first sighting of the Englishmen took place on October 15. That day, two slaves of Carvajal informed him that "a large number of people were in the port who seemed lost."[22] The news prompted him to urge the burghers of Tampico to join him to defending the port and village. But because some of them ignored the call, he had to use more forceful arguments:

> He notified Cristóbal de Frías, Diego Ramírez, and Antonio de Villadiego, and to the other burghers that under the penalty of death and permanent exile form this New Spain, they should follow him immediately because there were a large number of Englishmen in the port of this village.

Indeed, Carvajal put his coat of mail and went to the house of Cristóbal de Frías where he and others were eating and ordered them to get armed and go with him to defend the port.[23] According to an eye-witness they obeyed:

> Captain Carvajal, rapidly and with much diligence, gathered the burghers of the village and others who were there, made them get ready with arms and horses and with twenty men, more or less, went to the coast, to the mouth of the river of Tampico. And two or three leagues from the village, on the coast, they discovered many people on foot.[24]

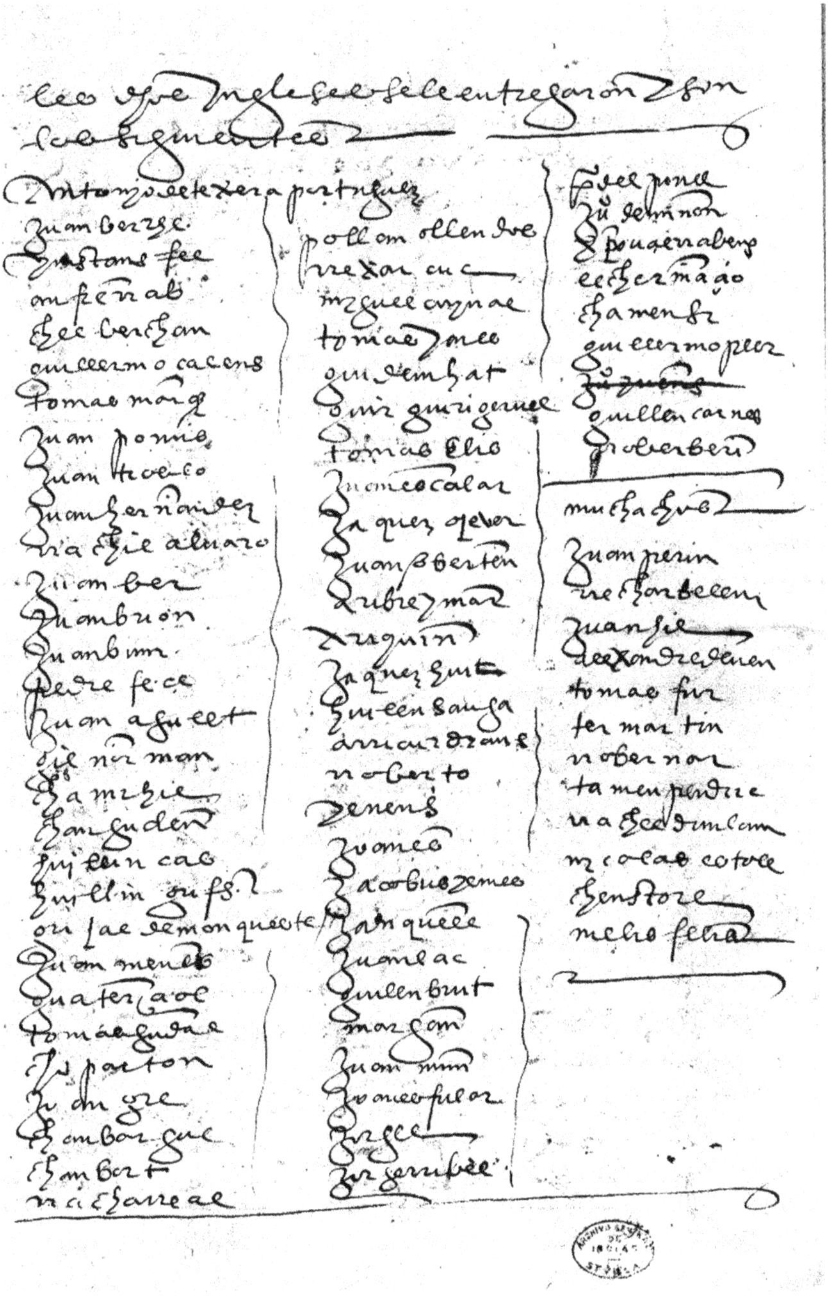
Los que Ingleses se le entregaron son los siguientes

Fig. 3.3. List of the 78 men taken prisoner by Carvajal in 1568. (*Courtesy Ministerio de Cultura. Archivo General de Indias.*)

And so, the Englishmen were taken to Tampico where they were given corn tortillas to eat and were allowed to rest a little before they were put in the local jail. The same day Carvajal started an inquest to try to obtain from them some information that might be useful to the Crown. As it turns out, Anthony Goddard, the man Phillips said was their captain, spoke Spanish and was the first to give testimony saying that his name was Antonio Texera, that he was born in San Miguel (in the Azores), and that his father was a Portuguese named Diego Días. Whether this was true is unknown because a year later, in Seville, he identified himself as Anthony Goddard and told the judges that he was born in London and that the Spaniards called him Antonio Tejera. In any event he gave Carvajal some information about the *Minion*, its weapons, crew, and about Hawkins' plans.[25]

Three days later the prisoners were handed over to Antonio Villadiego, *alcalde de la Hermandad*, who had offered to take them to the viceroy in Mexico City.[26] To do so, a list was made giving their names, which is shown in the next figure. The list has 78 names, one of which is crossed out because "that person stayed to die." Among those listed there were twelve *muchachos*, that is, young boys whose names appear at the end of the list. Incidentally, the last entry was for a Melis Felis, or Miles Phillips.

Carvajal's *Diligencias* also shows that before the prisoners left Tampico, all jewels and money were taken from them. The event is of some interest because it explains part of the heated arguments, mentioned above, between Diego Ramírez and Carvajal:

> Wanting to see if the Englishmen had some money, [Carvajal] asked Antonio Texera in the presence of Diego Ramírez . . . to show whatever money, or silver, or gold they had with them. And Antonio Texera took out a velvet purse he had in his shoes, which Diego Ramírez took. And the alcalde ordered Diego Ramírez to turn it over so that it could be deposited in a trustworthy person until H.M. ordered what to do with it. But Diego Ramírez refused saying that the purse and whatever else would be found should be divided, half and half, between him and said alcalde because they were the leaders of the people who went to take the Englishmen, because that was the manner in war.

This confrontation continued for some time, with Carvajal reiterating his order and Ramírez repeating that he did not want to turn the purse and its contents. In the end, Carvajal agreed that Ramírez could keep it in deposit until H.M. ordered what was most convenient. For that purpose, the money and other valuables taken from the prisoners were catalogued and listed in the document. That list indicates that Texera's velvet purse contained two gold chains, two jewels mounted on gold, ten or twelve pieces of gold, and 32 gold pesos. This closely agrees with what Goddard stated a year later in Seville. In addition, 209 gold pesos were taken from the other prisoners that were given to Carvajal to pay the expenses related to the prisoners.

There remains to examine Carvajal's claims about his actions during this episode. In this regard it is useful to cite several passages taken from the *Méritos de Carvajal*, written almost ten years after the events took place. In those passages several individuals who had participated in the capture of the Englishmen responded to the questions of an oidor of the Audiencia de México. For example, Pedro de Aguilera said that: "they saw that they were English and that they had no arms and were in poor conditions so that without any resistance or danger they were taken." Hearing this, the oidor asked him "if he thought the action was of any effect, given that those people were tired and without arms and could do no harm." Aguilera's answer was that

> It is true that ... said people had no weapons, were destroyed and did not re-
> sist. Nor was there any harm in taking them prisoners, but since they were of
> that kind [pirates] and could be armed to damage the towns along the coast,
> Captain Luis de Carvajal volunteered to the fight and to what might happen.[27]

The same issue was addressed by Luis Villanueva, who had been an oidor of the Audiencia when Hawkins arrived in New Spain. He said that:

> When he was in the Real Audiencia, governing in it, he knew ... that the English
> captain had left many men in the Tampico coast, where Luis de Carvajal was
> [alcalde] and had gone against the Englishmen with his people and had taken
> them prisoner. And that ... as a good captain, he had been shrewd and agile in
> war matters, and in the guard of that port, *taking risks if the opponents had come
> with bad intentions and armed* (emphasis added).[28]

These statements clearly show that the Spaniards did not know the intentions of Hawkins' men or that they were unarmed. In fact they were certainly worried that the Englishmen might harm the towns along the coast, as they had done elsewhere. In this regard, it is also useful to compare Carvajal's reaction to their arrival in Tampico, with those of the Spaniards in Río de la Hacha, Cartagena, San Juan de Ulúa, and Veracruz who, as the letters of Maldonado, Delgadillo, and Zegri show, had run away upon Hawkins' arrival.

4. THE HERETICS

The remaining Spanish accounts repeat, with slight changes, those given above and say little about what happened to the prisoners after they were sent to Mexico City. On the other hand, the English accounts, particularly those of Phillips and Hortop, continue at length, detailing the many troubles and vicissitudes experienced by them. Their stories, however embellished they might be, are compelling but are beyond the scope of this work. It should nevertheless be stated here that, at least initially, some of those left behind by Hawkins remained in New Spain, living freely, taking Spanish names and working on various enterprises. But on November of 1571 the tribunal of the Holy Office of the Inquisition was formally established in New Spain. Its first inquisitor, Archbishop Pedro Moya de Contreras, suspecting that most of them were Lutherans, had many of them rounded up soon afterwards, to be tried as heretics.[29]

After months-long trials, most were declared heretics, though not in equal degree, as their sentences reveal.[30] Those sentences were pronounced in the first *Auto-da-fé* that took place in New Spain. The date was 28 February 1574. Some, such as Miles Phillips, received benign punishments, probably because of their young age. However, most of those tried were sentenced to receive between two and three hundred lashes and to serve in the galleons for several years. Given the harsh nature of that service, it is likely that many died before completing their

Fig. 3.4. Archbishop Pedro Moya de Contreras.

sentences. Finally, three were burnt at the stake, though it appears that they were garroted before their bodies were burnt.

Not tried in New Spain were Anthony Goddard, Job Hortop, Robert Barrett, all of whom had been sent to Spain in 1568 to face the authorities there. It appears that Goddard was freed, for Miles Phillips, who managed to return to England in 1582, stated that Goddard was living there at that time. Some of the others were tried by the Inquisition in Seville. Three of them, including Barrett, were burnt at the stake. Hortop was luckier. After many years of forced service in the galleons, he returned to England at end of 1590, twenty-three years after he left it in one of Hawkins' ships.

4

Captain Carvajal

*I order Luis de Carvajal to go from the province of Pánuco to . . . Mazapil and
discover and look for a road. . . . In which journey he should be the captain of
the people going with him, who should obey him as such.*

Martín Enríquez, April 11, 1572.[1]

The viceroy's order excerpted above was written more than three years after the
Hawkins' incident. It is not known what Carvajal did during the intervening
years, but it is unlikely that he dedicated himself to raising cattle. In any event,
his actions in Tampico had made a positive impression on the viceroy. It is
therefore not surprising to see him naming Carvajal as a captain and ordering
him to carry out several important tasks. Among these was the *Discovery Journey*,
perhaps the most important undertaking by Carvajal prior to 1578.[2] This
chapter describes that journey as well as other events that took place soon after.

1. The 1572 Comisión

Before describing the ten-month-long Discovery Journey, it is useful to
consider the *Comisión* that the viceroy sent to Carvajal in April of 1572. In
essence, this was an order to carry out two tasks. The first was to explore a
certain region in order to find a road that could be used to go from Pánuco to
Mazapil. The second was to punish certain Indians living north of Tampico
who had robbed and killed many Spaniards.

It is puzzling to see such disparate tasks being ordered at the same time,
but a closer reading of the document explains the reasons: However desirable
the discovery of such a road might have been, the Crown did not pay for
the expenses incurred in the process. Rather, the money was to be obtained
from the sale of the service of Indians who supposedly had committed crimes
against the Spaniards. This procedure was remarkable because the viceroy had
expressed serious concerns about the abuses perpetrated by the Spaniards on
the Indians.

On the other hand, the Crown had for a number of years been trying to expand the northern frontier of New Spain, an action strongly resisted by the Chichimeca. An expansion was indeed taking place, but rather slowly; Indian *rancherías* would fall in the hands of the Spaniards, who would then distribute the Indians living there among the conquerors with the stated purpose that they should be evangelized. In reality, these "pacified" Indians would be used as servants, though in some cases, a meager salary would be paid to them.

From time to time, some of the peaceful Indians would run away from their towns, an action referred to by the Spaniards as an *alzamiento*, or uprising. Since these uprisings usually meant a return to their old rites, the rebelling Indians would also be accused of apostasy. To make things worse, the Chichimeca would occasionally attack the pueblos where the peaceful Indians lived, killing some of them and burning their houses and churches. Normally, any of these actions would initiate a punitive response, or *castigo*, from the Spaniards, who would take Indians that had "rebelled to the service of God and H.M." These practices benefited the poorly-paid Spanish soldiers, their leaders, and, of course, land and mine owners. However, aided by the epidemics that affected the Indians in New Spain in the second half of the sixteenth century, those abuses contributed to a drastic decrease of the Indian population in New Spain.[3]

Now, while Enríquez wanted to punish some Indians to prevent further Chichimeca attacks, he also wanted to prevent abuses by the Spaniards. Thus, after describing the reasons behind his order to Carvajal, he prescribed how should the punishment be carried out:

> I order said Luis de Carvajal that after returning from the discovery of the road he should . . . find who are the Indians responsible for murders, robberies and other atrocities. And those that would be found guilty he should take prisoner, and to their leaders he should do justice in the manner of war. As for the others found guilty, their service should be sold for ten years . . . provided that no Indian under the age of twelve can be sold in service. . . . And those Indians that can be sold in service he can bring to Spanish towns, so that they [the Spaniards], as Christians, can watch over their conversion and indoctrination.

The order adds that "And from the sale he should cover the cost of the expenses for said journey. And after the expenses are covered he should take for himself one-fifth of what is left and the remaining distribute among the people that accompanied him." This shows that the Crown did not cover the expenses incurred in carrying out either task. Instead, those expenses were to be covered from the sale of the service of those Indians that would be taken prisoner after the Discovery Journey was completed. However, since large amounts of money were required before the journey could begin, the question remains as to how was its cost paid. This is where Carvajal entered in the picture for he had the money to pay for the expedition and was more than willing to put out the required amounts. In fact, it is likely that it was he who convinced the viceroy to issue the Comisión.

When the order was signed, Carvajal was a *corregidor* in the town of Guejutla (presently Huejutla de los Reyes). There he received a number of letters from the viceroy. The first one, dated 17 April 1572, says:

> *Magnifico Señor*, . . . I was informed that none of the priests you suggested could go with you because all of them are convening here. . . . Since I so much wish to see this business completed and do not want to delay it, I want to trust you entirely and compel you to go with more rectitude than is ordered. And even though the Comisión . . . orders that you should not leave without taking with you a priest, by means of this I order you to leave soon on your journey without one, asking you again to see what you do, and that you should also see what your soldiers do. And do not depart from the righteous way, because if you do, you put me in a very difficult position. Do not wait any longer than you have to, because the time is passing rapidly and I do not want the opportunity to pass.[4]

It is clear that the viceroy wanted Carvajal to depart as soon as possible. But to do this he had to put his complete trust on Carvajal, even though he did not really know him. Furthermore, since no priest would be able to go on the journey, Enríquez felt it was necessary to re-iterate his concern about the Indians.

The viceroy wrote to Carvajal about the same topic on at least two more occasions before the journey began. The dates were 9 and 20 June, 1572, respectively. In the first of these, he told Carvajal not to forget the principal purpose of the expeditions and reminded him that he, the viceroy, had put his trust in him and that he should not change his good intentions of that which "you have promised me." It is likely that Carvajal made this promise to the viceroy in person.

The covers of these letters contain short summaries written by somebody other than the viceroy or his scribe. Comparison with documents written at later times shows that these summaries were written by Carvajal himself. The last point of interest in these letters is that the viceroy addressed Carvajal as *Magnifico Señor.* Keeping in mind the large repertoire of respectful titles used by the Spaniards in those days, not much can be read into this, but it is obvious that the viceroy regarded Carvajal as a man of some wealth.

2. The Discovery Journey

Although the province of Pánuco had been in Spanish hands for a long time, its northern frontier had remained essentially unchanged since Cortés' days. The reasons were simple. On the north, roughly across the river Pánuco, the Chichimeca continued to successfully prevent the Spaniards from increasing their territorial possessions. And extensions the east or to the west were not possible because of natural barriers. The extent of the Spanish-controlled area may be grasped from the historic map of the Guasteca, shown in Chapter 2. Although not entirely factual, the map gives an idea of the conditions in that area a few years before it was drawn. Incidentally, the name of the region did not imply a political entity. Rather it represented a region were the same language was spoken by the natives. It is noted that both Tampico and Pánuco (S. Esteban del Puerto) appear south of the river Pánuco, whereas Valles appears north of it. The map also shows that the Spanish settlements were quite sparse in the area north and west of the central region.

Consider now Carvajal's search for a road between the province of Pánuco and the mines of Mazapil. It is clear that this was not an easy endeavor. Among the difficulties were the long distance between the two places—more than 200 miles as the crow flies; the terrain; and the Chichimeca. Of course, exact distances were unknown because longitudes could not be determined with reasonable accuracy. Nevertheless, it was known that Mazapil was north and west of the Pánuco region.

Thus, it would seem reasonable to begin the journey from a place in the province as far north and west of Tampico as possible. Such a place was Tanxipa, or Tanchipa. The region north of this town had not yet been pacified and further west was the Sierra Madre Oriental. This sierra divides the coastal low-lands in the province of Pánuco, where Tanchipa was located, from the Mexican Plateau. The town of Mazapil is on that plateau, at an elevation of about 1900 meters, whereas the elevation of Tanchipa is only about 100 meters. However the problem confronting Carvajal did not end there because the sierra is made of high mountain chains that run nearly parallel to one another, roughly along a north-south direction. Thus, in order to reach Mazapil Carvajal would have to find several mountain passes through the range.

Although Carvajal prepared a description of the lands he explored during this journey that included a *pintura,* or Indian map, neither the description nor the map have been found. The map on the next page indicates the locations of the places he visited or explored, as well as others that are mentioned in contemporary documents describing his actions.

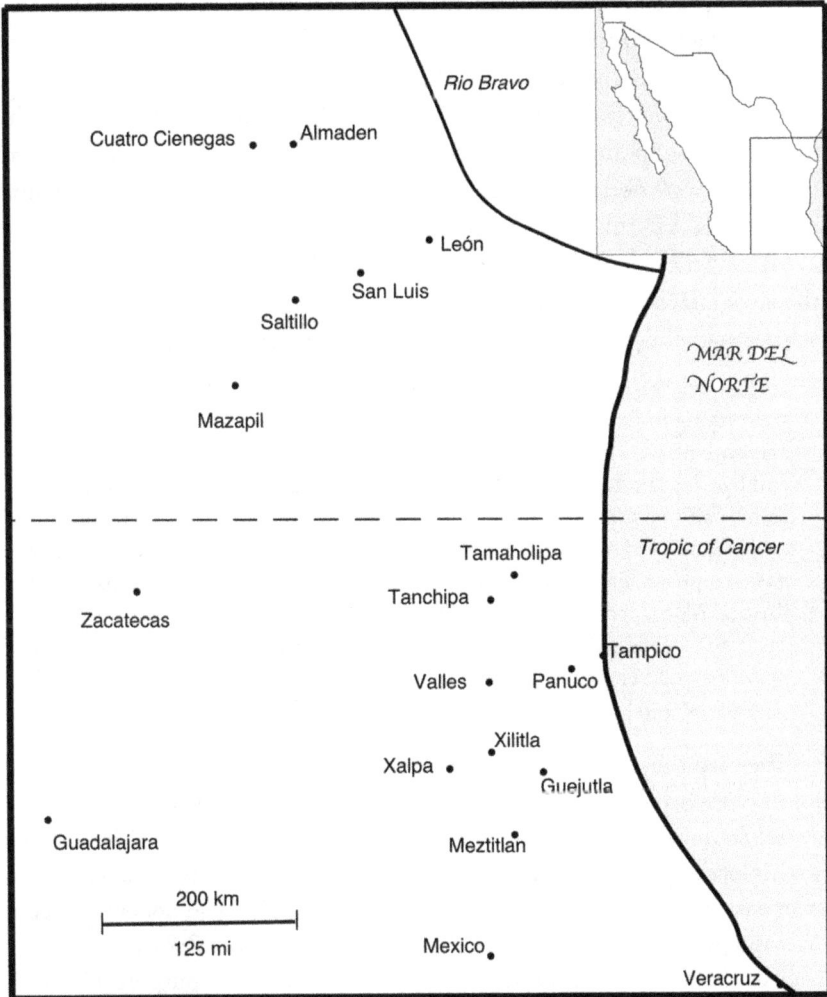

Map 2. Names of the towns, villages and cities that appear in the documents related to Carvajal. All names are as they were known in the sixteenth century

The arrival in Guejutla of the viceroy's order meant that Carvajal had to start getting ready for his journey. The first thing he did was to recruit as many soldiers as he could, as well as supporting personnel. The contingent he assembled included "forty men on horse . . . hundred eighty friendly Indian men, sixty five boys of service, and three hundred fifty horses, one hundred twenty of which carried provisions."[5] The large number of soldiers is easy to understand. The journey would have to be through *Tierra Adentro*, where the Chichimeca ruled. To them, the expedition would be nothing short of another attempt by the Spaniards to invade their lands.

As for provisions, Carvajal could not rely on any being available along the way and had to bring as much food as he could. For this purpose he "sent someone to Mexico City to purchase more than 150 *quintale*s (or 15,000 pounds) of *biscocho.*" Finally, according to Juan Lorenzo, the scribe who certified the appointment of Carvajal as alcalde ordinario of Tampico, all provisions were obtained locally and were gathered "in the town of Tanchipa, town of peace in this frontier of war."[6]

Among the many narratives about the Discovery Journey, that of Lorenzo is the most interesting as it contains several important details. For example, after stating that others had in vain attempted to find a road to Mazapil he said that:

> And he [Carvajal] departed from that place on 4 August of the year 1572, and went trying to find said road. . . . And Luis de Carvajal continued on that voyage working . . . very hard because of the big sierras, rivers and difficult passages, and fighting almost every day with the Chichimeca who wanted to do damage to him and to prevent the journey. But he attempted to befriend them, and to bring them to our Lord and to the obedience of H.M. And after *sixty four days* (emphasis added) we came to the road to Zacatecas, having finished all the provisions, and having lost many horses because they were exhausted. And the whole company stayed in that location more than twenty days where he provided it . . . at a great expense on his part, having for this purpose sold a black slave of his, and borrowed a large quantity of gold pesos, which he later paid.[7]

The road they came to on 4 October of 1572 was the famed *Camino Real*, joining Mexico City with Zacatecas.[8] The exact location was *Fuerte de las Palmillas*, located just south of Zacatecas.[9] Along a straight line, the distance to this location from Tanchipa is less than 375 km, or 235 miles. And yet it took over two months to cover it. To make things worse, they had not even reached Mazapil. Although this village was within easy reach from Zacatecas, the path they had followed so far was not adequate for the intended purpose. However, Carvajal was not ready to give up the search for a good road. Obviously he had to return to Pánuco, but he needed to find a different way. And so, twenty days after arriving in Las Palmillas, "he went to the mines of Mazapil inquiring how . . . to find a better road because the one he had followed so far had been too rough with sierras, mountains, wildernesses, rivers and, in some parts, extremely dry lands."[10] In Mazapil he remained ten or twelve days, recruiting more soldiers and replenishing his provisions before attempting, once more, to discover the desired road, this time in reverse, from Mazapil to Pánuco.[11]

Carvajal's big discovery

In 1572 Mazapil was a small but growing mining center in Nueva Galicia, north of Zacatecas. Its location was ideal for further exploration of the northern territories because it was then further north than any other European settlement in eastern New Spain. Only a few years earlier Francisco Cano, the lieutenant of alcalde mayor in Mazapil, had reached a lake which he called *Nuevo México*, now believed to be near Parras, in the western part of the Mexican state of Coahuila.[12] The memory of that exploration must have been quite fresh in the minds of Mazapil residents when Carvajal and his soldiers were stationed there. It is quite likely that he asked Cano, or others living there, about ways of crossing the sierras nearby. In fact he was told that towards the north there were some canyons that might enable him to find a pass.[13]

Fig. 4.1. Detail of a map made by Joseph Goldberg in 1846. (*Library of Congress, Geography and Map Division.*)

And so, Carvajal and his party went north, flanking the western slopes of the sierra, eventually reaching a valley, some 100 miles northeast of Mazapil, where Saltillo is located. Carvajal seems to have spent some time there exploring the area looking for the desired pass to the east, which he found in early 1573. The significance of the discovery may be appreciated from the following statement he made in 1578:

> I found a clear *abra* through which he crossed the sierra, which no one before me had discovered it, even by accident.[14]

This abra was an opening in the Sierra Madre, north and east of Mazapil, which enabled him not just to cross it but to descend from a high elevation to a much lower one in a short distance. It was this discovery that opened vast regions to the north for future exploration and expansion.

The location of that abra was determined in a recent work on the basis of a detailed study of the topography of the region between Saltillo, at 1600 meters above sea level and Monterrey at 535.[15] Those cities are now connected by both rail and car roads that parallel each other until the grade becomes too steep for a train. Starting from Saltillo, the elevation slowly decreases until the line dividing the Mexican states of Coahuila and Nuevo León. At that point and opening before the viewer is a deep ravine. To the left and to the right mountains raise to more than 2000 meters, but in front and beyond there is a low-elevation valley where Monterrey is located.

Seeing that valley from a high point Carvajal must have realized that he was facing the other side of the sierra he wanted to cross. Like Moses, he probably felt in front of the Promised Land. However, unlike him, Carvajal was able to reach the valley facing him. This he did following a canyon that circles a mountain as it descends.[16] That canyon is clearly marked in a survey map made during the Mexican-American war.[17] Figure 4.1 shows a detail of that map which includes a wagon road then existing between Saltillo and Monterrey, as well as several mule tracks made long before the map was made. The track on the north side of the ravine is the abra found by Carvajal. This identification follows from a statement, quoted below, made by Juan Lorenzo.[18] To better understand what he said, it is helpful to remember that Carvajal was traveling west to east, or from left to right on the map.

> And after passing said abra, *turning to the left* (emphasis added) following the mountain range he had crossed, captain Carvajal found extended prairies, with trees and delightful grasses, and with many rivers, almost each half a league in between, and very easy to pass. And the land such that made us wish to live in it.

Although the present city of Monterrey has obliterated much of this idyllic setting, there is no question that Lorenzo was describing the valley of Monterrey. This valley, called Extremadura in the sixteenth century, is a large area abutting the Sierra Madre on its south side.

Given that Carvajal prepared a map to accompany his report about the discovery journey, it is likely that he named various places along the way, particularly those that had salient features, including the name of that valley; the *Cerro de la Silla,* a peculiarly-shaped mountain on the western side of that valley that has become the symbol for the Mexican state of Nuevo León; the *Cerro de las Mitras*, on the same side as the abra; the river *Santa Catarina*; and a gorge called *La Huasteca*.[19] It is also likely that, being the first European to reach the valley where Saltillo is located, he named that valley as well.

Having found the passage he was looking for, Carvajal headed back to the province of Pánuco, which he reached in May of 1573, ten months after departure.[20] Although seemingly long, this duration included lengthy exploration stays in the valleys of Saltillo and Extremadura. The return journey was uneventful and direct, even if they were traversing previously unexplored regions that still were in the hands of the Chichimeca. The path he followed on this occasion would be used by him, in the reverse direction, nearly ten years later to explore regions further north.

With his return Carvajal seemed to have successfully carried out the main task given to him by the viceroy. Indeed, the discovery journey represented a very substantial contribution to the future progress of New Spain. First, the abra opened up vast territories in the northeast of present day Mexico. Second, Carvajal discovered and explored two valleys, both suitable for settlement. These places attracted many Spanish colonizers in the years to come. Also important was the path he discovered on his way from Tanchipa to Zacatecas. That is, Carvajal was also the first European to explore the eastern portion of the present Mexican state of San Luis Potosí.

To the punishment

The record is relatively brief about the second task given by the viceroy to Carvajal: the punishment of certain Indians who lived on the coast north of Tampico. However, if he obeyed his orders, the punishment took place shortly after the return from the discovery journey. There exists several brief affidavits by individuals that accompanied him on that occasion. One states that:

> Said Captain Luis de Carvajal went to punish those Indians to the Río Bravo and coast of La Florida. . . . And this witness went in his company to the ranch of the Chichimeca. . . . And with much industry he surrounded them, and killed the captain and apprehended thirty persons to whom he punished in accordance to the Comisión.[21]

Another affidavit shows that the punitive expedition reached the Río Bravo, and crossed it.[22] It thus appears that, in addition to those areas mentioned earlier, Carvajal explored the coastal areas north of Tampico. After the punitive expedition Carvajal returned to the province of Pánuco in the fall of 1573.[23]

The next recorded event in Carvajal's life took place late 1573 or early 1574. At that time, Carvajal was back in Tanchipa. Nearby, in *Tierra Adentro,* lived certain Indians who had not been vanquished. Thinking that it might be possible to bring them under Spanish rule, Carvajal entered their town with his soldiers, an action that ordinarily would be considered an act of war by the Indians. Juan Lorenzo, who also accompanied Carvajal this time, stated that:

> He went with Carvajal to the pueblos of the Capunoques and Palalueques, people of war who live more cleanly than the other Chichimeca and have houses and plant corn. . . . In said pueblos not a single Spaniard has entered but thanks to his industry, said captain Luis de Carvajal entered in them without alarming them and without making them any harm. Instead, he . . . gave them some things from Castile . . . with which they remained happy and in peace.

This shows that some of the Chichimeca tribes lived in houses and raised crops; that is, they were not nomadic but sedentary.

Aside from the details of these three expeditions, the record shows that Carvajal had obeyed the viceroy orders regarding the treatment of Indians, treating them well because he felt that was the only way to live in peace with them. As shown later, Carvajal displayed the same restrained manner when dealing with Indians who had rebelled against their Spanish masters, even though he was entitled to punish them. That benign treatment was very successful and gained him considerable respect from the Indians and from the viceroy. However, it also produced resentment among poorly-paid Spanish soldiers and encomenderos, all of whom benefited from harsher retaliation policies against the Indians.

3. THE QUIET YEARS

Having completed the tasks assigned to him by the viceroy, Carvajal prepared reports of his activities, including a description of the areas he had explored. Very likely he went to Mexico City to present his reports to the viceroy in person. In any event, the New Spain records about him are silent for nearly two years. It appears, however, that Carvajal went to Spain in the Spring of 1574 and returned to New Spain in the summer of 1575. The basis for this belief is a document, dated 10 November 1574, whose summary shows that Carvajal was in Seville on that date. That summary says:

> Luis de Carabaxal, master [of a ship] in *La Carrera* to the Indies, and burgher of Seville, in the Magdalena quarter, agrees to pay to Juan de los Reyes, lender to Doña Francisca de Carabajal, wife of Damián Aguirre, in the obligation she had made to join her husband in New Spain . . . .[24]

This brief catalogue entry shows that a master of a ship engaged in the back and forth travel to the Spanish New World (La Carrera), appeared on that date before a public notary in Seville. There is little doubt that this man was the protagonist of this work.[25] Therefore, it would appear that Carvajal traveled in a ship that left New Spain together with the official fleet that went to Seville in the Spring of 1574 and returned in July or August of 1575. The dates seem to fit well between Carvajal's discovery and punishment journeys and those events that took place in 1576, described later in this chapter.

The approximate dates given above indicate that Carvajal was in Spain 8–10 months. What did he do during that period? Of course, he probably visited his wife. More importantly, however, he must have spent some time discussing future business plans with his father-in-law, Miguel Núñez. An event supporting this speculation is that during the fall of 1575 Núñez appeared before the judges in the House of Trade to re-iterate his request that he be granted permission to do business in the New World.

But Carvajal's plans were far more ambitious than doing business with his father-in-law, and the news he heard upon his arrival in Seville must have pleased him. In July of 1573, that is, one year before he arrived there, the Crown had issued a set of cédulas that would henceforth rule all aspects related to the new discoveries and settlements in the New World.[26] The set consisted of 149 rules that dictated in the smallest detail how such discoveries, pacifications and settlements should take place. Included in it were rules that specified what those individuals making the discoveries were expected to do as well as the rewards that the Crown would grant them. There is no doubt that Carvajal read the rules with increased excitement. After all, they showed that his 1572-73 discoveries in the New World were potentially a good example of what the Crown wanted done. That is, what he had discovered was a large territory that seem to have all the necessary requirements to make it suitable for pacification and settlement. It was then that Carvajal begun to think how he could take advantage of the new rules which, as the next chapter shows, he did a few years later.

4. Xalpa's Rebellion

Soon after his return from Spain in 1575, Carvajal received another important Comisión from the viceroy. This one had to do with an Indian uprising in a mountainous area north of Mexico City, whose central focus was an Indian town called Xalpa, known today as Jalpan. The uprising was not unlike others that had occurred elsewhere in the northern frontier of New Spain: Some of the previously pacified Indians would abandon their towns, burn their churches and, in some cases, join the warring Chichimeca. As a result, the Crown would lose some income and the Spaniards in those areas would lose the services provided by the Indians, services without which they could not exist. The usual response would be to force them to return to their towns and service, severely punishing their leaders.

The Xalpa rebellion started sometime in 1575 and extended to many of the neighboring towns including Xilitla, Chapuloacán, Molango, Tamansunchal, Tlachinol and others. Some of these towns appear in one of the maps forming the *Relaciones Geograficas*, a collection of documents giving information about towns and villages in sixteenth century New Spain. The map in question was made in 1578. It depicts the region around Meztitlán from the imagined perspective of an observer placed above and south of that town, but facing north.[27] A portion of the map is presented in figure 4.2. This shows some Indians with bows and arrows, indicating that the region was not yet pacified.

Fig. 4.2. Detail of the Meztitlán map. (*Courtesy of the Benson Latin American Collection. The General Libraries. The University of Texas at Austin.*)

Before the uprising, the northern frontier of New Spain was protected by Spanish soldiers who served under D. Francisco de Puga. But on this occasion, the rebellion had spread over a wide territory that included the Camino Real. This prompted the viceroy to commission the pacification of Xalpa to Carvajal, allowing Puga and his soldiers to protect other parts of the frontier. Carvajal was notified of this decision.

To put Carvajal's actions in context, it is useful to quote here excerpts from the viceroy's Comisión, starting with the reasons to order Carvajal to defend Xalpa:

Having been informed that Indian Pamines, Chichimecas and Guachichiles of the province of Xalpa have risen and rebelled against the service to H.M., and have attacked the pacified towns that exist in that sierra as far as the village of Valles and the town of Tamaholipa . . . I had committed their punishment and pacification to D. Francisco de Puga. . . . And because of reports that he sent me, and because it is convenient that he should go elsewhere to deal with similar problems and that a captain remains in Xalpa with some soldiers and trusting that Luis de Carvajal will do and obey that which by me is ordered, by means of this Comisión I appoint him as such captain, and order him that with ten soldiers assist in said town of Xalpa.[28]

The number of soldiers mentioned by the viceroy deserves a comment. First, it only included soldiers paid by the Crown. Second, Puga himself had only twenty five soldiers, hardly enough to maintain the peace in the whole frontier. The reasons for these small numbers were that the viceroy had no funds to carry out even important tasks such as this, and that the salary paid to soldiers was so small that it was difficult to find Spaniards willing to enlist. In fact, as Enríquez wrote to the king on 31 October 1576, what motivated Spanish men to become soldiers was the hope of capturing some Indians and selling them.[29] Clearly, the viceroy was fully aware of this, and yet all he could do was to order his captains not to permit their soldiers to abuse the Indians.

The viceroy also ordered Carvajal to disregard past offenses committed by the Indians, adding that:

If from now on some Indians of that region . . . rise against the service to H.M. and do harm to the subjects and vassals of H.M., obtain . . . due information as to who they are and what harm they committed, and, if found guilty of such uprising and damages, he should pursue them . . . without harming or apprehending others.

The Comisión prescribed the types of punishments that those found guilty should receive: death to the leaders, body amputations to the warriors, enslavement to the rest of the Indians over eleven years of age, and the taking of small children away from their mothers for the purpose of indoctrination.[30] At the same time, however, the viceroy also wanted to protect innocent Indians:

And that he nor them do any harm to any Indian, nor use them, or take from them or their belongings anything without paying their normal prices. . . . Furthermore, said captain and his soldiers are not to enter any Indian town to take Indians unless they are guilty, having first determined their guilt.

The document also listed the salaries to be paid by the crown while the engagement lasted. Thus, Carvajal was to earn a yearly salary of five hundred gold pesos, and each soldier three hundred and fifty. While the soldiers' salary seem commensurate with that of their captain, it should be remembered that they had to pay for their horses, armor, and weapons.

Carvajal's actions

A few months before the 1576 Comisión was issued, Carvajal, then a magistrate in Guejutla, received a letter from the viceroy in which he was ordered to "stop doing whatever he was doing and go to the town of Xilitla to resist the Indians from Xalpa who had risen and rebelled against the service."[31] Once in Xilitla, Carvajal "made a made a big wooden palisade to defend the entrance of the rebelled enemies."[32] Two months later Carvajal was back in Guejutla, where he received the Comisión, perhaps late April of 1576.[33]

After receiving the order, Carvajal went to various places to recruit soldiers and friendly Indians. And on 26 May 1576 he wrote to the viceroy telling him he was getting ready to go to Xalpa.[34] This he did soon after, "passing through the towns in peace of that region, until he arrived in Xalpa, where the Indians were about to abandon their towns and haciendas because they were afraid of those who had rebelled."[35] Francisco de Aguilar, one of the soldiers who accompanied him, said that the day they entered in Xalpa:

> They discovered in the brush some war Indians, naked and with their faces painted. They attacked the Indians and took them prisoner and brought them to the town of Xalpa. And ... the captain spoke to them through an interpreter, had their faces washed, fed them and clothed them, and ordered them to tell other rebelling Indians in their land that he had come only to help them so that no harm would be done to them from either Indians or Spaniards, who could come to kill them.[36]

This good treatment seems to have worked:

> Eight days later many Indians who had rebelled came together with those he had sent. And to everyone he gave food. And to their principals and captains he gave blankets. And with good treatments and words that he used with them, he quieted them and brought to peace all of the Indians who had rebelled.[37]

These sworn affidavits by eye-witnesses appear to show that Carvajal continued to treat the Indians well. Not only did he not harm them but also established a good rapport with their leaders, committing "their names to memory and calling them by their name."[38] Very clearly, to Carvajal the Indians were human beings which, as pointed out by Viceroy Enríquez years later, was rather uncommon among Europeans in sixteenth century New Spain.[39] Carvajal also believed that only through such good treatment could peace be obtained. In fact, Carvajal transmitted that belief to the viceroy through D.

Francisco Puga, as the following excerpt from one of the letters that Carvajal received from the viceroy while Carvajal was in Xalpa:

> In a report that D. Francisco sent me I saw something you said, which I believe is very good, and that is that if the Indians are not treated well, war will result. ... Give me the pleasure, Sr., that you will do your best to pacify these Indians and tranquilize those who are in peace.[40]

Carvajal had also a genuine concern for the religious education of the Indians. For example, "he would gather the rebelling Indians so that they would hear the Christian doctrine in the Mexican language." Whether the Indians considered this education important is unknown; what mattered to them was that they were not taken to be sold. In the words of Pedro de Portes:

> This witness saw that even if by his Comisión he [Carvajal] had the power to proceed against said rebelling Indians and make them slaves and profit much from this, and even if some tried to persuade him to do that, he procured to insure the safety of the Indians, and pacified them without doing them any harm.[41]

It is therefore not surprising to learn that because of his good treatment, the Indians who had rebelled "wanted to return [to their towns] to meet said captain, who would keep his word," or that "It was so much what Captain Luis de Carvajal did [for them], that in all the towns the Indians would come out to see him and meet him." Incidentally, it was also D. Francisco de Puga who after consultation with Carvajal recommended that the viceroy should send a captain with soldiers to Xalpa and that a fort be built there. It was also he who stated that the viceroy, "*having notice of the prudence and good traits of Captain Luis de Carvajal* (emphasis added), sent him a Comisión so that he would assist with his soldiers in Xalpa."

In addition to showing the high regard in which Carvajal was held, the statement by Puga indicates that a decision had been made to build a fort in Xalpa. This fort is not mentioned in the 1576 Comisión but deserves to be considered here.

The Fort of Xalpa

In his 1589 self-defense, Carvajal stated that "he rebuilt the town of Xalpa and built there a fort made of stone, among the best in the New Spain." Although these actions have also been questioned by some authors, the evidence supporting Carvajal's claim is irrefutable. Thus, an order from Viceroy Enríquez, dated 28 May 1576, says:

> Because I have ordered Captain Luis de Carvajal ... to make a fort in the towns of Xalpa to resist the Indians who have risen and in war, where the people

can take cover in case of an attack, by means of this I order said captain to compel the Indians of said town, as well as those subject to it, and to those in the neighboring towns, to assist in building the fort.... And that the officers of H.M. make it so happen and obeyed.[42]

The decision to build the fort was, as Puga's stated, arrived through consultation between him and Carvajal, with Puga making the final recommendation to the viceroy. It is likely that one factor motivating the decision was the good defense provided by the palisade built by Carvajal in Xilitla a few months earlier.

The importance of the fort is made clear by several other documents, including a number of letters from the viceroy to Carvajal. Thus, in a letter written on 26 October 1576, Enríquez stated that:

> I very much want to see that fort finished because it would remove the infinite sorrows that often come over me. Put into it as much diligence as it is necessary, as I understand you have so far done. I am ordering the alcalde mayor that he should help you with Indians and officers.[43]

Among the people who were told to send Indians to help in the construction of the fort was the *encomendero* Francisco Barrón, who apparently had to be forced to help Carvajal. Thus, in a later dated 5 June 1576 the viceroy told Carvajal "And, Sr., make Barrón help in whatever is needed because he is obliged to protect the Indians." Nevertheless, it seems that Barrón continued to refuse to help, for three weeks later the viceroy wrote again to Carvajal telling him that:

> I have ordered Barrón to protect the natives living in his town and that . . . he should help in all that is necessary. And you, Sr., should tell him that since you are in Xalpa with soldiers on *his* (emphasis added) behalf, it is also fair that he also does the same. Make sure he obeys and keep me informed.[44]

It is likely that the strongly worded letter from the viceroy convinced Barrón to help. In any event, the fort was completed late 1576 or early 1577, for in a letter dated 10 November 1576 the viceroy wrote to Carvajal saying "I am glad to hear that the fort has been finished. . . .What is left, try Sr., to finish it little by little."[45]

In the Spanish archives there is the sketch of a fort, a copy of which is shown in figure 4.3.[46] Although the sketch lacks identification, the detail of Meztitlán map presented earlier in this chapter shows that it refers to the fort that Carvajal built. Near the map's top center, there is a fort-like structure, la- beled *Fuerte de Xalpa,* that has a strong resemblance to the fort in the sketch.

Also, the sketch has some features that match the description of the fort given by some of the individuals who participated in its construction. One of these individuals said that Carvajal "made a fort of stone where the Indians take cover if there is need. And inside it there is house and church for the priests who live there."[47] Another added that "a canal was built to bring water into the fort."[48]

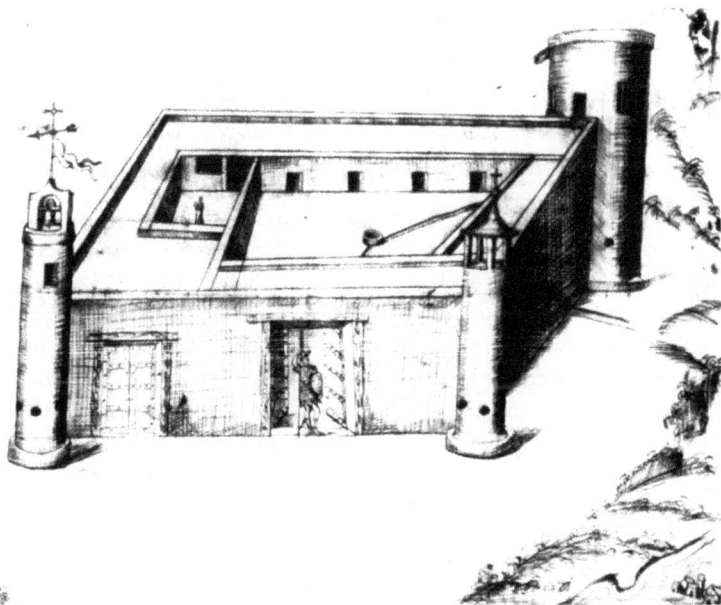

Fig. 4.3. Sketch of an unidentified fort found among the documents of Viceroy Enríquez. (*Courtesy of the Ministerio de Cultura, Archivo General de Indias, Seville.*)

The records also show that Carvajal worked to improve the town:

And because the town was not in a good location to defend itself from the enemies, he [Carvajal] made it change its location, and sketched the streets, and lots for the Indians with great desire, and they came to it.[49]

Of course, the Chichimeca were not happy with the construction of the fort:

One night, while the fort was being made . . . came upon the captain, his people and the friendly Indians with him, more than 400 Chichimecas to kill them and to prevent the completion of the fort, seeing that it was meant to subjugate them. And said captain, even though he was at the time sick and limping in one foot, gathered his people . . . and went to fight the enemies, making them run away without any harm to his people.[50]

A problem of a different kind seems to have surfaced while the fort was being built. Although Carvajal had for a long time understood that the only manner to prevent Indian uprisings was to treat them well, his methods were not shared by all Spaniards, particularly by the *encomenderos,* who needed free labor, and by the soldiers, who profited by taking Indians for the purpose of selling their service. To these Spaniards the rebellions provided an ideal excuse to achieve their goals. Nothing new in this, but it seems that while the fort was being built, other captains were entering nearby towns to take Indians. This must have upset the conditions in the Xalpa region for, on 30 July 1576, the viceroy sent an order to all of his captains who were in the area. The order is reproduced in figure 4.4 and says:

> D. Martín Enríquez, viceroy, etc., etc. I have been informed that some of the captains that I have named for the punishment of the Chichimeca Indians . . . enter in many towns that have been pacified by Captain Luis de Carvajal, which are those included from Sichu to Tamaholipa, and punish and agitate them, from which they return to rebel, fight, and abandon their towns. And because it is necessary to remedy this, I order every captain by me named, who ever he is, that from now on they should not enter in said towns to make any punishment *without first communicating and with the agreement of said captain Luis de Carvajal . . . which they should do and obey without any excuse* (emphasis added) . . .[51]

Among those receiving the order was Capt. Pedro de Herbiti, who said that:

> He saw the letters that to this witness (that is, himself) and to Captain [Francisco] Belver, who assisted with soldiers in those frontiers, in which the viceroy ordered not to get involved in anything related to war nor enter the Indian lands to take Indians, unless it was with the agreement of said Captain Luis de Carvajal.[52]

It seems that this order had no effect for a second uprising occurred soon after the pacification of Xalpa in 1576. That new rebellion was also resolved by Carvajal.[53] However, this resolution was also ephemeral.

A different account

The above pages describe, on the basis of several contemporary documents, the events that took place in Xalpa in 1576. However, a rather different version seems to appear in an Información that was obtained in Valles *nearly ten years later.* Extended parts of this document appear in a book by Velázquez.[54] According to him that Información shows that "None of the captains, none of the soldiers, none of the witnesses, nobody shows that Carvajal was truthful when he said that the war and rebellion of Xalpa was committed to him."[55]

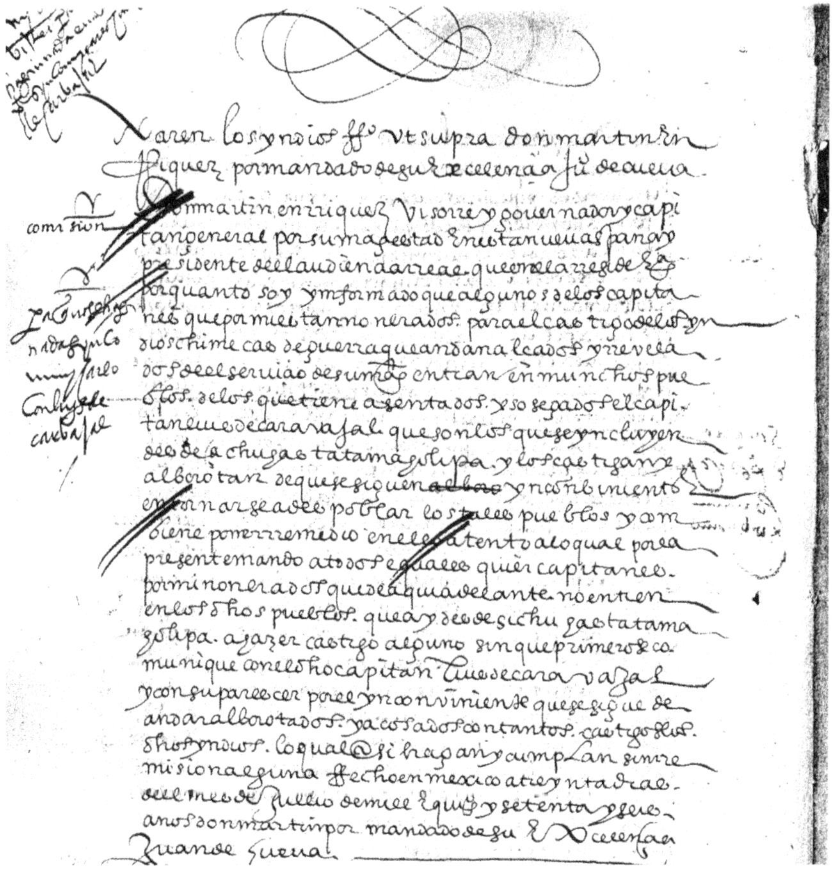

Fig. 4.4. Order of 30 July 1576 from Viceroy Enríquez to his captains in the province of Pánuco. (*Courtesy of the Ministerio de Cultura, Archivo General de Indias, Seville.*)

The Comisión given to Carvajal, the letters from Viceroy Enríquez , as well as the contemporary affidavits presented before the Audiencia de México and quoted in the above pages, shows that Velázquez statement is patently false. Also false are several other quotations that he includes in his narrative. One of them purports to describe the viceroy's order shown and transcribed above:

> Those [captains] sent by the viceroy gathered in the village of Valles, whose alcalde, Juan de Villaseñor, had received a letter, handwritten by D. Martín Enríquez, warning them not to take [Indian] slaves *"and that they should not trust Luis de Carvajal."* (emphasis added). . . . Without any doubt, the viceroy did not trust Carvajal.[56]

Comparison with the actual order issued by the viceroy shows that this statement is also untrue and that the quoted words within it do not appear in the order. That is, these words, like the rest of Velázquez' indictment of Carvajal, are fabrications.

Velázquez's book also contains other quotations from the Valles' *Información* that purport to show that Carvajal abused the Indians. The evidence provided for this purpose was, some statements supposedly made in Valles in 1585. One of those statements was ascribed to Capt. Francisco Belver who according to Velázquez said that Carvajal "swore by the Holy Gospels that even if the Indians would come in peace he would take them prisoner and would enslave them."[57] In fact, as the earlier statement by Capt. Herbiti shows, Francisco Belver was one of the captains in Valles who was disrupting the peace Carvajal had achieved in the region by entering some peaceful towns and taking Indians.

The reasons for the fabrications against Carvajal will become clearer in chapters 8–10, where certain events that took place in 1585 in Valles, are described in more detail. It should be stated here, however, that one purpose behind the Valles' *Información* was to clear Francisco Guerrero, its alcalde mayor in 1585, of the charge leveled against him by Carvajal, that he enslaved some peaceful Indians.[58] Another reason was to undo several rulings by the Audiencia de Mexico, which had given Carvajal some towns, including Valles. To achieve that goal, the officers in Valles included in their *Información* those allegations against Carvajal. However, the above quotations and the statements from Velázquez book shows how the record was distorted to achieve their goal.

The completion of the fort in Xalpa marked an important date in Carvajal's life. By then he had been in New Spain nearly ten years. During that period he had served the Crown in many ways, some of which had a lasting impact. Less obvious, but also important was his good treatment of the Indians. Although the frontier remained unstable for may years, that treatment was an important component of its eventual pacification. This was evident to Viceroy Enríquez and to others who knew Carvajal. And yet, the stories fabricated in 1585 by his enemies managed to create a different image. These issues will be considered in more detail in later chapters. But in 1577 Carvajal thought that his services to the Crown were significant and deserved palpable recognition. The steps he took to obtain it are considered next.

5

Taking Profit

*We confer upon you the title of Governor and General Captain of the provinces . . .
that are to be called Nuevo Reino de León.*

Philip II, May 31, 1579.[1]

Soon after completing his tasks in Xalpa, Carvajal went to Mexico
City to discuss his future plans with the viceroy. Since his arrival in
New Spain he had served the Crown in many ways and probably felt he
deserved a significant reward. However, what he wanted could only be
granted by the king. This chapter considers the events and reasons that
induced the king to give Carvajal the title and lands mentioned above.[2]

1. Obtaining a royal award

The normal path to request a special favor from the king was prescribed by
several royal cédulas that had been issued over the years.[3] These required that
an individual seeking a royal award should first request the audiencia closest to
him to gather information regarding the services he claimed to have performed
on behalf of the Crown. If the request was approved, the information would
be recorded in an official document. And if in the view of that audiencia those
services were meritorious, the document would be transmitted to the king via
the *Consejo Real y Supremo de las Indias* where, as the rules dictated, "it could
be examined to do whatever it was most convenient."

Consider now Carvajal's case. Given the events that took place afterwards,
it is obvious that the viceroy agreed that his activities were sufficiently
meritorious to proceed with an official inquiry about them. This meant that
Carvajal would be allowed to present before the Audiencia a petition that
listed his services, the names of individuals who might serve as witnesses, and
the endorsements from some Crown officers.

The first such endorsement, issued in Tampico on 4 June 1577, was a
resolution giving Carvajal power of attorney so that "he may appear before
H.M. and his Real Consejo de Indias; before the very excellent D. Martín

Enríquez, viceroy of New Spain; and before the president and oidores of the Audiencia, so that he can ask for privileges . . . useful and profitable to this village."[4] This shows that as early as June of 1577 Carvajal knew he was going to appear before the king; that is, he knew beforehand that his request would be endorsed by the Audiencia.

It is likely that Carvajal spent most of 1577 getting ready to make his case before the Audiencia. The most time-consuming task must have been that of finding witnesses willing to testify on his behalf during pre-assigned time slots. In any event, he was in Mexico City on December 4, asking that certified copies of some older documents be made. And a month later, he appeared before the Audiencia to request permission to present information about his merits and services. This petition heads the Información de Oficio required by the Crown of those seeking a royal privilege. This document was referred to in earlier chapters as the *Méritos de Carvajal.*

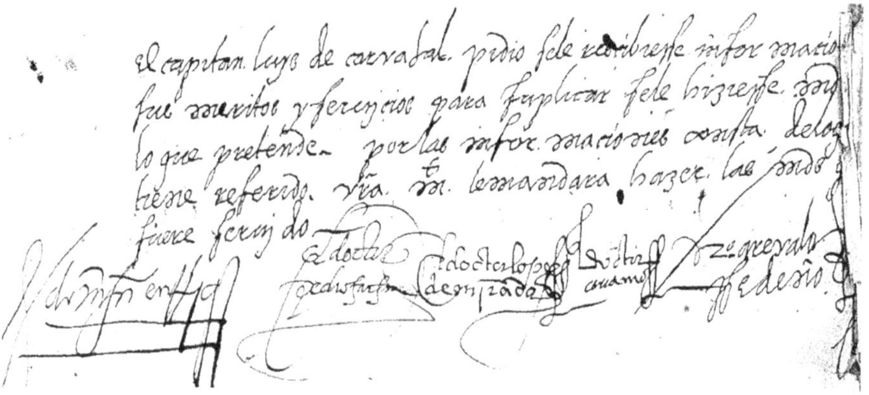
el capitan luys de carvajal pidio sele reçibiesse informacion de sus meritos y servicios para suplicar sele hiziesse merced en lo que pretende por las informaciones consta de lo que tiene referido. V.M. le mandara hazer la merced que fuere servido

Fig. 5.1. The transmittal letter from the Audiencia de México about Carvajal's merits and services. (*Courtesy of the Ministerio de Cultura, Archivo General de Indias, Seville.*)

After Carvajal's petition, the document states that "having seen said petition and questionnaire, said gentlemen (the oidores) forwarded them to the very excellent viceroy, who, as president of the Audiencia, ordered that the information offered by Luis de Carvajal be received before Dr. Arévalo Sedeño, oidor of this Audiencia." The first witness presented his testimony on 16 January 1578, and the last two months later. Between these dates, thirty three witnesses gave testimony before Sedeño in Mexico City, or before other magistrates in other locations. In addition to answering questions regarding Carvajal's claims, each witness was also asked to express his views about Carvajal's background, class (*calidad*), and his abilities to serve the Crown.

Not surprisingly most of them gave Carvajal glowing recommendations, but among them there were several whose reputations gave considerable credence to their opinions. These included D. Francisco de Puga, who had been the lieutenant of the viceroy on the Chichimeca border; Dr. Luis de Villanueva, a past oidor of the Audiencia and a special emissary of the king; Father Pedro de San Luis, who had been a friar in the province of Pánuco since the days of Andrés del Olmo, the spiritual founder of Tampico; and Alfonso Ortiz de Zúñiga, a past alcalde mayor of the province of Pánuco, all of whom were highly regarded in New Spain. Added to this list of trustworthy individuals was Viceroy Martín Enríquez, whose high regard for Carvajal made the inquiry possible.

After the document was examined by the other oidores of the Audiencia and the viceroy, it was transmitted it to the king together with their endorsement. The transmittal letter accompanying the document, shown in figure 5.1, informs the king that the Audiencia had received information about the merits and services of Carvajal and that it had verified what Carvajal claimed. Although the letter makes no reference to Carvajal's wishes, those wishes are noted in the Audiencia's condensation of Carvajal's petition:

> Captain Carvajal stated he had served H.M. in affairs important to the royal service, from which he wished H.M. and the gentlemen of his Real Consejo be informed so that he be granted royal privileges in works and honorable positions of importance, specially in the discovery and settlement of the provinces where he had served, or by some payment from his royal treasury or from rebelling Indians

This seems to indicate that Carvajal would be happy to receive, as a reward, anything the king would give him, but what he really wanted was the first item on the list: an important and honorable position in the Crown's system of government. The events that took place later show that what he wanted was to be named governor of the lands he had discovered and explored.

Carvajal knew that approval by the Consejo was not guaranteed. This council, set up to advise the king on all matters concerning the Indies, represented a serious roadblock no matter how strong would the viceroy's recommendation might be. Requests like his would often arrive in the Consejo from every colony in the Spanish New World and would cursorily be denied.[5] For these reasons, Carvajal had planned to go to Spain to argue his case in person, as allowed by the regulations then in existence. And so, a short time after the Información de Oficio about his merits was completed he went back to the province of Pánuco to get ready for the voyage to Spain. There he received another power of attorney, this one from village of San Esteban del Puerto. Soon afterward, he boarded one of the ships in the fleet going to Spain, arriving there in July.[6] Two years later he returned to New Spain, having, indeed, obtained from the king the position he desired.

2. In the Spanish Court

Immediately after his arrival in Seville Carvajal visited his wife, as well as other members of her family. He probably also took care of some business matters. But given the reasons for going to Spain, he probably spent most of the time in Madrid, lobbying the members of the Consejo. By the time he arrived there, this illustrious council had been active for many years, but in 1571 a new set of *ordenanzas,* or rules that stipulated its composition and function were ordered by the king.[7] The ordenanzas appear in the *Cedulario Indiano.*[8] The first of these shows that the Consejo consisted of a President and several *Consejeros* who, unlike the president, had to be *letrados*, and who should "be persons of good standing and of clean blood, fearful of God, and chosen for their knowledge and prudence."

Since 1571 the president of the Consejo had been Juan de Ovando, but after his death in 1575 the position remained open until July of 1580.[9] Following established rules Gómez de Santillán, the most senior member of the Consejo, had become its acting president, a position he still held when Carvajal arrived. The other members of the Consejo were then Alonso Martínez Espadero, Diego de Zúñiga, Lopez de Sarriá, and Lope de Vayllo. Also important was the secretary, Antonio de Eraso, whose name appears in many royal documents.

Carvajal had to follow a well-prescribed procedure to work his way through the Consejo. This was dictated by his desire that he be granted honorable positions of importance. Although he did not specify any such position, it appears that what he wanted was a semi-independent political entity in New Spain. And the mechanism by which this would be done was a *capitulación*, a type of royal grant that was rarely given. For example, during the last 25 years of Philip II's life, that is between 1573 and 1598, only six were granted, one of which, the penultimate, was for Carvajal.

A capitulación was a contract containing a number of *capítulos* or chapters, between two or more persons. But the capitulaciones between the king and his subjects were much more than that. Of course their contractual aspect was important, but more so was the fact that they were royal awards that enabled some selected individuals to pursue goals that were deemed important to the Crown. For example, the purpose of most of the capitulaciones granted during the reign of Philip II was to "discover, pacify, and colonize" some unexplored lands.

Who were the men who received their awards around the time Carvajal received his? Examination of the eleven royal capitulaciones that were issued from 1565 to 1574 shows that with rare exceptions the recipients were Spaniards who wanted to discover and conquer relatively small areas, for example the Islands of Puerto Rico, or Trinidad and Tobago, or to find a passage that was then believed to exist between the North (Atlantic) and South (Pacific) Oceans. It is likely that they had performed some meritorious activities, but the corresponding capitulaciones do not reveal any exceptional service to the Crown. On the other hand, all of them seem to have been able to finance the tasks they promised to the king.

Among the few exceptional individuals who received a capitulación in the period mentioned above was Pedro Menéndez de Avilés, a knight of the Order of St. James who had a well established reputation since the times of Charles V. The purpose of his capitulación, given in 1565, was to discover, conquer, and settle La Florida, a large territory whose coast extended from the Rio de las Palmas, north of Tampico, to Cape Santa Elena, in present-day North Carolina. Menéndez' capitulación also differs from those of others in the sense that it was the Crown that wanted him to pursue a task that had been attempted before but had not produced good results. As discussed below, Menéndez capitulación was instrumental in Carvajal getting his.

Regarding Carvajal, it appears that the Consejo had seen his petition by the end of 1578, for in February of 1579 that body elevated the petition to the king; a step that indicated endorsement.[10] The transmittal letter is one of several related to Carvajal that were written by the Consejo.[11] It contains his petition, and the king's response, which shows he was an active participant in the process. The cover of the document has a summary that says: "Captain Luis de Carvajal de la Cueba requests that in view of his services he be granted the territory [named] Nuevo Reyno de León." This short paragraph is the oldest known instance where the name of the territory given to Carvajal is mentioned. The statement is also the earliest known where Carvajal's name appears with the coda "de la Cueba." This addition was necessary to distinguish him from two other persons named Luis de Carvajal, both well known to the king and his council.[12] The text of the Consejo's letter includes the following introduction:

> Captain Luis de Carvajal says that by the Informaciones and other documents that have been seen in this Real Consejo, it has been verified for Y.H. that he has served Y.H. continuously, because of which he has supplicated that he be

gratified with some rent and to be commissioned the discovery and settlement
that he has indicated in his petition. He begs Y.H. that, in both Y.M. orders he
be given a reward in the same manner, he says, that Y.H. gave to the *Adelantado*
Pero Melendes (*sic* for Menéndez), together with La Florida, the land from the
Bay of S. Josepe to that of Pánuco. . . . And he not only did not colonize said
places, but did not even enter the land, nor did anybody else on his behalf. And
so the land is available to be commended to him by Y.H.[13]

Fig. 5.2. Chavez map of La Florida, The locations of S. Joseph and S. Helen are indicated by the arrowheads (added to the map). Tampico, not shown in the map, is
located about 60 miles south of teh Río de las Palmas, shown at bottom left.

Carvajal's petition follows the same pattern as that he presented before the Audiencia de México a year earlier but also requests
that the king grants him a rent of 3000 from the royal treasury.
Below this request there is an inscription written by a different hand, possibly
the king's, that says: "And give him a government or charge in which he can
serve." The next paragraph of the petition says:

> Also, in addition to the particular news he has of the land he has seen, he can say
> that the land he has seen . . . [is] yet to be explored and discovered from the end
> of what he saw, to the *Mar del Sur* (Pacific Ocean) to the northwest, and on the
> other part, to the north and northeast . . . of La Florida and Cape Santa Elena.

Here Carvajal was informing the king that the lands to the north of those
he had discovered were yet to be explored. In this he was nearly correct because, before his discoveries, there had been only accidental incursions into

parts of that territory. However, his idea that the territory extended from La Florida to the Pacific Ocean reveals the belief held at that time that the New World was much more narrow on the north than it actually is. At the end of the next paragraph in the Consejo's letter it is said that:

> [Capt. Carvajal] offers to discover, settle, and pacify . . . the provinces from the village of Tampico and river of Pánuco until the mines of Mazapil and all the other provinces from there to the northwest and south sea, and on the other side, until Cape Santa Elena.

Obviously Carvajal did not understand the implications of his promises. He had, of course, heard of the settlement in Cape Santa Elena, but had no idea how far it was from Tampico.

The rest of Carvajal's petition essentially repeated the services mentioned before the Audiencia. Obviously, the fact that the Consejo transmitted it to the king meant that those services were deemed sufficiently meritorious and that its members regarded Carvajal as a man of *calidad*, as required by the Crown of those asking for a capitulación. This implies that the Consejeros also considered Carvajal to be an hidalgo, as he himself claimed to be. In any event, the request was transmitted to the king, who decided the following:

> Give him a favorable recommendation, addressed to the viceroy of New Spain, that he should favor and honor Captain Luis de Carvajal, and should provide him in offices and charges in measure to his class, merits and services. And give him another cédula . . . that he [Carvajal] be given the discovery and colonization from the river of Pánuco and Mazapil until that land which he would colonize and discover from one sea to the other, so that in agreement with the demarcation of a map that accompanies this petition, pertaining to Pánuco, be all examined.

Evidently, the king was convinced that Carvajal deserved some compensation for the services he had performed and, therefore, ordered that a letter be sent to the viceroy of New Spain, telling him to give Carvajal a Crown position appropriate to his class, services and merits. However, thinking that the viceroy was in a much better position to evaluate the plan and determine whether something good could come out of colonizing the lands discovered by Carvajal, the king ordered the viceroy to inquire about those lands. But the most significant decision by the king was to order the viceroy that he should give Carvajal a capitulación.

Carvajal was informed of the king's decision shortly after it was made. Although he was probably pleased to see that the king had endorsed his requests, he must have been disappointed with the net result. For one thing, the king had said nothing about the stipend he wanted. More importantly, his ambitious plans about a government in New Spain would have to wait until the viceroy answered the questions raised by the king. And so, Carvajal appealed the king's decision.[14]

Carvajal's new arguments must have been convincing for less than a month later the Consejo forwarded his plea to the king.[15] That document offers some insight into the kind of negotiations that took place between the king and Carvajal. In his plea, Carvajal first acknowledged how great was the privilege [merced] already given to him, re-iterated the need for a stipend from the royal treasury, and then bluntly stated that "It is a big inconvenient that H.M. does not give him said government. Carvajal's backed this by stating that if he had to go to New Spain first more than three years would pass before he could start his project. Also, the recruitment of settlers, soldiers, and officers would have to wait until he returned to Spain. Furthermore, his having to go to New Spain would consume part of the assets that were required for the proposed discovery and colonization.

The following paragraphs in the appeal dealt with the Chichimeca Indians whose attacks continued to hamper the colonization efforts. Those attacks, Carvajal stated, would end sooner if a new government could be established north of the current frontier, and would result in an increase of the amounts of silver that could be extracted from the mines there. This implied, of course, that the king's coffers would receive their due sooner if the capitulación would be issued in Madrid. Having made his case, Carvajal stated that:

> Because of all of this he returns to implore that . . . Y.H. should be served to immediately issue an order that he (Carvajal) be given the government of those lands through the usual capitulación, so that he can make his journey with the people he has to take from these kingdoms

However, realizing that the king was concerned about granting him a territory in New Spain without consultation with the viceroy, Carvajal also proposed that "a letter could be sent to the viceroy informing him of what was agreed in Spain, and telling him that he, the viceroy, could add or remove whatever he wished from the agreement." This statement concluded Carvajal's appeal.

Apparently the king and his advisors were convinced by Carvajal's arguments, and ordered him to see Consejero López de Sarriá to review the conditions under which the enterprise was to take place. A few days later, on 14 April 1579, the Consejo sent another letter to the king informing him of Carvajal's desire to change certain stipulations in the contract.[16] This haggling is surprising, just as it is surprising to see the king giving in to some of the requests. Thus, in the first paragraph of this letter, the Consejo stated that:

> Captain Luis de Carvajal says that . . . so that he can start getting ready to make the journey, he begs Y.M. to order provide the following points:

> Firstly, he says that he had begged Y.M. give him a permit so that for ten years he could take each year a ship with provisions, arms, and other necessary things . . . without paying taxes, and that Y.M. has granted him only four years. And . . . he begs again that a permit be given for . . . eight years, and that in each he can take two ships.

The response by the king, written on the margin of this paragraph says "Let it be for six years, and one ship, as it has been ordered." Carvajal also requested to be allowed to bring with him one hundred slaves, which he says were need to work in the mines and the land. Apparently his earlier request had been reduced to thirty. The king's response to this new request was "Let it be forty." The next issue was more delicate:

> He also says that Y.H. has ordered that he should pay ten thousand ducats in bonds, which if he has to fulfill he will certainly do. And because paying them in these kingdoms would be very difficult . . . he begs Y.H. order that it should be sufficient to have him promise to pay said ten thousand ducats, as it has been permitted to others in similar cases. And that if he had to pay them, that they be commensurate to the licenses given to him, and that he can pay them in New Spain.

The king's response was: "Let it be eight thousand ducats in bonds, to be given in Mexico [City], to the satisfaction of the viceroy and Audiencia." Carvajal also asked to be permitted to take lands for himself and for those who would settle in his territory, to which the king responded that the viceroy should grant this request. Finally, he asked to pay to the Crown a smaller percentage of the gold, silver, and precious stones that might be found in his territory than the fifth, as was normally required. In response, the king ordered "Let them pay the twelfth for ten years."

On the surface, it seems surprising that Carvajal had the guile to bargain with the king. But inspection of similar grants shows that Carvajal was only requesting the same privileges granted to others before him. Perhaps more surprising was the king's willingness to participate in the bargaining. Also remarkable is the fact that only a small number of issues had remained in contention, namely those mentioned above; others had already been decided. These included the title conferred to Carvajal, its duration, the territories given to him, the number of colonizers he could take to New Spain, the duties assigned to him, and the help he would receive.

The matter of the bonds requires further comments for several modern authors have stated that Carvajal suborned the Crown in order to obtain his capitulación. The previous sections show that these speculations are incorrect. But, in addition, the amounts requested in bonds by the Crown shows several important facts. One is that the only money the Crown wanted from Carvajal was to insure that Carvajal would fulfill his promises. Requesting that bonds be paid in advance was a standard requirement. Also, the amounts required, eight thousand ducats, were miniscule from the perspective of the Crown. Another important fact is that Carvajal had little money at his disposal in Spain. These points show, conclusively, that money had nothing to do with the award given to him.

And so, towards the end of April of 1579 all the details had been worked out. Therefore, the Consejo scribes began to prepare the capitulación and other documents related to it. These were several royal cédulas that were meant to help Carvajal to carry out his duties. The capitulación was signed by the king on the last day of May of 1579. It is possible that it was given to Carvajal on that date, perhaps by the king himself.

3. The Capitulación

Although the original capitulación given to Carvajal has been lost, a copy of it, prepared at nearly the same time, exists in the Spanish archives whose contents have come to light only recently.[17] Because of its historical value a translation into English is included in Appendix A.

Generally speaking, Carvajal's capitulación follows the same pattern as others issued by the Crown in the last third of the sixteenth century. A preamble is followed by a set of obligations, which in turn is followed by a set of privileges and by a concluding paragraph. The particular obligations and privileges differed from other capitulaciones, but the preamble and the closing paragraphs have much in common with them. This is particularly true of the concluding paragraph, where the king promises to help Carvajal carry out his tasks, or to punish him should he fail. Clearly these promises and threats were pro-forma and were not designed for Carvajal alone.

Figure 5.3 shows a copy of the first page of Carvajal's capitulación. That page contains part of the preamble and, on the left margin, an inscription that begins with a statement that says: "Seen by Captain Luis de Carvajal." This shows that the document was approved by him.

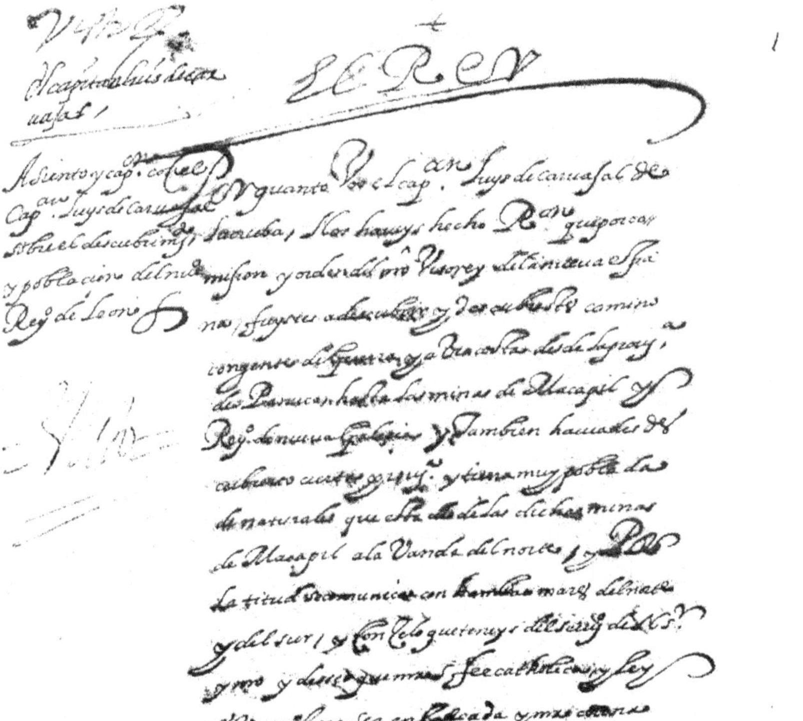

Fig. 5.3. First page of Carvajal's capitulación. (*Courtesy of the Ministerio de Cultura, Archivo General de Indias, Seville.*)

The following discussion presents the essential contents of those chapters in the document that require clarification, starting with chapter two of the obligations.

> 2. Discover, pacify and indoctrinate the Indians living in Chichimeca territory within five years.

The time allotted was unrealistic, given that the Spaniards had not been able to subdue the Chichimeca Indians since their conquest of the Aztec Empire more than 50 years earlier.

> 3. Build and colonize as many towns as needed between Tampico and St. Joseph.

As discussed before this obligation was absurd. Also absurd was the next.

> 4. Continue to colonize the land, Tierra Adentro, until reaching La Florida, and on the north and northwest, so that from them it is possible to connect his territory to New Spain and New Galicia.

As if the settlements along the coast did not already represent an enormous task, Carvajal was told to settle as many towns as needed to facilitate linking La Florida with Nuevo Reino de León and other provinces in New Spain.

> 6. Colonize a village where cochineal can be farmed.

The Crown was interested in cochineal because it could generate income to its treasury. That business, incidentally, followed silver in the amounts generated in the colonies.[18]

> 7. Build a fort at the mouth of the river Pánuco, at the beginning of your Government.

The need for such a fort was prompted by Hawkins' landing in New Spain ten years earlier, as well as by the news that Francis Drake had been assaulting Spanish ports in the Caribbean.

> 8. Within eight years bring to peace, again, the Indians of the towns of Tampasquín, Tamotela, Sanct Miguel and from there, those that exist until the towns of Xalpa and Sechu.

These towns were in a region previously pacified by Carvajal. Their appearance here is related to privilege number 12.

> 9. Take to New Spain up to 100 men, sixty of whom farmers, married, with their wives and children, and the others soldiers and officers.

It is obvious that the number of colonizers would be insufficient to carry out the tasks listed in the capitulación. This probably means that Carvajal anticipated that some people already in New Spain would join him.

11. Obey the Instructions for the Discovery, Pacification, and Population of New Settlements, which will be given to you.

The instructions mentioned here had been put into effect in 1573 and decreed the kinds of settlements that could be founded.[19]

12. Pay, soon after arriving in New Spain, up to 8,000 ducats in *fianzas* (bonds) *legas, llanas y abonadas.*[20]

As discussed before, this item was one of those negotiated by Carvajal.

13. Show the capitulación to the viceroy, who is ordered to keep that part which he does not find inconvenient, and remove those which he does.

Most, if not all of the jurisdictional problems that Carvajal encountered later would have been avoided if the viceroy in New Spain had paid attention to this item.

Capítulo 13 concludes the obligatory part of the capitulación. The privileges section begins immediately after.

1. We confer upon you the title of our Governor and General Captain of the provinces and lands that exist *from the port of Tampico, Pánuco River, and in the mines of Mazapil* (emphasis added), until the limits of Nueva Galicia and Nueva Vizcaya, and, from there to the north, what is yet to be discovered, from one ocean to the other, so long as it does not exceed two hundred leagues in latitude and other two hundred in longitude.

This important chapter is discussed later.

4. We appoint you as *alguacil mayor* for your life and that of one heir, with the additional right that you and him can name and remove judges from places already colonized, as well as those which you will colonize.

This clause was important. By it Carvajal was given the right to name and remove judges as he pleased, both in existing towns and in those he might settle in the future. This privilege was also the cause of much litigation in the years to come.

12. We order thta from this moment the towns of Tampasquín, Tamotela, Sanct Miguel and, from there, the others that have rebelled against our service, until Xalpa and Sechu, be of your jurisdiction provided that all of them be pacified and brought to our obedience within said eight years.

By this order the king awarded Carvajal a region that included towns to the south of the territory granted to him in the first chapter of this section. Apparently, the reasons for this inclusion is that a few years before Carvajal had pacified that region, and because the first part of the capitulación, required him to pacify it again. However, the towns mentioned in the order already belonged to the Crown.

Chapter 12 is the last in the privileges and honors section of the capitulación. After that the document concludes by stating that if Carvajal keeps his promises the king will fulfill his, but that otherwise he will be punished. These promises and threats were part of the template used in most capitulaciones and were not unique to Carvajal's. Years later, however, Carvajal would be accused of not having fulfilled the promises he made. In this he was not alone; most other recipients of such awards also failed to fulfill all of the requirements imposed on them. More importantly, Philip II also failed to fulfill his promises to help and support Carvajal's efforts.

Carvajal's Territory

The first chapter in the privilege section of the capitulación played a most important role in the jurisdictional disputes that took place in the mid 1580s, as will be described later. To provide some background for these disputes it is useful to discuss this chapter in some detail.

First of all, although the chapter seems to specify the territory's limits, its interpretation is unclear. It is true that it states that the territory was limited to a square having 200 leagues on each side, except that on the west it was limited by Nueva Galicia and Nueva Vizcaya. However, nothing was said about the southern boundary. Furthermore, the inclusion of Mazapil makes it difficult to understand the meaning of the paragraph. As it turns out, that reference was transcribed incorrectly.[21] The intended wording appears in the first chapter of the obligations section and in the 28 February letter from the Consejo, both of which say that "from Tampico and river Pánuco *until* (emphasis added) the mines of Mazapil." Of course, this correction makes it clear that the town of Tampico corresponded to the southeast vertex of the square and that Mazapil was some distance away. More troublesome was the absence of any statement about the southern boundary, although the reference to the river Pánuco seems to imply that it marked that boundary. However, privilege number 12 gave Carvajal certain towns that were well to the south of that river.

Now, Carvajal's territory was, in principle, a square having 200 leagues on each side, placed so that Tampico would fall on its southeast vertex. However, the western frontier was less than 200 leagues from the eastern edge because Nueva Galicia and Nueva Vizcaya had settlements that were considerably closer to Tampico than that distance. To the north of Tampico there were no prescribed limits; therefore along that direction the northern boundary was 200 leagues away. And on the northern edge the western boundary was also 200 leagues long because there were no Spanish settlements there.

To get an idea of the extent of Carvajal's territory, it is necessary to express the length of a league in miles. However, that equivalence is uncertain because, in the sixteenth century, the Spaniards used several types of leagues. Nevertheless, a recent study indicates that the league used in the capitulación was probably the *Legua Castellana*.[22] This corresponds to 5.572 km, or 3.47 miles.

Thus, a distance of 200 leagues corresponds to nearly 700 miles, so that the northern boundary of Carvajal's territory would have been a few miles south of present-day Dallas, Texas, whereas the western most location along that boundary would have fallen near present day Roads Fork, New Mexico, close to the Arizona border. Howver, on the south the border extended only as far as Mazapil. This means that Carvajal Territory was not a square but, roughly speaking, an irregular polygon whose area was about 15% larger than Texas.

The Cédulas

One of the promises kept by the king was one to issue several cédulas to help Carvajal carry out his tasks. Not counting those that were written after Carvajal arrived in New Spain, the Crown issued a total of twenty one cédulas whose summaries are given in Appendix B. Nearly all of the cédulas were written in Toledo on June 14, 1579, that is, two weeks after the capitulación was issued. The first six contain an acknowledgment signed by Carvajal.[23] These were obviously hand-delivered to him so that he could carry out some tasks while still in Spain, the most important being the recruitment of colonizer, considered in the next chapter.

6

Carvajal's People

Asked if all those people presented proof of not being of the forbidden to go to the Indies, he said that they did not because the king ordered, by a cédula, that they could go without showing such proof.

Inquisition trial of Gov. Carvajal, April 19, 1589.[1]

Two weeks after the king signed the capitulación, Carvajal received some cédulas that were intended to help him carry out certain tasks in Spain. One was to recruit a number of colonizers for his Nuevo Reino de León. Another was to acquire a ship in which to take them there and to prepare it so that it would be ready by the spring of 1580, when the next fleet was scheduled to depart for the New World. This departure date meant that he had less than a year to complete all of the preparations that were necessary to undertake the voyage. This chapter considers these activities in some detail and includes a discussion of the people he took to New Spain, as well as a short account of the voyage.

1. Recruiting people

The recruitment of the colonizers who left Spain with Carvajal in the Spring of 1580 started soon after he received the cédula that enabled him to do so. The task was not a small one. Most of the Spaniards who emigrated to the New World in the sixteenth century had done so already. However, facilitating Carvajal's task were the many relatives he had in Spain and Portugal. In fact, while negotiating his capitulación in Madrid, he had written to his brother-in-law Francisco Rodríguez de Matos, offering him an official position in Nuevo Reino de León. Apparently Francisco had initially rejected the offer thinking that it would be better for him and his family to go to France, where his older brother, Diego, lived at the time. Nevertheless, Carvajal felt that his sister and her family would be better off in New Spain. Also, her oldest son, Gaspar de Carvajal, was already there, which meant the family would be reunited. And so, Carvajal and a young relative of his named Felipe Núñez went to Medina del Campo, where Francisco lived, to attempt to convince him to join the colonizing effort in Nuevo Reino de León. His arguments obviously succeeded, for not only did Francisco agree to join him, but also helped recruit others.

Also living in the same city at the time were the families of Álvaro de León and of his sister, Isabel de León. As shown later, some of her children were recruited by Carvajal. After Medina Carvajal went to Benavente where other descendents of the León family lived, and then to Astorga where Isabel Rodríguez, one of the daughters of Carvajal's sister, lived with her husband Gabriel de Herrera. Although Gabriel had agreed to go to the New World, he died soon after Carvajal's visit. Nevertheless, Isabel joined her parents in the journey, a decision that was to have serious consequences later on.

From Astorga, Carvajal went to Portugal, probably entering that country after visiting Alcañizas, where his grandfather's brother, Alonso Núñez, had lived. In Portugal he visited Mogadouro, his birthplace, as well as Miranda, Cortiços, and Mirandela, where several other members of his family still lived.[2] He then returned to Spain, probably through Fermoselle, where his paternal ancestors originated. Finally, he headed south toward Seville, traversing the Spanish province of Extremadura, where he seems to have recruited more people. It should be noted that, except for Medina del Campo, the entire recruiting path fell in La Raya de Portugal.

Carvajal's excursion into Portugal should not be surprising because Philip II had made clear his intentions to annex that kingdom to Spain, claiming he was the heir to its throne after the death of his cousin, Cardinal Henry. In any event, crossing the border was a simple matter for anybody living in La Raya. More difficult, however, was to take Portuguese-born people to New Spain because they would have to pass an inspection that required all emigrants to be Spanish. This requirement would not alone be sufficient to prevent any person born in the Portuguese side of La Raya to go to the Spanish New World because their speech and manners differed little from those of the Spaniards living on the other side of the border. However, the inspections included a more serious roadblock, namely the royal order that no one should be allowed to go to the New World unless he had proved not to be "of the forbidden." The largest group among the forbidden were descendents of Jews who had converted to Christianity within the last three generations. Since Carvajal and his relatives were New Christian, they could not, at least legally, obtain certificates of limpieza de sangre. As the epigraph at the beginning of this chapter shows, Carvajal stated that the king had ordered that his coloniz-

ers could go to the New World without being required to show such certificates. Indeed, that is what the first cédula said. Here is the complete text of
that important order:

> The King. To our officers that reside in Seville, in the House of Trade. We order
> you to allow Captain Luis Carvajal de la Cueva to return to New Spain, taking
> with him one hundred men, sixty of whom married farmers with their wom-
> en and sons [and daughters], and the remaining soldiers and officers for the
> discovery, pacification and colonization of the provinces that will be entitled
> Nuevo Reino de León, which is in that land, about which we have made with
> him an agreement and capitulación, *without asking any of them any information*
> (emphasis added), because by means of this we charge said Captain Luis de
> Carvajal that he should be very careful that they be clean persons and not of
> the forbidden to go to those lands, and that in particular he makes sure he does
> not take with him any married man who leaves his wife in these kingdoms. All
> of which I order you to obey without putting impediment of any kind. Made in
> Toledo on 14 June of 1579. I the King. Verified by Antonio de Eraso and signed
> by the members of the Consejo.[3]

This was a most remarkable order. By it, Philip II allowed Carvajal to take
to New Spain anybody he wanted. Of course, the permission was conditional;
the king insisted that those taken by him to the New World should not be "of
the forbidden." But instead of letting the officers in Seville certify that each
person in the group met that requirement, he transferred that delicate function
to Carvajal. The cédula proves what Carvajal said before the Inquisitors, but
its discovery, in the 1970s, only added more fuel to the idea expressed by some
authors that the Crown had been suborned.

What could have prompted the king to issue this decree? The answer is
twofold. First, it is clear that the king regarded Carvajal as an hidalgo and
therefore trusted him. Second, time was short. The issue of trust is proven by
the great honor that the king had bestowed on Carvajal. The timing question
requires a longer explanation. After receiving his cédulas, Carvajal had to do
many things prior to departing for the New World, including equipping a
vessel to transport his people; supplying it with provisions for a long voyage;
and, most importantly, to recruit up to one hundred men to join him. Knowing
that time was short he must have argued that recruiting such a large number
of people would be a time-consuming effort that would leave little time to
obtain the necessary certificates of their limpieza because each certification
required a lengthy process.[4]

But even with this dispensation the recruiting task was not easy. For one
thing, the number of men willing to go to New Spain at that time had been

significantly reduced by previous emigrations.[5] Spaniards who still wanted to go to the New World preferred places where silver and gold had already been found, while all that Carvajal could offer at this stage was hope. Also, the king had specifically insisted that married men recruited by Carvajal should not leave their wives behind, a requirement that implied the relocation of entire families and further limited the number of those willing to leave Spain. Nevertheless, Carvajal managed to enlist a large number of men to accompany him. One factor that helped him was the fact that those he recruited were not required to provide certificates of limpieza.

The 1580 List

The names and origin of the people who joined Carvajal on his 1580 voyage are found in the list of the persons he declared in Seville in 1580, and in the list he made before the inquisitors in 1589. For simplicity, the Seville document is referred to here as the *1580 List*.[6] The Inquisition list is of limited value because it only mentions the names of some colonizers.[7] The *1580 List*, on the other hand, is substantially more detailed. In it appear the names of the individuals who Carvajal declared in Seville, their places of origin, and the names and origin of their parents. This information is most useful in any attempt to ascertain the background and religious practices of those recruited by him. The first page of the list includes Carvajal's declaration, the first cédula, and the entry for one of the recruits and his family. The introductory paragraph reads:

> Declaration of the persons that I Luis de Carvajal de la Cueva name to take with me to the discovery, pacification and colonization of the provinces that will be called Nuevo Reino de León, which is in New Spain, in conformity with the capitulación that H.M. ordered be taken with him, about the above. Which persons have to be one hundred, sixty of whom married farmers with their wives, sons and daughters, and the remaining soldiers, as it appears in a cédula by H.M., which reads as follows.

This statement is followed by a copy of the first cédula, after which there begins a listing of 83 men, clearly short of the allotted number. However, the list probably included only those who did not have their limpieza documents.[8] Those who had them did not need be declared. This means that there were other recruits. In fact, among those who were not declared in Seville are ten men whose names were mentioned by Carvajal in 1589, five of whom were not colonizers, and a certain Diego de Villalobos, who is mentioned in another cédula.[9] In any event, the *1580 List* mentioned all of those who did not have proof of their limpieza, and therefore included most of those who were "of the forbidden."

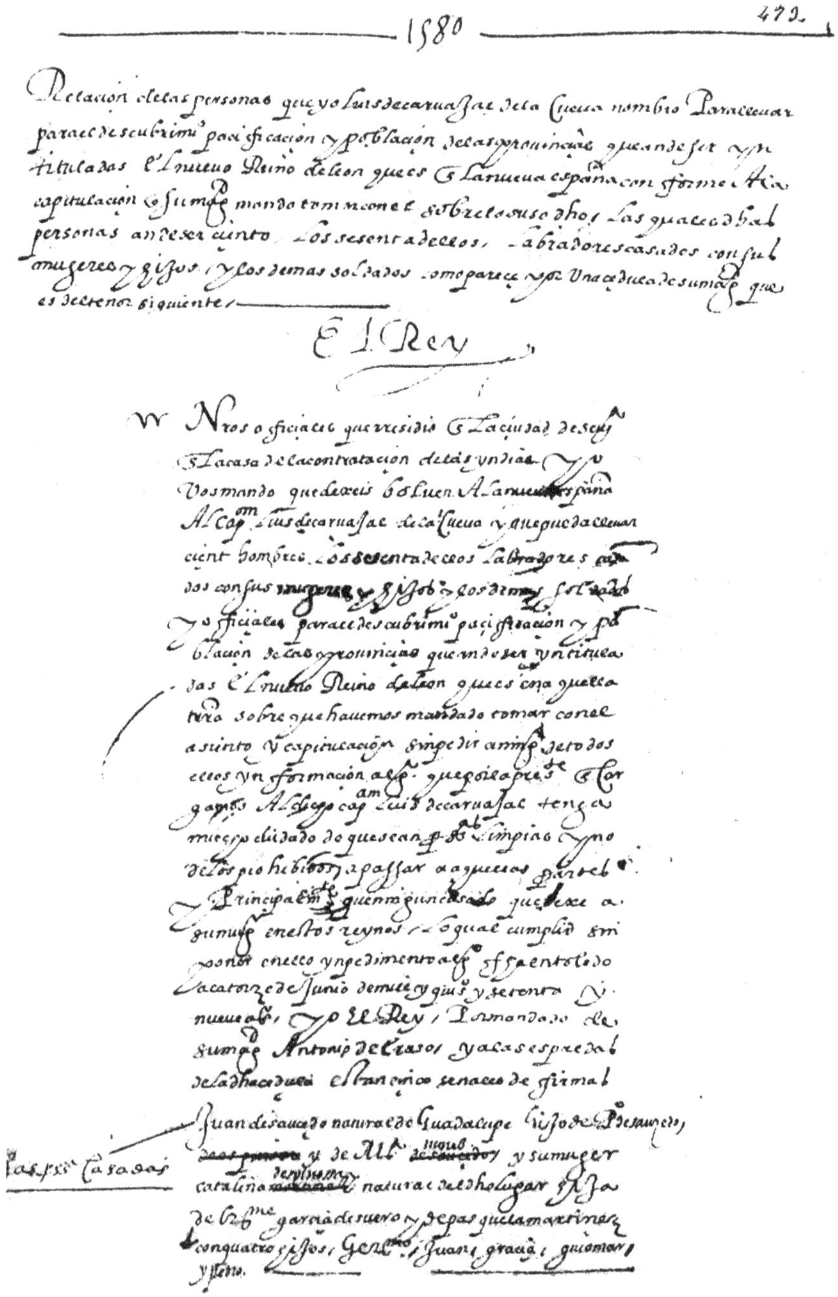

El Rey

Fig. 6.1. First page of the *1580 List*. (*Courtesy of the Ministerio de Cultura, Archivo General de Indias, Seville.*)

Excluding Carvajal himself, the total number of individuals appearing in the *1580 List* is 196, 117 adults and 79 minors. Adding those mentioned years later by Carvajal gives a total of about 200 colonizers. While this number seems small, it in fact implies that thanks to Carvajal's recruits, the year 1580 experienced a several fold increase in the migration rate to New Spain. For example, in the last two decades of the sixteenth century, a yearly *average* of only 15 individuals emigrated to New Spain.[10] Even more significant was the large number of females brought there by Carvajal. According to the *1580 List* that number was 69, 35 of whom were single, whereas the average number per year was less than five. It is clear that Carvajal's people must have had an enormous impact on the demographic and cultural development of that colony.

The recruits

The main question raised by the *1580 List* is whether Carvajal fulfilled his obligation to insure that none of the people going to the New World were of the forbidden. The evidence indicates that he did not. For one thing, all of the relatives who came with him were New Christians. This does not mean that Carvajal knew that fact, or that he purposefully ignored the king's charge. Rather, it means that thinking himself an hidalgo he must have assumed that all other members of his family were as well. On the other hand, several of his adult relatives certainly knew that they, and he, were New Christians. However, they also knew about his upbringing and realized that it would not be safe to inform him, or the authorities, of that background.

What about the other recruits? Although in some instances the *1580 List* seems to point to a Jewish background, the documentary evidence shows that Carvajal did not pay any attention to the limpieza of those willing to join him. What mattered to him was to recruit farmers, soldiers, and officers. But as late as January of 1580 he had not yet recruited as many as the capitulación stipulated. In an attempt to speed the process, he asked others to help him. Among these were Alonso Rodríguez and Diego Ruiz de Ribera, both of whom were empowered to "receive as colonizers ... *any persons, so long as they are married farmers* (emphasis added)."[11] This does away with the idea that he was careful, as ordered by the king, in making sure those enlisted were not of the forbidden.

The Seville archives contain some contracts that Carvajal made with several recruits between late January and early February of 1580. These contracts are of considerable interest because they describe what he offered to, and expected from, those joining him. Among the contracts with married men were those of Diego de Madrid, a mason from Seville, and of Juan de Saucedo de

Espinoza, a carpenter from Guadalupe.[12] And among the contracts with single men, there is one with Domingo Martínez de Cearreta, and another with five men from Espinoza de los Monteros, in León.[13] Each of these individuals was promised free passage to the New World; release from having to provide proof of his limpieza; and a promise to be treated preferentially in the distribution of lands and of other privileges granted by the king.

The contracts stipulated that each recruit should go to Sanlúcar de Barrameda with his family and belongings before the yearly fleet would depart to the New World. In addition, the contracts also stipulated that these men would have to live in Nuevo Reino de León for at least five years, working on whatever Carvajal ordered, and that they could not go elsewhere, even temporarily, without his consent. To guarantee that the contracts would be fulfilled, those recruited had to promise to pay 50,000 *maravedis* if they broke any of the clauses in the contracts. Also, each married men had to give Carvajal 30 ducats in bonds that would be returned once they had boarded the ship that was to take them to New Spain. The corresponding figure for single men was 20 ducats, an amount equal to the price of passage to the New World. All of these requirements show that these people were selected simply because they were willing to join Carvajal and that their nationality, ethnicity, or religious background did not come into the picture.

The above conclusions are not meant to imply that Carvajal did not bring with him people who were either New Christians or who still practiced Judaism under cover. He obviously did, but who were they? Of course, the *1580 List* does not directly answer that question. There are, however other markers in it that provide some help in this task. It should pointed out that the personal information given in that list cannot be entirely trusted because it contains some factual errors. These may have been made intentionally to hide the Portuguese origin of some of those listed. For example, the document states that Carvajal was born in Benavente, which was not true. Also intentional is the listing of Ginebra Márquez as the wife of Jorge de León, when, in fact, they were siblings. In addition, some individuals appear with changed names. For example, Carvajal's sister was named Francisca Núñez, but appears in the list as Francisca de Carvajal. Some conflicting information also exists in the names or places of origin of non-relatives. For example Diego Martínez de Valladares is listed as Diego de Valladar, born in Isla, near Laredo, whereas in the contract he signed with Carvajal it is said that Isla is in the diocese of Burgos.

These points bring up the question as to how was the list prepared. While it might be thought that each individual gave his own personal information at the time the fleet departed from Seville but this was not the case because the recruits were waiting in Sanlúcar. Instead, the document shows that Carvajal declared the names and family information of seventy five men—31 married and 44 single—in the *nao mayor*, in Seville, before the fleet's departure. The names declared by him appear first in the list, after which there appears Carvajal's own name and information, followed by two addenda that give the names of some people declared by Guiomar's brother, Nuño Álvarez de Ribera. The first, dated 1 June 1580, contains the names of two married and five single men. The second is dated 6 May 1580, possibly a mistake by the scribe for it appears below the June entry. It and contains the name of an additional married man, thus making a total of 34 married and 49 single men. Incidentally, these additional entries show that the voyage to the New World did not start before 1 June 1580.

Consider now the names of the people declared by Carvajal or by his brother in law. The *1580 List* first gives that information for the married men and their families, and then for the single men. For example, the first entry refers to a married man and says:

> Juan de Saucedo, born in Guadalupe, son of Pedro de Saucedo and María Núñez; his wife Catalina de Espinosa, born in the same place, daughter of Bartolomé García de Suero and Pascuala Martínez, with four (*sic*) sons and daughters: Geronimo, Juan, Gracia, Guiomar, and Pedro.

A complete list of the adults is presented, in tabular form, in Appendix C. The names are ordered alphabetically by surname, with the number of sons and daughters of each married man added at the end of his entry, split by gender. The first names of these minors are not included because their surnames were not given. The information thus provided can be used in a variety of ways, such as the count of the females given at the end of the last section.

Table 2 Regional origin of Carvajal's colonizers

Region	Married	Single Men	Minors	Totals
Andalucía	30	15	16	61
Extremadura	18	4	41	63
León	12	13	20	45
Other	8	17	2	27
Totals	68	49	79	196

Another use of the data is to classify, by region, the origin of the people who joined Carvajal. That information is presented in Table 2. Listed under "other" are those who originated in Vizcaya, Galicia, Castilla-La Mancha, and Aragón. As it is seen, the list does not include a single person from Portugal. This is unlikely. Carvajal spent a good deal of time there and must have managed to convince some Portuguese men to join him. On the other hand, the table shows that the number of people who originated in León and in Extremadura was 108, or 55% of the total. This is remarkable given that between 1580 and 1600 these two regions contributed less than 20% of the Spanish emigrants to the New world. In fact, the 108 figure probably underestimates the number of individuals originating in those two provinces because many of those listed as having originated in Andalucía may have also been born in them. This would mean that the majority of those listed originated in towns located near La Raya de Portugal, which was the home of many Portuguese crypto-Jews. An implication of these facts is that many of the individuals who came with Carvajal were New Christians of Jewish descent who wanted to avoid persecution from the Inquisition and did so thanks to the cédula that allowed them to leave Spin without showing proof of their limpieza. A rough estimate based on various factors such as family and surname type indicates that about 50% of those joining Carvajal belonged to that category.

Also important is the number of recruits that practiced Judaism under cover at the time they left Spain. This is, of course, impossible to ascertain. However, given that many had a Portuguese New Christian background and that they chose to go to the New World at that time, makes it likely that most of the adults counted in the above group were practitioners. Minors were normally told about these practices only after they reached a certain age or displayed a level of maturity such that they could be trusted with that secret. For example, El Mozo, Carvajal's well-known nephew told the inquisitors that he did not know about his parents' religion until after they arrived in New Spain "because his father had not wanted to tell him until then because he was a young boy."[14] It is likely that the same restrictions applied to children in the other New Christian families that joined Carvajal, which means that many of the other minors in other New Christian families joining him were also converted to Judaism after their arrival in New Spain.

3. The voyage home

Whether Carvajal had been able to recruit as many people as he was allowed, he had to carry out other tasks, such as making sure that his ship would be ready to join the fleet going to the New World in the spring of 1580. In addition, his father-in-law, Miguel Núñez, had died early that year, an event that increased Carvajal's responsibilities.[15] Nevertheless, most of his time was spent making arrangements for the voyage. For example, on 21 May 1580 he promised before a public notary to pay a certain Francisca de Castro 1,100 *reales* to cover the cost of 27 quintales, or 2,700 lbs, of *bizcocho*. The interesting point about this promise is that the stated amount was to be paid the following year, on the return of the fleet. This shows, once more, that Carvajal had little money in Spain. Also relevant is a document, dated 2 January 1580, that describes a legal transaction between Carvajal and a certain Hernán Benitez about a ship called *Nuestra Señora de la Luz*.[16] Some authors believe that the document shows that Carvajal purchased that ship, and that it was in it that he took his colonizers to the New World. However, a closer reading of the document shows that it simply was a transfer of power over the use of the ship—from Carvajal to Benitez.[17]

But Carvajal did own a ship, an *urca*, as El Mozo told his inquisitors.[18] The ship had to join the fleet that was to depart from Seville in the Spring of 1580. After being loaded, fleet ships would be inspected by officers of the House of Trade to insure that all cargo was registered and that the passengers had the necessary documents. Only after these tasks were completed, would the fleet be allowed to leave. The first leg of the voyage, from Seville to the Mediterranean, was over the waters of the Guadalquivir. While the distance was short, ships normally took a few days to cover it because that river had to be navigated carefully, particularly if the ships were heavily loaded. The difficulties did not necessarily end when the open sea was reached because a sand bar at the mouth of the river presented additional obstacles.

Whether Carvajal's ship left Seville with the fleet is uncertain. In a letter that he sent to the king in October of 1580 he said that the ship departed from Sanlúcar de Barrameda, a statement he repeated before the inquisitors in 1589.[19] These statements seem to be in conflict with that of El Mozo, who said that he and his family left Seville aboard his uncle's ship on the day of the *Santisima Trinidad* (Pentecost), and that they stayed four days in Bonanza, waiting for his uncle to join them.[20] Carvajal's statements are corroborated by the contracts that were drawn with the colonizers. As stated before these stipulated that the recruits should go to Sanlúcar before the fleet's departure, to board his ship. Having traveled the waters of the Guadalquivir several times, Carvajal knew that the weight of a fully loaded ship would make it difficult to safely navigate those waters. It is therefore possible that he decided to load only part of the cargo in Seville, and leave the rest for Sanlúcar. If so, his immediate family, which had been staying in Seville, probably boarded the ship there, as El Mozo said.

The date when the fleet left Seville is not known exactly, but it probably was soon *after* June 1, when, as the *1580 List* shows, a colonizer was declared before the Seville authorities.[21] On the way towards the Mediterranean, one of its ships foundered.[22] After reaching the open waters, the fleet encountered a severe storm that forced it to take cover in Cádiz until the 10th of that month. On that day a list was prepared that shows the names of the ships in the fleet.[23] The list, presented in Appendix D, shows that none of the fleet's ships had a master named Luis de Carvajal. The reason for this was that his ship did not go to Cádiz but stayed in Bonanza, where the colonizers came on board.

After the storm passed, the fleet left Cádiz and headed toward the New World. Carvajal's ship joined the convoy as it passed by Bonanza. The voyage was described by Francisco de Luján, the general of the fleet, in his report to the king.[24] Nine days after leaving Cádiz the fleet reached La Gomera, one of the Canary Islands. Some of its ships entered in the port of that island to get firewood and fresh water; others, including the *Capitana* did not because of strong winds. Luján said he waited for those that had entered until nightfall, after which he decided to continue the voyage, leaving them behind.

One month later, on 20 July, Luján's ship and several others that had left La Gomera at the same time arrived in the port of Ocoa in the Island Hispaniola. Ten other ships arrived there during the next two days. Five or six days later the fleet left that port reaching Cape San Antón on 11 August, which indicates they were doing good time. But afterwards, the winds ceased almost completely and the fleet was not able to make much progress for six days. In fact, some ships were dragged by ocean currents, with the result that on the 20th of August one ship, the *San Salvador*, foundered in the Isla de Arenas. Thanks to the fast rescue ordered by Luján, nobody died and the cargo belonging to the king—mostly mercury to be used in the silver mines—was saved. Finally, the fleet arrived in the port of San Juan de Ulúa on August 25 of 1580, two and a half months after having left Spain.

Traveling in the *Capitana* was the new viceroy of New Spain, Lorenzo Suárez de Mendoza, Conde de Coruña. His arrival in New Spain was also reported to the king by Luján: "The viceroy, Conde de Coruña, is [in] good [health] and is now in his government." Luján's letter does not mention Governor Carvajal, which is somewhat surprising. The reason was simply that he was not aware that the newly appointed governor was traveling in one of the ships accompanying his fleet. More surprising was the fact that Carvajal was not aware that a new viceroy had been appointed, much less that he was traveling in the same fleet. To complicate matters, the fleet arrived in New Spain without any official documents from the Crown, including a copy of Carvajal's capitulación.[25] This presented some problems for the Audiencia and for Carvajal, as it will be discussed in the following chapter.

Carvajal's Urca

Two questions remain about Carvajal' voyage to New Spain: the name and type of his ship, and whether it traveled to New Spain with the fleet. The search for the ship's name was motivated by a desire to learnthe names of the people that had joined him as colonizers and thus acquired an importance of it own. The initial search was based on something that Carvajal said in 1589, namely, that the *pilot* of his ship was named Pedro Sánchez.[26] A contemporary document cited by Eugenio del Hoyo indicates that a man by that name was the *maestre*, or master, of a ship named the *Santa Catalina*. This led him to speculate that this was Carvajal's ship.[27] However, the speculation is incorrect on several grounds. One is the vast difference between pilots and masters of a ship in a Spanish fleet. Another is that this *Santa Catalina* was not an urca, as stated by Carvajal's nephew, but a small *zabra*, that is, a very different type of ship. Furthermore, the document cited by Hoyo shows that this Pedro Sánchez and his zabra were in Seville on 30 August 1580, only five days after Luján's fleet arrived in New Spain. This would imply a *round-trip* duration of less than 90 days, more than a month shorter than normal, and ignores the statement made by Carvajal that his ship foundered in Tampico shortly after his arrival.[28]

As it turns out, contemporary documents confirm that Carvajal's ship was an urca that went to New Spain with the 1580 fleet. In addition, one of those documents includes the name of the urca. Consider each of these points separately. Confirmation that Carvajal's ship accompanied the fleet appears in a letter from Philip II to Moya de Contreras, written a few days after the departure of the fleet, in which he informs the Archbishop that "Captain Luis de Carvajal . . . is leaving in the present fleet."[29] And confirmation that Carvajal's ship was an urca appears in a cédula dated May 3, 1580, in which the king ordered "that despite previous orders, Captain Luis de Carvajal be allowed to take his people . . . to New Spain *in a new and light urca of about 130 tons, that he has purchased* (emphasis added)."[30]

The last issue is the name of the urca. This appears in Luján's letter to the king. There, he reported the arrival in Ocoa, on July 20, of the ships that had been left behind in La Gomera, using in all but two instances the names of their *maestres* to identify the ships. The two remaining ships he identified by their names, one of which was Carvajal's urca. Here is what Luján said:

> I arrived in the port of Ocoa on 20 July and anchored there at noon. And on 21 days of said month entered in that port the *Urca de Pánuco*, and the naos maestres Manuel Díaz, Hernán García, and Francisco Bernal y Nufio Rodríguez. And on the next day, at three in the afternoon, entered the naos maestres Francisco Salvago, Nicolas de Rodas, Juan de Atibar; and after the prayers, the *Almiranta*, and the naos maestres Esteban de la Zubieta, and Juan de Micina. And so, blessed be the Lord, the complete fleet was gathered, except a *nao* from Cádiz of burgo novo that . . .[31]

Thus, the day after Luján's ship arrived in Ocoa, ten other ships arrived there, two of which were not identified by the names of their masters, but by their names. One was the *Almiranta,* and the other was a ship named the *Urca de Pánuco.* The latter could be no other than Carvajal's urca, obviously named that way in honor of the region where he had lived for the past 23 years and where his Nuevo Reino de León would commence.

While the final destination of the fleet was San Juan de Ulúa, Carvajal's ship did not go there. His destination is mentioned in the first letter he wrote to the king after his arrival in New Spain:

> I left the port of San Lucar in the company of the fleet that arrived in New Spain, *from which I separated in Ocoa* (emphasis added). And from there I took the route that would take me to Tampico and river of Pánuco, which is in the beginning of the Nuevo Reino de León, where I anchored and disembarked the 100 colonizers that with me traveled, as it can be verified by the testimony that I send with this.[32]

The arrival in Tampico took place on 24 August 1580, a day earlier than the fleet's arrival in San Juan de Ulúa. This ended the voyage of Carvajal and his people to the New World, and marked the beginning of an entirely new life.

7

Arrival

After I disembarked the people, I came to this City of Mexico to present my credentials to Viceroy D. Martín Enríquez, whom I found was no longer in charge of this New Spain, which was no small inconvenience.

Luis de Carvajal, October 15, 1580.[1]

The arrival in Tampico of Carvajal's urca with a large number of people must have been surprising to the Spaniards living in the northern regions of the province of Pánuco. Although the towns of Tampico, Valles, and Pánuco had been founded many years before, the number of Europeans living in them had remained small.[2] While several reasons accounted for this, the most important were the warring Chichimeca and the rebellions of some of the previously conquered Indians. This chapter describes the salient events in the period immediately after Carvajal's arrival, including his meeting with the new viceroy and the first Indian rebellion he faced as a governor.

1. LIFE IN THE FRONTIER

The arrival of the new settlers in Tampico could not have come at a better time. The province was in turmoil because of the damages that the Chichimeca had been causing. Because of this, many Europeans living there wanted to leave. However, The arrival of so many people gave them renewed hope because, as Carvajal put it in his October 1580 letter to the king: "from that action follows the security of all of [the province of] Pánuco."

The reaction of the new settlers was probably quite different. Although they were well received, they must have been disappointed by what they saw.[3] They had expected to see rich Spaniards living as lords in magnificent houses, but what they encountered was a small number of poorly built houses. After the grandeur of Seville, which they had seen only a few months earlier, the appearance of Tampico and Pánuco must have shocked and worried them. Also, the heat and the humidity were unbearable and the hurricane season was upon them. Worse yet, they saw that life in that part of New Spain was hard, probably harder than any of the had experienced. Most worrisome to them, however, were the news that some of the pacified Indians who lived in the province had rebelled once more. This deprived the Spaniards of the labor provided by those Indians and increased the danger to their villages.

The conditions in other parts of New Spain were better as the departing viceroy described in his instructions to his replacement.[4] That document also contains a lengthy discussion about the harm that the Chichimeca continued to inflict on the Spaniards who lived near the frontier. Since his arrival in New Spain in 1568, Enríquez had tried to defend the European settlements and roads from the Chichimeca. Apparently, nothing had changed by 1580, for in chapter nine of those instructions he stated that:

> Some Indians, who are called Chichimeca, and others from other nations that have joined them, none of whom have yet been conquered . . . continue to be a serious problem in this kingdom. . . . And even though I have tried to remedy the situation, the problem continues, and I believe it will continue until H.M. determines that the Indians be attacked relentlessly, *a fuego y a sangre* (emphasis added), until they are defeated. . . . And what Your Lordship can do in the meantime is to continue to secure the roads with soldiers so that the damages are diminished.

Obviously, Enríquez had concluded that the only way to solve the Chichimeca problem was to pursue them in earnest but had not taken that path. Presumably he had asked the king's permission to proceed in that manner and was waiting for an answer. In the mean time, he recommended to continue to protect the roads with soldiers, but without abusing the Indians. To this end, he gave the incoming viceroy some advice:

> I advice Your Lordship that Luis de Carvajal, who came in this fleet as governor of Nuevo Reino de León, is the person who, in my opinion, can provide the best help in this because he has lived among these Indians for many years and knows their ways and their leaders, and they know him. And he has dealt with this problem for a long time, particularly in bringing them to peace. And because I see him more inclined to that goal than to shed their blood, I always valued his help in this, and believe that Your Lordship would be right in doing the same.

It is clear that Viceroy Enríquez believed that Carvajal was the best qualified European to deal with the Chichimeca problem, both because of his knowledge and of his good treatment of them.

2. Presenting Credentials

The first thing Carvajal had to do after his arrival in the New World was to present his credentials to the viceroy. Therefore, after ordering that certain tasks be carried out near Tampico, he went to Mexico City accompanied by some of his men and by the son of the viceroy, D. Diego Enríquez, who had traveled from Spain with him. As the governor of a new entity in New Spain, Carvajal probably expected a warm reception from Viceroy Enríquez. After all, Enríquez knew him well and had given him a great deal of support and encouragement. But instead of Enríquez, he found that Lorenzo Suárez de Mendoza, Conde de Coruña was now the viceroy. Carvajal's reaction can be surmised from the epigraph at the beginning of this chapter. Furthermore, while the new viceroy had landed in New Spain late August, he was installed more than a month later, which meant that Carvajal had to wait in México City some time before presenting his credentials. However, his main concern was far more serious than waiting:

Fig. 7.1. Viceroy Lorenzo Suárez.

> And because the success of my tasks depends on the support I should get here, and since the viceroy has just arrived and does not understand their importance, and the ministers . . . think they stand to lose some of their jurisdiction, the need for that support is not attended as promptly as it is required. I humbly ask Y.M. that he orders the viceroy to give me all the favor and help I need.[5]

Very clearly the viceregal change was a major blow to Carvajal. Martín Enríquez, probably one of the most able viceroys that served in New Spain, understood well the land, its people and its problems. On the other hand, the new viceroy had a rather limited knowledge of the colony and had to rely on what his ministers told him.

Lorenzo Suárez was installed as viceroy of New Spain on 8 October 1580. Among the first things he did afterward was to review Carvajal's capitulación and cédulas. In fact, three days later he swore to obey one of those cédulas. This was cédula numbered six in Appendix B. In it, Carvajal was given some Indian towns that he had pacified previously. The document says, in part:

In Mexico City, on October 11 of 1580. The very excellent Viceroy Lorenzo Suárez, Conde de Coruña . . . having seen this royal cédula from H.M., obeyed it with due reverence and respect, and ordered it be kept and obeyed, as H.M. has ordered, and that the officers who have jurisdiction in the towns declared in said cédula leave the jurisdiction to said Luis de Carvajal. Conde de Coruña.[6]

The obedience ceremony must have also included the other cédulas that ordered the viceroy to help Carvajal.[7] However, no record of those actions has surfaced. In any event, as Carvajal's letter also shows the viceroy did not provide any help to the governor. Furthermore, the letter shows that some jurisdictional issues had already arisen in 1580 because some ministers of the Audiencia were upset by the losses they would experience because of the capitulación. Those ministers must have been quite influential for a month later the Audiencia wrote to the king saying that:

This royal Audiencia has received notice of the capitulación that H.M. ordered be taken with Captain Luis de Carvajal. . . . And on the excuse that one of its chapters says that the towns of Tampasquín, Tamotela, S. Miguel, and all others until Xalpa and Sechu belong to his government . . . he has insisted that they fall in his district, not being that the case as his documents show, because what is included in it is the land that is to be discovered and pacified from the river Las Palmas and beyond, as this Audiencia mentioned in reference to a cédula given to the Adelantado Pedro Menéndez. . . . Because of this we have forewarned him not to take jurisdiction until Y.M. orders what is convenient. Conde de Coruña, Dr. Pedro de Farfán, Dr. Lopez de Miranda.[8]

The merits of this claim and its subsequent development deserve a detailed discussion that is left for a subsequent chapter. For now it should be noted that these issues were decided years later in favor of Carvajal, a decision that was re-affirmed twice. But in 1580, at the beginning of the controversy, the Audiencia's letter shows that Carvajal was forewarned not to take over certain areas. One of these, the largest, was the territory between the rivers Pánuco and Las Palmas; the other included the pueblos specifically mentioned in the capitulación, which the Audiencia argued should not have been given to Carvajal because they were already settled and pacified. Although the viceroy signed the Audiencia letter, it is unlikely that he understood the issues. More likely, those ministers who stood to lose some lands had convinced him to include that paragraph in the Audiencia's report to the king.

From Carvajal's perspective the warning was not acceptable. After all, his capitulación clearly stated that his territory started in Tampico and included an extensive region to the north and west of that town. That the Audiencia had in the past objected that the Crown had granted those lands to Menéndez hardly mattered for that objection had been disregarded by the king. As for the already-settled towns, Carvajal had both a cédula from the king giving them to him, and a document signed by the new viceroy which ordered the officers in those towns to give their jurisdiction to Carvajal. Nevertheless, at least temporarily, Carvajal did not attempt to take them over.

During his stay in Mexico City, Carvajal also took care of other legal matters, such as giving power of attorney to Hernando de Medina to represent him in whatever financial or legal cases might occur, and paying the 8,000 ducats that the Crown required in bonds. In two of the letters he sent to the king, Carvajal mentioned having paid those bonds, an action that was witnessed by Felipe Núñez and others.[9] Incidentally, Medina was one of the single men who had gone to New Spain with Carvajal, presumably as a soldier or an officer. In reality, however, he was a businessmen of some means.

The Audiencia's report mentioned earlier contains a chapter that might have been related to Carvajal. That chapter states that:

> In our letter of 19 October of 1577, we stated that Y.M. has ordered that . . . those who come to these parts should bring with them proof of their limpieza . . . particularly those who come as public officers and as royal dignitaries. And because such information has not been obtained from some who have arrived here, it is not possible to trust them in the same manner as it would be if there was no suspicion about their limpieza.[10]

It is evident that the somebody in the Audiencia suspected that some of the people who arrived in New Spain were New Christians. The particular concern expressed in the report was about some high level public officers that had arrived that year. It is not possible to ascertain who were those suspected by the Audiencia. However, among those who arrived in 1580, only the new viceroy and Carvajal fitted the description. The viceroy was a member of the Spanish nobility and did not have to prove anything. On the other hand, Carvajal should have shown proof of his being an Old Christian before leaving Seville, but as discussed in the previous chapter he did not. It is therefore likely that some ministers in the Audiencia suspected that he had a New Christian background. Of course, his origins could not be questioned at this time, but the suspicion must have remained.

After finishing his business in Mexico City, Carvajal returned to Tampico some time in November of 1580. There, he had to fulfill some other obligations stipulated in the capitulación, such as the construction of a fort at the mouth of the river Pánuco. Although in his letter to the king of October 15, he had stated that he would begin the construction immediately after arrival, he did not because the viceroy had not given him the help promised by one of the royal cédulas. Nevertheless, there were other tasks that had to be carried out. One was the founding of a village on the north side of the river Pánuco, which he named Santiago del Puerto.[11] More important, however, was the pacification of some Indians that had rebelled prior to his arrival. That rebellion was a surprise to Carvajal because prior to his leaving for Spain in 1578 he had pacified the province. But given the promises he had made in the capitulación, he felt it was his responsibility to pacify it again. He therefore left Tampico and went to take care of the uprising.

3. The Pacification of 1581

The rebellion was centered around an Indian town called Tamapache, or Tamapatz. Although its exact location is unknown, reference to other towns mentioned in the documents points to a place half way between Xalpa and Valles. As in other uprisings, the rebelling Indians had abandoned some of their towns and encomiendas, and had reverted to their old rites, abandoning the newly acquired Catholic religion. The reasons for the uprising were the same as in previous instances: mistreatment by the Spanish encomenderos; the continued practice by Spanish captains and soldiers of taking Indians for insignificant reasons and selling them as slaves; and the Chichimeca, who continued to press them to rebel.

In a letter to the king dated 18 February of 1581, Carvajal wrote to the king saying, in part, that:

> And because my arrival in this province of Pánuco . . . put fear in the rebelling Indians . . . some of them showed that they were happy because of my arrival and wanted to return in peace. . . . And not to let the opportunity pass, I went to tend to the pacification and conversion with 20 Spaniards of my company and a priest of the order of San Francisco. . . . And having spent many days in discussions with them, they decided to leave the sierra where they had been and come in peace to settle where I would tell them.[12]

The pacification is described in a long, unnamed document written between January and March of 1581 that contains several other legal documents that are not related it. For simplicity, the complete document will be referred to here as "*La Pacificación de 1581.*"[13] This record of the pacification is of interest because it contains the Indians' side of the argument—at least as expressed by the Spaniards— and because it shows how Carvajal addressed the uprising. The document's narrative includes the time consuming dialog mentioned by Carvajal, some of which is repeated below.

The narrative begins on January 21, 1581, when Carvajal arrived in Cuzcatlán, a town near Tamapache. After appointing Hernán Pérez as scribe, Carvajal stated that:

> In obedience of what he is compelled by the capitulación ... [I] came to this town ... so that from here, the closest town to those of Tamapache, Tanpasquitán, Tamolen and the other rebelled town of this region, [I can] do what is necessary to pacify said Indians ... and to bring them to the obedience of H.M. and into the Holy Catholic Church, from which they have separated.[14]

The Indians had heard about Carvajal's return to the region from Matheo García, the majordomo of a hacienda near the town of Huehuetlán, who later said that:

> One night of the month of August of last year of 1580 ... he saw an Indian with many arrows, which made him jump thinking that they wanted to kill him. And the Indian said that he was a messenger of the leaders of Tamapache, who were nearby. ... And [after they came] they asked ... if it was true, as they had heard, that Luis de Carvajal had arrived in the port of Tampico with many Spaniards.[15]

Carvajal's first step in Cuzcatlán was to ask D. Tomas, the Indian governor of Huehuetlán, to serve as emissary between him and the Indians of Tamapache. The choice was dictated by the fact that D. Tomas and his people had been among those that had rebelled. And so, Carvajal ordered him:

> To go to Tamapache to tell the Indians there that he had arrived to Cuzcatlán and to tell them that H.M. had appointed him as governor of their town, and that they should come to see him and that he would show them the royal provisions, and would show them friendship ... and that he had brought with him Father Juan Patiño, from the order of S. Francis, so that he could teach them the doctrine of our Catholic faith, and baptize their children.

Five days later, Carvajal received a letter from D. Lucas Suche, principal Indian from Tamapache, in which he said that they would come soon to see him. In fact, the very next day he and the principal Indians of two other towns came to Cuzcatlán,

> and with them some Indians from Tamapache, their bodies naked, with loin clothes [*pañetes*] worn as evidence of their infidelity and without their dress that they used to wear when they were Christians. And they came to said town with their bows and arrows, as people of war. And having left them in a house, they came before the governor who received each in friendship, embracing every one.

And . . . he showed them his title of governor and each of them took it in their hands, making comments as they were told what it said, and kissed it and put it over their heads saying that they would obey it. And the governor told them that H.M. had given him the territory and had ordered him to bring to peace the Indians in it so that with more safety they could leave in peace and return to the holy Catholic Church and . . . leave their pagan rites and ceremonies . . . and that in that manner they would live in peace, free of those captains and soldiers that had left Mexico City in pursuit of the Maceguales. And that should they not obey him, he would punish them and would gather as many Spaniards as possible as well as peaceful Indians from Meztitlán and Molango.

This started an exchange between D. Lucas and Carvajal.

And D. Lucas said that they would be in peace and that they had come as such. . . . The governor responded that since they said to be of peace, that he wanted to go to their town . . . and call to peace the other rebelling Indians. D. Lucas, answered that it couldn't be because the roads were in bad conditions and they (the Spaniards) could not pass.[16] The Governor told them that by the same roads they came, he and his people could also pass, and they would open a road even if the land was mountainous, as he had done when he went to Mazapil, as they knew well.[17] To this they said that there was no food for them to eat if he went there. And the governor said that he would bring food from here and that they should not feel bad.

At this point the Indians "made other excuses saying that if they would allow some Spaniards in their town, those of Tamolen would kill them in Tamapache because the Indians of Tamolen did not want the governor to enter their town or others." This seems to have exasperated Carvajal, for he decided to issue an ultimatum:

The governor then asked why did they say they were in peace if they did not want him, or any Spaniard, to enter in their town; that this was not peace . . . . that they should do one of two things: The first was to get down [from the Sierra] to live near Huehuetlán, where they would be safe from the attacks of said enemies; or, second, agree that the governor and Father Juan Patiño . . . enter their town to give them doctrine. . . . And that if they wanted that the governor and his people stay there, or leave men to protect them and make them a fort, that he would do it.

Obviously not convinced, D. Lucas stated that "it was enough if they would come when the governor and other justices would call them." The give and take continued for some time, as the following narrative indicates:

In spite of reasons, gifts and good words, the Indians . . . remained obstinate and would not, by any reason, of their own free will, do as told, and tried to make the governor be afraid telling him that he could well go to Tamapache, but if . .

. those of Tamolen and other Chichimeca ambushed him and his soldiers and some died, that the Spaniards should not be surprised. . . . And because of this the governor asked Father Patiño to . . . preach to them to move them in the direction of what was needed. And said Father went with them and talked to them for over two hours . . . reporting to the governor . . . that he found them very hard.

But the very next day a change of mind seems to have occurred:

And on the 28th they of January of 1581, Father Patiño told the governor that he had again preached to D. Lucas and to the other Indians . . . and had convinced them to get down from their town of Tamapache and come, with their women and children, to live near Huehuetlán, where they could be indoctrinated. . .

One wonders what did Father Patiño tell the Indians to make them change their mind. In any event, some celebrations took place.

. And before the governor and other Spaniards and Indians of this town left, he called D. Lucas Suche and the others who came from Tamapache and . . . embraced them, giving many thanks to God for having done this, and the same was done by the other Spaniards. And this being done Father Patiño said mass with solemnity and music.

A few days later other Indians came in peace to see Carvajal.

And on February 4 there came 15 Indians sent by their leaders. . . . And the governor received them happily. And he and Father Patiño exhorted them to leave their sierras and come in peace. . . . And they said they would. . . . .And so that the Indians would feel more contented and secure . . . he sent with them some wine for their leaders.

The good news were confirmed a few days later, when Francisco Barrón, the encomendero who had been unwilling to help Carvajal in the construction of the fort in Xalpa, came "very happy because the Indians wanted to come in peace" and told Carvajal that:

More than 600 Tamapache Indians wanted to settle in said pueblo because governor Carvajal had treated them well and had not done any harm to them and that they had rebelled for the harm that other captains had done to them and because of the fear that other captains who had gone to fight them and to punish them.

Barrón carried a letter from the Indians to Carvajal in which they said that:

That they would, as ordered, settle in Tamazquo, where they would gather and build their houses, and begged the governor to go to their pueblo in 25 days, when said houses would be finished, to tell them where they should build the church.

This concludes the document's description of the pacification. Although the Indians had been pacified this time, many other rebellions would take place in the years to come. For now, however, Carvajal felt he had fulfilled one of his promises to the king.

4. Jurisdictional problems

In his 1580 letter to the king Carvajal had complained that some ministers did not help him because "it appears to them that the capitulación takes away from them some of their jurisdiction." Part of the problem was that the province of Pánuco had been conquered years earlier by the Spaniards and was, since then, administered by an alcalde mayor whose jurisdiction included some of the towns that had been given to Carvajal by the king. In 1581 that officer was Juan del Trejo who in spite of the order issued by the viceroy had decided to contest Carvajal's jurisdiction. Of course, Trejo could not do this on his own. Someone in the Audiencia was supporting his actions. In a letter dated February 18, 1581, Carvajal told the king that:

> The alcalde mayor, who by my capitulación loses the lands north of the river [Pánuco], tries to impede all that I do in the service of Y.M., contradicting the limits of my jurisdiction. And if in every instance I had to go to Mexico City . . . . it would be to spend more time and money than in the settlement. And I have nobody there who can defend my position.[18]

Another officer causing problems was the alcalde of Tampico:

> After my return from Mexico city, I founded the first village in the best place for the defense of the port . . . but after I left, an alcalde mayor called Gonzalo Jorge went there and without an order from the viceroy or from the Audiencia destroyed what was built and ordered others not to help me. He dares do this because of a minister [in the Audiencia]. Because of this several of the colonizers I brought with me abandoned the area. . . . This happens because the ministers inform [the viceroy] as they wish and as it is best for them.

Carvajal would have been within his rights to resort to force to make both Gonzalo Jorge and Juan del Trejo stop harassing him, but felt that this was not the way to solve the problem.

> Because I don't want to defend the limits by force, as I don't think this would be in the service of Y.M., I tolerate all I can until Y.M. remedy all by means of a royal cédula. . . . I beg Y.M. orders that the officers who had jurisdiction over said pueblos and limits let me have free jurisdiction over them. And with this all differences and expenses will cease and I will better fulfill my obligations. And since viceroy D. Martín Enríquez, who knew very well how necessary was the

order that H.M. gave regarding this government, left this New Spain, I am left without help. And if the [new] viceroy . . . understood the land, I am sure he would help and favor me. But until he does, there will be no remedy.

Carvajal also informed the king that he had removed four *presidios* that existed in his jurisdiction, which he said were costly and unnecessary because he could cover the frontier with 20 soldiers of his own. This decision proved to be wrong on several grounds. One was that the extent of the frontier was too large to be secured by a few soldiers. Another was that by this action he deprived the Crown soldiers and captains that served in those presidios from having a steady income. Carvajal also cited another difficulty with the presidios, namely that "if there were soldiers who served other jurisdictions, they would be against those I have, *because I want peace and they go against it so that they can sustain themselves* (emphasis added)." While this statement was correct, the removal of the presidios was also not welcome by those officers in Mexico City since, as he stated in the same letter:

And now it appears that some officers had, because of their interests, advised the viceroy to put those presidios and soldiers, which results in more expenses and problems with the Indians. . . . And since the viceroy has just arrived he does not know what is, or is not, convenient. I beg Y.M. to write to the viceroy and Audiencia to favor me.

Obviously, Carvajal could not count on the viceroy for help and had to seek support from the king. The king did respond, but his response, shown in figure 7.2, was written on 19 April of 1583, more than two years after Carvajal's request.[19] The text of the letter says:

The King. Conde de Coruña, relative, our viceroy . . . in New Spain, and in his absence, to the person, or persons, in charge of the government in that land. From letters of Luis de Carvajal . . . and from other persons, we have learned about his work in said settlements and that he is satisfied and continues to work with diligence and care, from which news we are contented. And because we very much desire that the effort continues in the best manner . . . we charge you and order you that for that purpose you give said Luis de Carvajal all the necessary favor and help that is possible, because from it we shall be served. And that which you will do and learn about said province you will inform us. Written in Madrid on 19 October 1583. I the King.

The order could not be clearer. Unfortunately, it arrived after the viceroy died.[20] Furthermore, in spite of the king's clear order that those who followed him should obey it, nobody did. Rather, those who had sought to prevent Carvajal from fulfilling his duties, continued to oppose him.

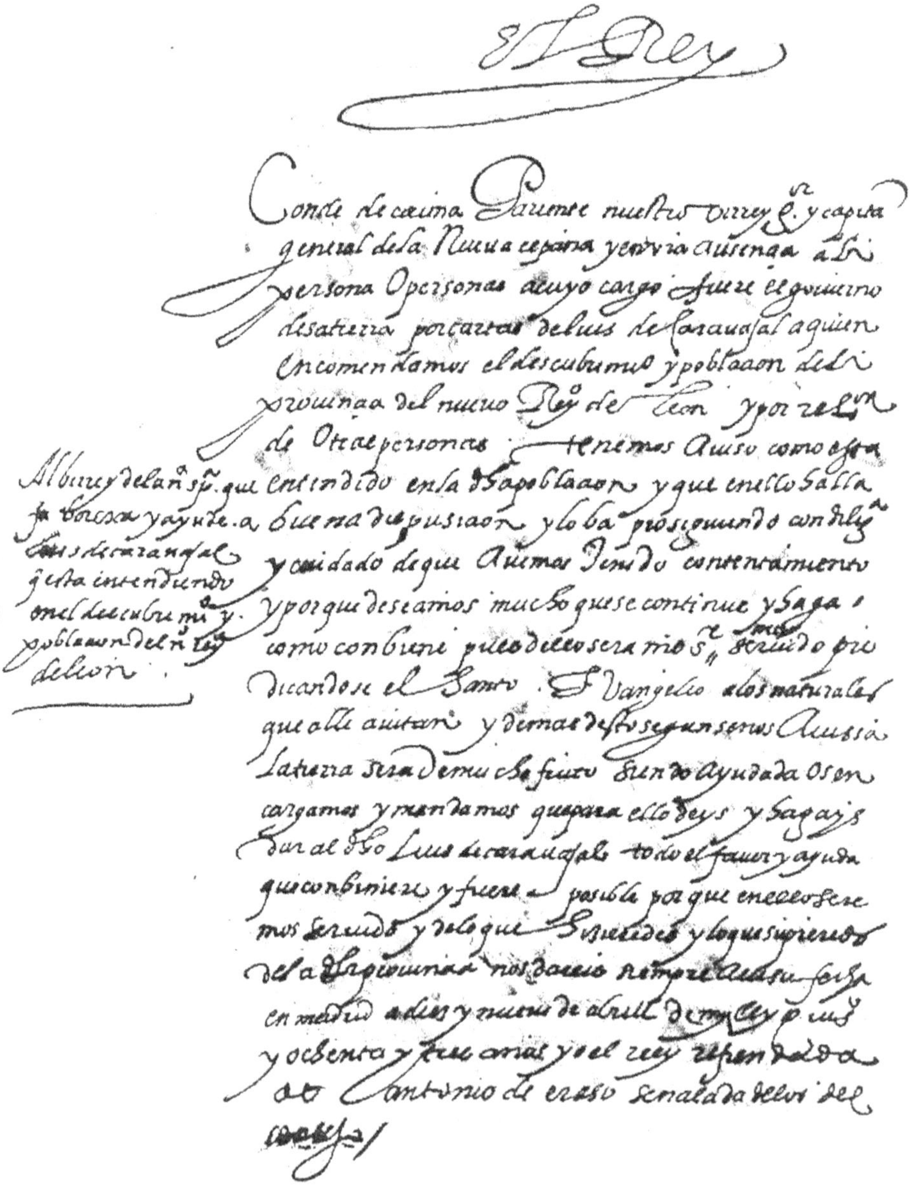

El Rey

Conde de Coruña Pariente nuestro Virrey gobernador y capitan general de la Nueva España y en vuestra ausencia a la persona o personas a cuyo cargo fuere el gobierno de esa tierra por cartas de Luis de Carvajal a quien encomendamos el descubrimiento y poblacion de la provincia del nuevo Reyno de Leon y por relacion de otras personas tenemos aviso como esta entendido en la dicha poblacion y que en ello halla buena disposicion y lo va prosiguiendo con diligencia y cuidado de que avemos tenido contentamiento y porque deseamos mucho que se continue y haga como conviene pues de ello sera Dios nuestro señor servido predicandose el Santo Evangelio a los naturales que alli habitan y demas desto segun se nos avisa la tierra sera de mucho fruto siendo ayudada os encargamos y mandamos que para ello deis y hagais dar al dicho Luis de Carvajal todo el favor y ayuda que conviniere y fuere posible porque en ello seremos servidos y de lo que sucediere y lo que supieredes de la dicha provincia nos dareis siempre aviso. Fecha en Madrid a diez y nueve de abril de mil y quinientos y ochenta y tres años. Yo el Rey. Refrendada de Antonio de Eraso, señalada de los del Consejo.

Al Virrey de la Nueva España que favorezca y ayude a Luis de Carvajal que esta entendiendo en el descubrimiento y poblacion del nuevo Reyno de Leon.

Fig. 7.2. Royal order to Viceroy Lorenzo Suárez. The note on the margin says: "To the viceroy of New Spain. That he should favor and help Luis de Carvajal, who is working on the discovery and settlement of Nuevo Reino de León." (*Courtesy of the Ministerio de Cultura, Archivo General de Indias, Seville.*)

Realizing that a long time would pass before the king would answer his letter of February of 1581, Carvajal decided to appoint somebody to represent him in legal matters before the Audiencia, freeing him to pursue other tasks. A few months earlier he had given wide powers to Hernando de Medina to represent him in all sorts of legal and financial matters. But Medina was a businessman, not a lawyer, and could not, therefore, argue cases before the Audiencia.

Apparently a person who could was found quickly. On April 6 of 1581, Hernando de Medina transferred some of those powers to Pedro de Vega, a solicitor before the Audiencia.[21] Some time later Vega appeared before that body to request that an order be issued to all officers in New Spain to obey Carvajal's capitulación and cédulas. The date of his appearance is unknown but must have been toward the end of 1581 for on January 18 of 1582 the Audiencia issued the following order in the name of the king:

> D. Phelipe, etc., etc. To the magistrates, alcaldes mayores, alcaldes ordinarios, and to any other judges and justices of all cities, villages and places in our kingdoms, and to every one of you in all jurisdictions and to those to whom the contents of this corresponds in any manner . . . that after you read said title and cédulas here incorporated, given by us to said governor and captain general Luis de Carvajal . . . you will obey, and make others obey what is contained in them without impeding in any manner in what is in his district, limits, and jurisdiction, so that he can freely administer it. . . . Given in México City on 18 January of 1582. Conde de Coruña, Dr. Pedro Farfán, Dr. Lope de Miranda, Dr. Robles, Dr. Palacio.[22]

The cédulas mentioned in this order were those labeled 6 and 14. Cédula number 14 stated that Carvajal could name and change justices and other officers in towns that already existed in his jurisdiction, whereas cédula number 6 specifically gave Carvajal some towns already settled. This cédula had been obeyed and put into effect by the viceroy on 11 October 1580. Now, a little more than a year later, the Audiencia issued the same order in the name of the king. Although the order should have put an end to all jurisdictional disputes, Carvajal's enemies simply ignored it. The enemies were, of course, the ministers that stood to lose the income associated with their possessions in the area that had been under contention.

Nearly seventy years later, Alonso de León wrote that the Viceroy Lorenzo Suárez, Conde de Coruña, resented being forced by Pedro de Vega to issue the order, a resentment that, according to him, caused Carvajal's downfall.[23] But this is incorrect. The viceroy responsible for that event was Álvaro Manrique de Zúñiga, who become viceroy in 1585. The Conde de Coruña, the viceroy in charge in 1582, was not an enemy of Carvajal, nor did he object to Carvajal's territorial claims in any manner, for if he did he could have easily changed the terms of the capitulación, as the king had authorized him.[24] Also, although he had promised to obey the king's cédulas, he did not really care about such issues. That apparent indifference enabled Carvajal's enemies to continue their opposition to Carvajal. This opposition gained strength with the arrival, soon after the 18 January order was issued, of the newly appointed *fiscal* of the Audiencia de México, Eugenio de Salazar.[25] The arrival of a new prosecutor at that time provided a good opportunity for Carvajal's enemies to bring into their fold a most powerful ally. In fact, soon after the viceroy's death, Salazar brought charges against Carvajal about the same jurisdictional issues. That legal suit, referred here as the *Salazar-Carvajal pleito*, is an important component of the forces that brought Carvajal down and will be described later, after considering Carvajal's attempt to explore, conquer, and settle the northern parts of his territory.

8

Discoveries, Foundations, and Pacifications

I discovered a serranía which I named Nuestra Señora de los Remedios . . . and in its vicinity I founded the village Cueva de León and the city of León.

Luis de Carvajal, April 1582.[1]

After giving his power of attorney to Pedro de Vega in the Spring of 1581, Carvajal felt that his jurisdictional problems in the province of Pánuco were in good hands. This meant that he could proceed with the settlement of other parts of his territory. The activities that followed are the focus of this chapter.

1. To the North

The area that Carvajal was eager to explore and settle was that which he had discovered nine years earlier. As he had stated in his petition to the king, that area had silver, good lands and many Indians. Now that he had somebody representing him in the Audiencia he felt he could begin its settlement And so, some time in the summer of 1581 he started making preparations to go there. The departure took place on October 25 of 1581 from the town of Tamaholipa, some twenty five leagues northeast of Valles.[2] Accompanying him were an undisclosed number soldiers and settlers, as well as Juan de la Magdalena, a friar of the order of San Francisco.[3] Given the purpose of the journey, they took with them cattle—large and small, seed for planting wheat and other plants, and large amounts of provisions to sustain themselves for some time. Of course, the provisions had to be carried on horses and mules; transportation by wagon would have to wait a few more years.

The region to be settled was northwest of Tampico, entirely in Chichimeca's hands. Rather than crossing the long sierra west of Tanchipa, as he had done in 1572, Carvajal followed a route that flanked its eastern slopes. He knew that route well for he had traveled it, in the opposite direction, in 1573 in order to return to Pánuco from the valley of Extremadura. And except for the warring Chichimeca, the road presented no serious obstacles.

The path followed by Carvajal on this occasion was probably close to the modern railroad between Tampico and Monterrey. Before reaching the latter, this road passes through Victoria, Linares, and Montemorelos. After the valley of Extremadura, Carvajal continued towards Saltillo, reaching the "mouth of the river Nacataz, six leagues from Saltillo and then returned" to that valley before proceeding north.[4] It is likely that on this journey he learned that Saltillo had been founded in the name of New Vizcaya by Capt. Alberto del Canto.[5] Feeling that the town was in his territory, Carvajal replaced its existing officers with others of his own.[6]

In any case, Carvajal returned to the valley of Extremadura, but did not stop there, even though at the time of its discovery he thought it would be an ideal place to start a settlement. It is true that two years later he ordered that a village be founded there, but at this time he was looking for silver and knew that the mountains around that valley had none. And so, he turned north, where he discovered a mountain range which he named *Nuestra Señora de los Remedios*. Although this name no longer exists, it is likely that this range is now called Sierra de los Picachos, located to the southwest of present city of Cerralvo, previously known as León.[7]

This newly-discovered mountain range differed from others Carvajal had seen in his previous journey through the region in that it had silver. After making sure that the metal they found was indeed silver, the settlers embarked on a wider search that resulted in the discovery of many mines. These become known as the mines of San Gregorio, the name with which they appear in several contemporary records. These discoveries required official records of ownership. Therefore, on December 10 of 1581, Carvajal named Andrés del Águila as *Escribano de Gobernación* (government scribe) whose duties included the registration of the mines. The naming document contains a reference to the foundation of a village: "And I signed it in my own name in this village Cueva de León, which was founded on this day, December 10 of 1581, as witnessed by Felipe Núñez, Manuel Fernández and Diego Barbosa."[8] The village was located on the slopes of the newly discovered serranía, in a place convenient to the miners.

By April of 1582, Cueva de León had many settlers engaged in the extraction of silver. In a letter to Pedro Moya de Contreras, the Archbishop of Mexico City and Inquisitor of New Spain, Carvajal stated that sixteen other discoveries had been made and that more than 600 mines had been registered.[9] In that letter he expressed optimism about the future of the village because the area had silver and plenty of water and ". . . is surrounded by many towns and *rancherias*, where more than 8,000 Indians live, all in peace and in obedience to H.M." If true, these Indians were very different from those that had previously prevented the Spaniards to conquer the areas north of the river Pánuco. Although it is possible that the Indians of the region were initially peaceful, it is even more likely that Carvajal was exaggerating things in order to attract additional settlers to the area. As described later, these peaceful Indians rebelled several times in the following years, eventually destroying all he had built.

While the location of Cueva de León was convenient for the miners, it was not adequate for other purposes. Therefore, a few months after its foundation, Carvajal founded the city of León. In the same letter to Moya Contreras, written on 20 April of 1582, he stated that:

> Three days ago I founded this settlement, with the title of city, in a valley, the best for farming . . . in which there are many farmers, cattle, and wagons with provisions. And the farmers work the land which will produce a great quantity of provisions for the city and for the village [Cueva de León]. And I have named officers for the royal treasury and justice.

Denoting the new settlement as a city meant that Carvajal intended to make it the capital of his territory. Supporting this idea is the fact that he brought there the *Caja de Tres Llaves*. This was to hold whatever silver would be paid to the Crown by the settlers, as well as the tools needed to mark it. Also, according to Juan de la Magdalena, he and Carvajal set aside a block-size lot in the central area of the city "for the temple of S. Pedro."[10] By 1583, the city appeared to be functioning well, for as a visitor stated: "When this witness arrived in said city of León, it was already populated, and around it there were farms growing corn and wheat . . . and the houses in the city were of adobe."[11] The city also had "a *casa fuerte* where the treasurer lived. And in it there was artillery for its defense. . . . And the city had an alcalde mayor and captain, two alcaldes ordinarios, and regidores."[12]

Before describing other activities that Carvajal carried out during this time, it is useful to return to the letter he sent to Pedro Moya de Contreras, the powerful archbishop and inquisitor who later become viceroy of New Spain. Moya's acquaintance with Carvajal went back to the 1570s when he appeared as a witness in the Inquisition trials of some of the men left behind by John Hawkins. And in 1580 the king had written to Moya telling him that "He has ordered Captain Luis de Carvajal, who is leaving with the present fleet for the conquest of Nuevo León, to take the remaining Indians under his care and to make the roads safe with his new conquest."[13] In fact, it seems that a rapport existed between Carvajal and the archbishop, for in the letter cited earlier, Carvajal informed the archbishop that he had appointed Juan Batista de Olid, *criado* of Moya, as the first alcalde ordinario of Cueva de León, adding that "I am of the house of your illustrious lordship."

Given that long-standing connection, it is not surprising to see Carvajal writing to the archbishop. However, the letter covered several matters that were not about religious or personal matters. For example, Carvajal asked the archbishop to help him get back some carpenters he had in Tampico who had run away. Such matters should have been dealt via the Audiencia. It is likely that Carvajal did not trust the secretaries of the viceroy and that his mistrust was so deep that he was afraid that his letters would be intercepted by them. But he knew that the archbishop would transmit his letter to the king, as in fact happened later, when Moya wrote to the king: In that letter he said:

> Luis de Carvajal de la Cueva, governor of Nuevo Reino de León, and friar Joan de la Magdalena . . . wrote letters to me which I send to Y.M. so that Y.M. learns what happens here. . . . And about this all I can say is that it is very important that the governor continues the settlement of *Tierra Adentro*, with which the peaceful Indians will be safe and those of war will leave. And in this manner Y.H. will be served to help and favor him so that this cause goes forward. And to that effect I have sent him, on his request, an exemplary priest who will keep me informed of all that might happen there.[14]

It was this letter by the archbishop that prompted the king to write to the Conde de Coruña, ordering him to help Carvajal. But, as already noted, the king's letter arrived in Mexico City after the viceroy's death.

2. OTHER ACTIVITIES

Carvajal's letter to Moya de Contreras shows that he was trying to fulfill the obligations stipulated by the capitulación. Not only had he founded both Cueva de León and León but by the end of 1582 he had managed to put in them mills and foundries to refine and melt metals extracted from the mines; had brought to the area cattle of various kinds; and had distributed lands to the colonizers who were growing wheat and corn in them. The settlers in León lived in adobe houses that had flat roofs supported by *vigas*, that is, pueblo-style houses, commonly found in parts of the American Southwest. Some of these houses had look-out decks on their roofs. The city also had a church and a casa fuerte that housed soldiers as well as the royal chest.

Among the other activities that Carvajal carried out while he was in León was the continuation of the pacification effort. By the end of 1582 he had pacified many Indians who lived in the vicinity of that city. Thus, in his letter to Moya he claimed to have baptized more than 8,000 Indians. While this number was probably inflated, it must have been nevertheless large for the records show that he had assigned three encomiendas before the end of that year. That is, he had distributed many Indians among three Spaniards who profited from their service. The encomenderos were Hernán Ramírez, Manuel de Mederos, and Diego de Montemayor.[15]

However, as in other instances, this pacification did not last. Within a few years two uprisings took place there, with the second one ending in the destruction of what had been done by Carvajal. Nevertheless, that early pacification was said to have been miraculous because Nuevo Reino de León was located in Chichimeca territory, a territory that the Spaniards had failed to conquer before.[16] How was this pacification accomplished? It appears that at least two factors enabled Carvajal to achieve it. First, his good treatment of the Indians and his insistence that his soldiers should not abuse them. Second, most of the soldiers that Carvajal brought with him were people who obeyed him and acted accordingly. Later on, however, the news that he had discovered and settled new lands brought many others whose allegiance and obedience to Carvajal did not exist and who sustained themselves practicing the same abuses that had prevented the peace in other parts of the frontier. Their presence in Nuevo Reino de León disturbed the precarious peace that Carvajal had achieved and produced the rebellions that the territory was to witness in the following years.

Several of those abuses took place while Carvajal was in Cueva de León. Not far from that village, two captains who were responsible for the safety of the Camino Real, had entered Nuevo Reino de León—more than 80 leagues from that road—supposedly pursuing some Indians who had assaulted Spanish travelers. In reality, however, their purpose was to take some *piezas*, as the captive Indians were then called. Together with their soldiers, those captains had entered the ranchería of Pesquería, some 12 leagues from Cueva de León, and had taken 40 docile Indians. According to the testimony of Felipe Núñez, their *cacique* informed Carvajal about the capture, saying

> Thou tells us that the soldiers should not do any harm to us. How is it possible that they have captured many of my people and many others? Go and free them because thou has told us we should never be taken.[17]

On hearing this, Carvajal went after the transgressors using the cacique as a guide, finding them near the Nacataz river, where he disarmed them and released the captive Indians. This was but one of many such incidents. What makes this one interesting is that those captains were not part of Carvajal's group but were under the command of Rodrigo del Río Loysa, the lieutenant general for the viceroy in Nueva Galicia. Also interesting were the statements made about the incident by the inspector general of the presidios and roads of Nueva Galicia and by one of the captains who had entered Nuevo Reino de León to take Indians. This captain was Francisco Leyva Bonilla, who as pointed out in note 4, was one of the leaders of an expedition to Nuevo México.[18] In his testimony about this incident he said that:

> He and Captain Cristóbal Caldera, with his soldiers, were following certain Indians who had caused harm and found many of them, and captured them to take them before General Rodrigo del Río. And this witness went to capture other Indians, remaining Captain Caldera with those we had already taken. . . . And afterwards he returned and found said Governor Luis de Carvajal and his people, but did not see the prisoners . . . And Captain Caldera told him that they had been freed because said governor had so ordered.[19]

Confirmation of these events was provided by Matheo del Río, the inspector for Nueva Galicia's presidios, who stated that:

> About four years ago he learned that Governor Luis de Carvajal had released a number of Indians taken prisoner in his jurisdiction by captains Cristóbal Caldera and Francisco de Leyva Bonilla, and that he had disarmed them. And later he saw that Rodrigo del Río Loysa, lieutenant of captain general in Nueva Galicia, had arrested said captains because they had allowed Governor Carvajal to take their weapons.[20]

Whether Leyva and Caldera were following Indians who had assaulted travelers along the Camino Real is uncertain. What is certain is that they had entered Nuevo Reino de León, and had gone to the valley of Extremadura, much too far from the road they were supposed to protect. Another important point is that according to all reports Carvajal let those Indians go free because they were peaceful and had done nothing wrong.

A similar incident took place six months later, when Diego Ramírez Barrionuevo was returning to León bringing food and other supplies. Not far from that village, some Chichimeca Indians who lived near Paraje de los Papagayos assaulted him. Although he was able to escape, the Indians killed his mules, most of his horses, and stole the supplies he was taking to León. After learning about this Carvajal ordered Capt. Melchor de Herrera to go after those Indians who had assaulted Barrionuevo. Reportedly Herrera found six of them, whom he took prisoner and brought to Cueva de León, where they were sentenced to forced service. After examining Herrera's report, Carvajal let all six go free, thinking this might bring peace. But the release was not well received by Herrera's soldiers because they had counted on some additional income from the sale of the service of the Indians. To resolve the issue, Carvajal paid the soldiers 300 pesos, which was the assessed value of that service. For comparison, a horse owned by the governor that had been killed by some of his own soldiers, was assessed in the same amount.

The abuse of the Indians by his soldiers was a problem that Carvajal had time and again tried to eliminate. Ironically, years later, it was repeatedly stated by Carvajal's enemies that it was he who was abusing the Indians. As pointed out earlier, that charge was fabricated by his enemies in the province of Pánuco and in the Audiencia, apparently to regain that which they had lost by legal means. In this they succeeded, as described in chapters 10 and 11.

After having founded Cueva de León and León, Carvajal decided to continue the exploration of his territory and to make settlements where desirable. Some of these tasks were undertaken by him, but most were commissioned to others. Among his own explorations was a search for a place along the coast that could serve as a port. Of course, he had already explored the coast in the 1570s, during the punitive journey described in Chapter 4. This time he was joined by captains Agustín de la Saca and Cristóbal de Heredia as well as by many soldiers. Carvajal and his group traveled towards the northeast through previously unknown regions until they reached the mouth of the Río Bravo, which they had hoped could serve as a port. Instead, they found that the waters were too shallow and that the currents were so strong that the sand bars would continuously shift under their effect. The search continued beyond the Río Bravo, but no suitable place was found.[21]

More fruitful was Carvajal's commission to Diego de Montemayor, given towards the end of 1582, to explore the region northwest of León. According to the reports of soldiers who accompanied him, Montemayor discovered, some forty leagues away, the province of Quahuila (Coahuila), and in it silver mines that he named *La Trinidad*. One of those soldiers reported that Montemayor returned to Cueva de León twenty days later.[22] Given the long distance he had to travel, it is unlikely that he accomplished much on that journey, although his having discovered silver in them apparently induced Carvajal to found there a village at a later time.

Antonio de Espejo

One of the earliest explorations of Nuevo México was led by an interesting individual named Antonio de Espejo.[23] His journey is relevant to this narrative because it was apparently commissioned by Carvajal, who in his Inquisition trial stated that:

> And from there [Cueva de León], by my Comisión, were discovered the provinces called Nuevo México, and Antonio de Espejo did it with my Comisión.[24]

Espejo's expedition to Nuevo México took place between November 10 of 1582 and September 20 of the following year, that is, it lasted ten months. On his return to New Spain, he wrote a report of his journey to the viceroy, but nowhere in it is a reference to Carvajal, a fact that brings into question the governor's statement.[25] Adding to the idea that Carvajal's claim was false was Espejo's statement that he and fourteen others started their journey from the valley of San Bartolomé, nine leagues from Santa Bárbola.[26] Thus, Espejo and his companions did not depart from Cueva de León, as a superficial reading of Carvajal's statement seems to imply.

However, Carvajal did not claim the expedition left from Cueva de León, or that he handed the Comisión to Espejo in person. What he said was that the document was *issued* there. Supporting this interpretation is the testimony of Juan González who years before Carvajal's self-defense in the Inquisition was written said that he saw that "the governor *was sending* (emphasis added) a Comisión to Antonio de Espejo to enter the province of Nuevo México."[27] That is, Carvajal's Comisión was *sent* to Espejo from Cueva de León. While this may clarify a point about Carvajal's claim, it does not confirm it, particularly since Espejo mentioned other Crown officers as having commissioned the expedition. It is possible that Espejo, in need for official permission to undertake his exploration of New México, sought one from several Crown officers including Carvajal, but got another from a Capt. Ontiveros, a lower-ranked officer in Cuatro Cienegas, a settlement in Nueva Vizcaya.

There is, however, contemporary support for Carvajal's contention. First of all, several witnesses appearing before the Audiencia in Guadalajara stated they saw the Comisión that Carvajal gave Espejo.[28] Others reported having seen letters that

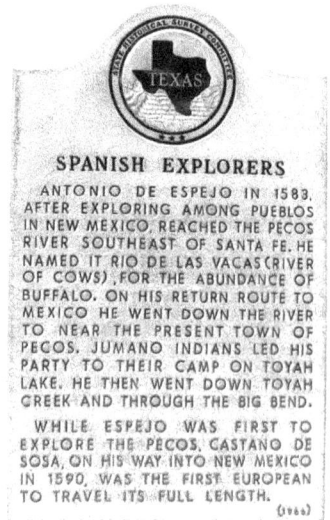

SPANISH EXPLORERS

ANTONIO DE ESPEJO IN 1583, AFTER EXPLORING AMONG PUEBLOS IN NEW MEXICO, REACHED THE PECOS RIVER SOUTHEAST OF SANTA FE. HE NAMED IT RIO DE LAS VACAS (RIVER OF COWS), FOR THE ABUNDANCE OF BUFFALO. ON HIS RETURN ROUTE TO MEXICO HE WENT DOWN THE RIVER TO NEAR THE PRESENT TOWN OF PECOS. JUMANO INDIANS LED HIS PARTY TO THEIR CAMP ON TOYAH LAKE. HE THEN WENT DOWN TOYAH CREEK AND THROUGH THE BIG BEND.
WHILE ESPEJO WAS FIRST TO EXPLORE THE PECOS, CASTANO DE SOSA, ON HIS WAY INTO NEW MEXICO IN 1590, WAS THE FIRST EUROPEAN TO TRAVEL ITS FULL LENGTH.

(1966)

Fig. 8.1. Plaque in Pecos, Texas.

Espejo wrote to Carvajal, informing him of what had been discovered.[29] More convincing is the testimony of Pedro Hernández de Almanza, who said that:

> And this witness knows that said governor commissioned Antonio de Espejo to go to discover the province called Nuevo México. *And this witness went with him* (emphasis added) and was present in the discovery of said Nuevo México and discovered many pueblos of clothed Indians. . . . And that said discovery lasted ten months.[30]

Conclusive evidence that Hernandez was telling the truth is the fact that he appears in Espejo's list of the men who accompanied him.[31] This corroboration of Carvajal's statement does not mean that the Comisión he sent to Espejo was the only instrument that made the expedition possible. Espejo was a man of some means and did not need Carvajal's money to carry it out. But he was running away from the authorities in Mexico City, accused of murder.[32] However, regardless of his wealth, he could not enter an unexplored territory without official permission, which Carvajal and others provided.

It remains to address the most difficult point: If it was true that Carvajal commissioned him, why did not Espejo acknowledge that fact? After all, Carvajal's position as governor carried much more weight than that of Capt. Ontiveros. Several reasons may account for this: Espejo knew that Carvajal wanted to be given the province of Nuevo México on the basis that it was contiguous to Nuevo Reino de León.[33] Nevertheless, he wanted that privilege for himself. And so, soon after his return to New Spain on September of 1583, he initiated a petition to be given that province.[34] However, by then, the fiscal of the Audiencia had started a pleito against Carvajal, a fact that was well known in New Spain. Obviously Espejo must have realized that mentioning that Carvajal had commissioned him would not have been advantageous to his own plans.

San Luis

After returning from his search of a suitable location for a port north of Tampico, Carvajal was informed that the Indians of Tamapache, and those of other towns near it, had rebelled once more, killing some Spaniards and causing many other damages, all of which had made the Spaniards in the area want to abandon it. Convinced as he was that the rebelling towns were within his jurisdiction, he felt it was his responsibility to pacify them again, and so he started making preparations to go to the province of Pánuco. Prior to his departure he named a lieutenant to administer the León area in his absence, and commissioned others the continuation of the exploration and settlement of the northern areas of his territory. The settlement task was of considerable importance. Cueva de León and León were, so far, the only towns he had successfully founded in Nuevo Reino de León.[35] More settlements were needed to fulfill the obligations stipulated by the crown.

Thus, before leaving León in the Spring of 1583, Carvajal decided it was time to found a village in the valley of Extremadura.[36] For that purpose he commissioned one of his captains to do so. Among those who witnessed the foundation was Capt. Diego González, who said that "this witness saw that by commission of said governor, Captain Gaspar Castaño de Sosa founded the village of Sanct Luis de los Ojos de Santa Lucía, and this witness was present at its foundation."[37] This event marks the first official foundation of the town that was to become known as Monterrey.[38] Prior to that time there had been several visits to the place, which were no more than "*asentamientos*," or temporary camps made by European explorers. The first occurred in late 1572 or early 1573, when Carvajal discovered the valley of Extremadura. A second is said to have been made by Alberto del Canto in 1577, although this information is based on hearsay statements appearing in a document written 67 years later.[39]

Although there was no silver in the mountains near the valley of Extremadura, the location of San Luis was ideal for other purposes, as it was between Saltillo and León, not far from the mountain pass discovered by Carvajal. That pass enabled the transport to León and San Luis of goods from Nueva Galicia, to the south, and from Nueva Vizcaya, to the west.

3. New Rebellions

Having delegated the tasks mentioned above, Carvajal went to the south regions of his territory with a large number of soldiers, as he normally did when traveling through Chichimeca territory. The exact date for the departure is not known, but it was before May of 1583, for some documents place him in the province of Pánuco at the beginning of that month, attempting to take over the jurisdiction of certain towns. However, he first had to deal with another Indian uprising. Contrary to the Tamapache pacification of 1581, which was of limited extent and was achieved by peaceful means, this one covered a more extensive region and was not achieved by words alone:

> The Indians of Tamapache, Tampasquín and Tamotela . . . had once more rebelled. . . . And the governor tried to talk to them about peace, offering them a pardon for their crimes, which they did not want. Instead, they came to the governor in war saying that the tribute they had to give would be in arrows. And

seen this by the governor, he went to their serranía with many soldiers . . . and said Indians came out to fight. . . . And said battle lasted more than four days. And the governor defeated them, taking some prisoner who confessed their crimes. . . . And the governor condemned some [of them] and returned the rest to the service of God, our Lord, and H.M. . . . And with this the province of Valles and Pánuco, and the serranías of Meztitlán and Molango remained safe.[40]

This pacification took place between July and December of 1583, although some of the time was spent in the reconstruction of the churches that had been burnt. It also appears that the rebellion extended further south to Xalpa, for in August of that year Carvajal was in that town. There, as discussed in Chapter 4, Carvajal had built a fort in 1576 that served to protect the area against the attacks of the Chichimeca. Since Xalpa was one of the towns given explicitly to him in the capitulación, Carvajal now appointed Capt. Francisco de Abreu as its magistrate and as the leader of the soldiers that served there.[41]

It was during this time that a serious difference seems to have occurred between Carvajal and Francisco Barrón, the encomendero mentioned in the pacifications of 1576 and 1581. The only reliable information about those differences stems from two letters that the Audiencia wrote, years later, to the king. The first, dated 25 February 1586, was written by Eugenio de Salazar, the fiscal of the Audiencia, and says:

> The *pleito* with Francisco Barrón about the Indians from Tamapache, which Luis de Carvajal, governor of Nuevo Reino de León, had reduced to the service of Y.M., and which Barrón has pretended, after their pacification, that they are of his encomienda, was decided in favor of Barrón. And thinking that the cause cannot be won here, I sent the pleito to the Real Consejo de Indias . . .[42]

The second letter, written more than two years after the first, was motivated by the Crown's insistence to get an answer about the Indians pacified by Carvajal. Thus, in November of 1588 the Audiencia wrote to the king saying that:

> We received another cédula dated August 8 of 1587 in which we are ordered to punish those who are found guilty of having sold as slaves certain Indians that Captain Luis de Carvajal pacified in Xalpa. . . . About this there has been a pleito in this Audiencia and there have been some conclusions which will be necessary to see.[43]

Clearly, somebody other than Carvajal had enslaved the Indians that he had pacified in and around Xalpa.

Although a detailed account of Carvajal's activities in the Pánuco-Xalpa region is missing, it appears that he remained there from May of 1583 to the end of 1584. The first half of that period was taken by various tasks that included the pacification of the region, the reconstruction of some Indian towns, and the completion of certain documents he needed for the jurisdictional pleito that had started in the Audiencia. It was also during this time that he visited, for the last time, his sister's house in Tampico. It was during this visit that Isabel Rodríguez, his oldest niece, approached him and told him that he should follow the Law of Moses, a suggestion that according to Carvajal's trial greatly upset him. It was this conversation that, as described in chapter 11, was the basis for the inquisition trials that the Carvajal family would experience years later. Although as a Catholic Carvajal should have denounced his niece, he did not, claiming that he had to take care of an Indian uprising and that afterwards he forgot the incident.

Also keeping him busy at that time was the naming of officers in several towns he thought were included in his jurisdiction. But by August of 1584, the jurisdictional pleito had extended to the area around Santiago de los Valles, which meant that Carvajal had to give up, at least temporarily, his desire to take over that town.

In any case, Carvajal stayed in the province of Pánuco until the end of 1584, when a certain Capt. Melo arrived there from León bringing bad news: in the governor's absence, the Indians of the region around León had killed some Spaniards and had done many other damages.[44] The reason for the uprising was that some captains and soldiers, taking advantage of Carvajal's absence, had taken many Indians. On hearing the news Carvajal and his soldiers departed Pánuco and went to León. This was the first time those Indians had rebelled and it was not difficult for Carvajal to pacify them without using force.

On the way to León, Carvajal and his soldiers encountered a *caudillo*, or leader of a group of self-appointed soldiers, named Juan Trujillo, who had taken more than a hundred Indians and had condemned them to forced service for no apparent reason. As in past occasions Carvajal released the Indians. Of course, this helped him obtain peace in the region without recourse to arms, but, at the same time, continued to fuel a strong resentment among those soldiers who had hoped to profit from the capture and sale of Indians. In fact, the releases of captive Indians by Carvajal "had caused some soldiers to hate him" to the point that some, like Juan de Zayas raised against the governor.[45]

Carvajal's refusal to punish Indians who had been caught with stolen property prompted a curious incident. Thinking that the governor would not be so lenient if his own property was stolen or damaged by the Indians, some soldiers killed his favorite horse with arrows, so as to make it appear that the Indians had done it. Realizing what had happened Carvajal ordered that "from now on no Indian can be condemned of any charge unless caught *infraganti.*" Although well intentioned, it is doubtful that the order was obeyed.

Almadén

Having completed the 1585 pacification of the area around León, the governor commissioned Lucas de Linares, to found the villa del Almadén in the mines of Coahuila. The foundation date is uncertain because in 1589 Carvajal stated that "and now, lately [*ultimamente*], I settled a village in the mines of Coahuila, which I discovered and named Almadén." This has been taken to mean that Carvajal founded that village just before he made that statement, but what he meant was that Almadén was the last town he had settled. A more reliable date was provided by Felipe Núñez, who in September of 1587 stated that "More than two years ago, Lucas de Linares and other soldiers, settled, by order of the governor, the village of Almadén in the mines of Coahuila."[46] Thus, the foundation took place in 1584 or 1585.

The reasons for founding a settlement there are unclear. Of course, it could simply be that Carvajal wished to profit from the silver that Diego de Montemayor had found there in 1582, but why at this time? One possibility is that a group of soldiers led by Capt. Martín López Palomo had entered his territory from Nueva Vizcaya, supposedly to start a settlement there but having no commission to do so. The real reason was to take some Indians. It was after this incident that Carvajal commissioned Lucas de Linares to found Almadén, fearing that further incursions could take place from the west, where the Nueva Vizcaya village of Cuatro Cienegas was located. Since that province was only a short distance from Almadén, it would appear that this village was founded at that time in order to protect the northwest borders of Nuevo Reino de León.

With the foundation of Almadén, the northern provinces of Nuevo Reino de León included four towns that lived from mining, cattle ranching, cochineal, and from the raising of some basic crops such as wheat and corn. But other things were needed that were not produced locally. Therefore, Carvajal decided it was time to tackle an important problem that affected the growth of his kingdom: the transportation of goods and supplies to and from León.

Since the early days the provisions and supplies that were needed for the sustenance of Cueva de León and León, had come via Saltillo. This village was the door through which people and merchandise from Mazapil, Zacatecas, and Mexico City could reach San Luis and León. However, other parts of Nuevo Reino de León, namely the Pánuco region, could not easily trade goods with the northern settlements. Thus, in the spring of 1586, Carvajal turned his attention to the opening of a road from León to Tampico that could be traveled with *carretas*, or wagons. For that purpose he rented a number of them from a settler named Alonso Ruiz, and together with some of his soldiers went to Tampico, opening the desired road. One of those soldiers stated that:

> Governor Luis de Carvajal rented 13 carretas for 1400 gold pesos, which he took from said city of León to the province of Pánuco to open the road, and in them he took a large quantity of slag (*greta*) . . . for some mines he wanted to find in said province and this witness went with him with said carretas until Tanchipa, which was always believed to be impossible, and they were taken very easily.[47]

This statement shows that Carvajal had planned to explore some mines that he had discovered in the province of Pánuco. Whether he was successful is unknown. All that the documents show is that Carvajal got involved with the construction of the fort he had promised to build at the mouth of the river Pánuco, where the Chichimeca still reigned. Together with some of his people he first built a fence that would enclose the fort, so that those working in the fort could feel safe. But soon after the completion of that fence he received word that Viceroy Álvaro Manrique de Zúñiga, Marqués de Villamanrique, wanted to see him to talk about certain unspecified issues related to the government of New Spain. The order was received in September of 1586, and was to become the beginning of Carvajal's downfall as described in the following chapters.

9

Salazar *v.* Carvajal

Be informed that before . . . our Real Audiencia . . . there has been a pleito
between, on the first part, Licentiate Eugenio de Salazar, our fiscal . . . and,
on the other, Luis de Carvajal, our Governor of Nuevo Reino de León.

Royal Ejecutoria, June 7, 1585.[1]

Reference has been made in the previous chapters to the jurisdictional disputes that Carvajal faced during the first year of his tenure as governor. To resolve the conflicts he had, through Pedro de Vega, asked the Audiencia to order all Crown officers in the province of Pánuco not to interfere with his tasks, a request that was granted in early 1582. Nevertheless new and more troublesome problems arose the following year that resulted in a long-lasting pleito in the Audiencia de México. While the pleito was decisively ruled in favor of Carvajal, it set in motion the forces that eventually brought him down.

1. Confrontation in Pánuco

Although the Audiencia de México had, in January of 1582, ruled that certain towns in the province of Pánuco belonged to Carvajal, he could not take advantage of the ruling because he had left the Pánuco area in the fall of 1581. However, on his return in May of 1583, he decided it was time to take over those towns. To do this he would have to appoint magistrates and tax collectors in them, replacing those that existed at that time, all of whom reported to the viceroy via the alcalde mayor of that province. The changes wanted by Carvajal meant, if implemented, that these officers would lose considerable income. Because of this Carvajal's attempt to take over the areas under their control met strong resistance, as described below.

On the last day of May of 1583, Carvajal began the process to establish his authority over some Indian towns in that province. For this purpose he appointed Gaspar Delgado as scribe and made a long statement about the king's grant, adding that he wanted to obtain an Información regarding the "towns, places, and valleys that are included in the limits of the territories given to him by the king."[2] The task of obtaining that information was delegated to Diego Ramírez Barrionuevo, who heard the sworn testimonies of several long-time residents of the region, each of whom stated the population of several Indian towns.[3] Not surprisingly, all of them stated that each of those towns was in Carvajal's territory.

After the testimonies were taken Carvajal summoned the Indian governors of Tamecín and told them to relinquish their positions, elect new officers, swear allegiance to him, and to bring before him all cases of justice that might occur. Of course, the Indian officers did as told, saying that "they welcomed him as their governor." The transfer of power also meant that whatever tribute the Indians were required to pay to the Crown would be now paid to Carvajal.

In the next few days Carvajal repeated the same transfer ceremony in other towns, including Tantoyuca and Tancolol. Initially there was no resistance to his actions. However, on June 4, while in Tancolol, there arrived Juan de Villaseñor Alarcón, who at that time was the alcalde mayor of the province, and, as such, regarded these towns to be his. He therefore entered the town with "*vara alta*," that is, as the highest magistrate. It appears that he had been informed of Carvajal's activities and wanted to assert his authority. For that purpose he went to see the governor. In the lengthy exchange that followed, Villaseñor was shown copies of Carvajal's capitulación, cédulas, and copies of the viceroy's order of 1580 and of the royal order issued by the Audiencia in 1582, but this did not cause the desired result:

> Having shown the royal order . . . to Juan de Villaseñor Alarcón . . . who held it in his hands and kissed it and put it over his head saying that he obeyed it . . . and that he would respond what he would consider convenient. And regarding the towns which the governor asks, he, as alcalde mayor . . . will obey what the Audiencia orders in the name of the H.M.[4]

For his part Carvajal was no less insistent and told Villaseñor that:

> He requires him, one and more times, not to interfere in the execution of his duties in those parts and places he has been told . . . and that he should stop acting as the highest magistrate in this town.

Villaseñor's next step was to order that an Información about the events in Pánuco be made. Its opening statement, dated 6 June of 1583, says:

> Luis Carvajal de la Cueva, governor of Nuevo Reino de León has entered with more than 30 soldiers in the towns of Tamecín, Tancolol . . . and others that belong to both the Crown and to the encomenderos, all of which are in the

jurisdiction of the alcalde mayor of this province. . . . And without respect to this, he took away the titles of the [Indian] governors that administered justice in those towns saying that H.M. had given them to him . . . all of which has been against the wishes of H.M. and his viceroy, because even if he has declared those towns, they are not his. . . . By means of this, these events will be known to H.M. and his excellent viceroy of this New Spain so that the situation is remedied in the most convenient manner.[5]

Villaseñor's Información included the testimonies of six witnesses, three of whom were associated with Carvajal, which shows that the encounter was not a violent one. These three witnesses simply confirmed what Carvajal had done. The remaining witnesses, all Villaseñor soldiers, stated that Tancolol was not part of Carvajal's territory.[6] The document was concluded on 9 June 1583, after which Villaseñor stated that since the issue fell under the jurisdiction of the viceroy and the Audiencia, he was sending the Información to the viceroy. For his part, Carvajal also had his Información certified and sent to the Audiencia, most likely through Pedro de Vega. The date was 14 June of 1583. A few days later the two sets of documents arrived in Mexico City, starting a pleito that lasted over two years.

2. Reasons for the dispute

Before describing the events that resulted in several rulings in favor of Carvajal, it is useful to review the claims made by both him and Villaseñor. Of the two, the clearest was Villaseñor's. Simply stated, he said that the viceroy had named him as the alcalde mayor of the province of Pánuco, which for a long time had included the Indian towns that Carvajal was now claiming to be his, and that while he was shown the capitulación, the cédulas, and the orders from the viceroy and the Audiencia, he felt that those towns were his, and that he should not relinquish them without a direct order from the viceroy.

Carvajal's arguments were that the king had given him the lands north of the river Pánuco and that the capitulación and cédulas specifically gave him the right to name officers in every town that fell within the limits of his territory. He also insisted that the viceroy had obeyed the king's order and had ordered that it be obeyed by others, and that the Audiencia had issued, the previous year, a royal order giving him those towns.

The first point to be noted is that Villaseñor had received his appointment *after* October 11, 1580, when Viceroy Conde de Coruña signed an order to the officers of the Crown that they should not interfere with Carvajal. This means, of course, that the viceroy had not been alerted that the appointment of Villaseñor contradicted an order he had issued earlier. It is true that he should have connected the two orders, but the Conde de Coruña was not a very competent administrator. Of course, he was not the only one that contributed to the problem. The Audiencia also confused matters the first time they ruled in favor of Carvajal. That ruling would have prevented the dispute had it not been for the interference of Sancho López, a powerful secretary in the Audiencia, and for the omission, in the ruling, of a precise description of Carvajal's territories.

It thus appears that the most important reasons for the jurisdictional pleito were: The fact that the viceroy had ignored the chapter in Carvajal's capitulación that enabled him to change whatever he did not like; the unclear description in the capitulación of the lands that were given to Carvajal; Carvajal's interpretation of the limits stated in that document; and the personal opposition of the alcalde mayor of Pánuco and of someone in the Audiencia, both of whom stood to lose some lands.

Consider now the documentary sources for the dispute. Undoubtedly, the most important among these was the capitulación, which in the first chapter of the privileges part described the limits of Carvajal's territory. Carvajal's understanding of what was granted to him can be seen in the opening statement in the Información he obtained in Tamecín, where he declared that:

> H.M. named him Governor and Captain General from the port of Tampico, river of Pánuco, and mines of Mazapil until the beginning of the Nueva Galicia and Nueva Vizcaya, and from there to the north, 200 leagues, or more, of longitude and latitude, form one sea to the other.[7]

This statement, like the capitulación, says nothing about the southern limit of Carvajal's territory. Later on, however, Carvajal added that his jurisdiction included the "land north of the river Pánuco." It is evident that he believed this was the southern border of his territory, for in his letter of 18 February 1581 to the king he had asked that the whole province of Pánuco—north and south of the river by that name—be given to him. But that belief was also troublesome. For one thing, the river Pánuco had different names in different places. Furthermore, its source was in the eastern slopes of the Sierra Madre, whereas Mazapil was on its western side, far from Tampico.

In addition to those issues, the order given by the Audiencia on 18 January 1582 ruled in favor of Carvajal, it did not state the limits of his territory. Instead, it left the interpretation of the royal documents to the very people who were being ordered not to interfere with Carvajal, certainly a prescription for trouble.

And so, soon after 14 June of 1583, the pleito was referred to the Audiencia for resolution. But the viceroy died on the 19th of that month. His death left that royal body without a president, and New Spain without a viceroy. More than a year would pass before Pedro Moya de Contreras, the Archbishop-Inquisitor, would be appointed viceroy. In the mean time, the Audiencia tried to rule the colony.

In the absence of a viceroy, the authority resided in the oidores and the fiscal. By royal order, the oidor with longest service would take the role of the president.[8] The fiscal, whose position was below the most recently appointed oidor, was also a powerful member of the Audiencia, not only because the implied tasks of his charge, but also because the regulations required him to mediate between the viceroy and the oidores in those cases where differences occurred.[9]

At the time of the viceroy's death, the fiscal of the Audiencia was Eugenio de Salazar, a distinguished individual who is much better remembered because of his literary works.[10] For unknown reasons it appears that he acquired additional responsibilities and power after the viceroy's death. In fact, in the letter where he informed the king of the death of the viceroy, written of 30 June of 1583, he hinted that the oidores delegated some important responsibilities to him.[11] As it turns out, this prolific writer played a very important role in the life of Carvajal. For this reason, it is necessary to interrupt the discussion of the jurisdictional pleito and present a brief description of Salazar's accomplishments up to 1590, when he was promoted to the position of oidor. The source of that description is a letter he wrote to the king in 1596.[12]

3. Eugenio de Salazar

Eugenio de Salazar was born in Madrid around 1530. He studied law, first in Alcalá de Henares, then in Salamanca, and finally in Sigüenza, where he obtained the title of Licentiate. After completing his education he started a distinguished career in the service of the Crown, which was to end in Spain as a Consejero in the prestigious Real Consejo de Indias.[13] That service is described in his letter to the king.

As stated at the end of the previous chapter, Salazar arrived in Mexico City in early 1582, after serving nearly six years as oidor in the Audiencia de Guatemala. It is likely that he was installed as fiscal of the Audiencia de México soon after his arrival, beginning immediately to tackle many important issues, which he described at length in his letter to the king. It is interesting to note that his description of his activities contains a gap that corresponds to the period between the death of the Conde de Coruña and the appointment of

Viceroy Álvaro Manrique. Perhaps coincidentally, this was also the period that covered the long pleito with Carvajal.

Salazar's own summary of his services makes it clear that he was a zealous and tenacious Crown officer who was guided by the idea that the Crown's financial interests were paramount. This is shown by the zeal with which he prosecuted new pleitos as well as old ones that had been ruled against the Crown, apparently without profiting personally from them.[14]

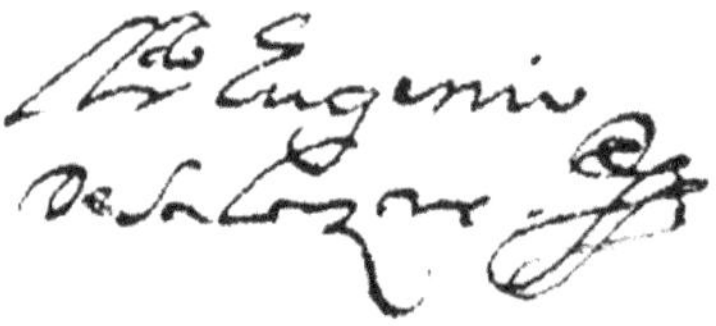

Fig. 9.1. Signature of Eugenio de Salazar.(*Courtesy Ministerio de Cultura, Archivo General de Indias, Seville,*)

This stubbornness was undoubtedly useful to the Crown but seems to have driven Salazar to press issues that were of little importance.[15] Perhaps he was right in doing so, but his relentless pursuit of them shows that compromise was not acceptable to him. In addition, Salazar also pressed charges on many individuals, regardless of who they were. It is not surprising to read that his pay, as he put it, "was a large number of enemies."

It is difficult to reconcile this portrait of Eugenio de Salazar with that of the writer of so many literary works in which he displayed a keen sense of humor and an understanding of the human condition. The man who went after Carvajal was not the sensitive writer, but a cold prosecutor who saw the issues in black and white, and who also told the king that he "was the best prosecutor that had ever served in New Spain."

Salazar's service included prior appointments that may have played a role in his forming an opinion of Carvajal. Thus, early in his career he had served as a judge along La Raya de Portugal. As such, he must have been aware that many New Christians from Portugal were returning to Spain. There is little doubt that he must have met many of them, and that he was well acquainted with their background, manners, and slightly different speech. Although Carvajal appeared to be an upper class Spaniard, it is possible that Salazar may have suspected him to be a Portuguese New Christian. In addition, as described in Chapter 3, Salazar was a governor of the Canary Islands in 1567, when Hawkins arrived there. That appointment lasted until 1573, when he was sent to Santo Domingo as the fiscal of its Audiencia. He therefore knew, first hand, that many Portuguese ships used the Canary Islands as a point of departure for the Spanish New World, as Carvajal had done in 1567, only a few months before Salazar arrived in those islands. Salazar was well aware that the practice was illegal and that Carvajal's voyage had originated in La Palma. It is therefore possible that this knowledge may have supported his suspicion about Carvajal's background. It is likely that these points may have played a role years later, when Carvajal was brought before the Inquisition, as will be discussed in due time. But it should be now stated that none of them played, at least openly, a role in Salazar's pleito against Carvajal.

5. THE PLEITO

The pleito between Eugenio de Salazar and Luis de Carvajal is described in a long document that the Audiencia issued on 7 June of 1585, which opens with the epigraph at the beginning of this chapter. The document, a royal order called an *Ejecutoria*, contains a narrative of what was argued before the Audiencia, going back to 4 July of 1583. To guide the discussion, it is useful to include a table that lists the pleito's main events in chronological order.

Table 2. Chronology of the pleito Salazar-Carvajal

1983	4 July	Pedro de Vega presents a petition in name of Carvajal. Eugenio de Salazar brings charges against Carvajal.
	25 October	The Audiencia rules in favor of Carvajal (in degree of *Vista*). Salazar appeals the decision.
1984	6 July	The Audiencia rules, again, in favor of Carvajal (*Revista*). Vega petitions that an Ejecutoria be issued.
	13 July	Salazar appeals for the second time the Audiencia's ruling.
	18 July	Oidor Sánchez Paredes orders that the Ejecutoria be issued. Salazar requests that the order be voided.
	14 September	The Audiencia orders Carvajal not to take possession of Valles until it completes its review.
1585	20 May	The Audiencia rules against Salazar's second appeal.
	7 June	The Audiencia issues the Ejecutoria in favor of Carvajal.

The Ejecutoria contains several certified copies of documents placed in evidence by both sides, as well as reference to certain others that seemed relevant to either Salazar or Carvajal but which were not included in it. One of these was another Ejecutoria from an earlier dispute about the town of Tamaholipa, which had been ruled in favor of Carvajal. Another is a 1584 order to Carvajal, to be discussed later, not to take the village of Valles until the Audiencia would conclude its examination of all facts.

As the table shows, the pleito started when Pedro de Vega appeared before the oidores of the Audiencia in the name of Carvajal. In the voice of the king the Ejecutoria states that Vega said:

> That we knew well what was the district promised to his part in Nuevo Reino de León. And even though we had issued orders that all officers in New Spain respect his territory, they still disturb him. . . . And he begged that our royal person keeps what had been promised to him for district, with all the towns in it, and that we impose serious penalties to the alcalde mayor of Pánuco and Valles. And he pleaded justice and presented certain *recaudos* and Información.[16]

The recaudos, or supporting documents, mentioned by Vega included two cédulas, numbered 5 and 6 in Appendix B; Viceroy Conde de Coruña's order of 11 October 1580; the 18 January 1582 order issued by the Audiencia in the name of the king; several documents relating to the discoveries and foundations made by Carvajal; and, of course, the Información that Carvajal had obtained in Pánuco.

After the opening by Vega, the Audiencia ordered that copies be made of the documents introduced by him and sent to fiscal Salazar together with the Información that Juan de Villaseñor had prepared. Salazar response is also recorded in the Ejecutoria:

> And our fiscal presented . . . a petition in which he accused Governor Luis de Carvajal, saying that he had entered many Crown towns in the province of Pánuco and had expelled our alcalde mayor and other magistrates . . . with the purpose of extending his jurisdiction and obtaining from those towns the salary promised to him in his titles, in all of which he had committed enormous atrocities against our royal person. And because of them he deserves to be severely punished. . . . And our fiscal begged us to order that Governor Luis de Carvajal be taken prisoner and brought to the royal jail . . . so that he can be punished for his crimes. And that we should reinstate all the officers he had removed and that we also order that he not be allowed to enter said towns.[17]

It is noted that Salazar did not simply ask that the jurisdiction of the contested towns be given back to the alcalde mayor, as might have been expected from Villaseñor's Información. Instead, he wanted the Audiencia to order that Carvajal be taken prisoner and be brought to México City and put in jail as a common criminal.

To add weight to his charges, Salazar presented another accusation against Carvajal:

> After which our fiscal said that Governor Luis de Carvajal, exceeding the powers we had given him … had entered in other towns … that had been subject to the Crown, and *had ordered that a fort be built there* (emphasis added), as shown in the documents he presented, which the governor had signed.

The documents mentioned by Salazar were copies of the commission, mentioned in the previous chapter, that Carvajal gave to Capt. Francisco de Abreu in the town of Xalpa. Of all the charges Salazar brought against Carvajal, this was the most absurd, for his own statement shows that he had not read the documents he introduced to support his case. Specifically his additional charge was that Carvajal had entered into the town of Xalpa, which was peaceful and belonged to the Crown, had ordered that a fort be built there, and had appointed Abreu as its main magistrate.

Indeed, Carvajal had built a fort in Xalpa, but that had been in 1576, when viceroy Martín Enríquez had ordered him to do so, as described in Chapter 4. Further, Xalpa was one of the towns explicitly given by the king to Carvajal in the capitulación, a fact that Viceroy Lorenzo Suárez had acknowledged and which Salazar should have known.

The first and second set of remarks made by Salazar concluded what was to be the first round of the litigation. The Ejecutoria then states that:

> And our president and oidores ordered that all documents entered in this pleito be added to those of another that our fiscal and Gaspar Jorge, our alcalde mayor in the province of Pánuco, had tried against Governor Luis de Carvajal about the jurisdiction of the town of Tamaholipa, which contains the titles and cédula by us *given in favor of said governor* (emphasis added). And having seen all documents, they pronounced and signed the following *auto*.

Auto de Audiencia

In Mexico City, on 25 October 1583, the president and oidores of the Audiencia Real of New Spain, having seen this and other autos in this pleito between … Licentiate Eugenio de Salazar, fiscal of H.M. in this royal Audiencia, and Luis de Carvajal, our governor of Nuevo Reino de León and Pedro de Vega in his name, about the jurisdiction of his territory and what the fiscal asked, declared that, despite what the fiscal argued, all towns that are on the other side of the river Pánuco, towards the north, belong to the government of said Luis de Carvajal, and are included in it, and that they belong to his jurisdiction so that he can use it and govern them in accordance with his titles and capitulación. . . . And they released and freed said Luis de Carvajal of the charges made against him by said fiscal. . . . And they so pronounced it and ordered that the auto by the fiscal be removed.[18]

Thus, based on the presentation of both parties and of the documents introduced by them, the Audiencia decided the pleito in favor of Carvajal, voiding Salazar request to take him prisoner, and ruling that all contested towns belonged to the governor.

Of course, Salazar was not to yield so easily. The first thing he did was to appeal the decision, as shown below. Secondly, perhaps anticipating another defeat, he included his views of the issue in his next report to the king.[19] In that report he repeated his arguments against Carvajal adding: "However, the pleito has been concluded in his favor, adjudicating to him those towns. I have supplicated the ruling, and that is how the case remains." Thus, sometime between October 25 and November 1 of 1583, when Salazar's report was written, he appeared again before the oidores to appeal their ruling in favor of Carvajal:

> And our fiscal begged us, in writing, that . . . said auto in favor of Governor Luis de Carvajal should be revoked because the documents, cédulas and agreements introduced in the pleito showed that . . . we had not given him said government . . . because they said that 'you will be Captain General of those provinces that you have discovered or will discover and settle'.[20]

As before, the Audiencia sent copies of the appeal by the fiscal to Pedro de Vega, who responded that the resolution should be ordered because:

> From the record of the pleito it was clear that the government of his part included the towns that were on the other side of the river Pánuco, towards the north . . . regardless of whether those areas were settled or not.

To this, Salazar answered that "the proofs . . . that [Vega] was presenting were made before suspect and impertinent witnesses." This response is interesting because all but one of those witnesses he considered suspect were the same as those used by Villaseñor.

Although the Ejecutoria stated that certain other documents were introduced by Carvajal, and that some orders were issued, none of these documents appear in it. However, more than a year after the pleito had begun, the Audiencia decided, once more, the pleito in favor of Carvajal stating that:

> And in said pleito passed other autos and certain other documents were introduced. And having our president and oidores seen the pleito, they gave

and pronounced another auto, in degree of *Revista* [review], signed by their names, which is as follows:

Auto de Revista de la Audiencia de México

In Mexico City, on 6 July 1584, the president and oidores . . . said that despite the supplication made by said fiscal, they confirmed in degree of Revista the auto pronounced, about this cause, on 25 October of the last year of 1583, in which it was declared that all the towns that are on the other side of the river Pánuco belong to the government of Luis de Carvajal . . . . And said Luis de Carvajal was freed of all the charges brought against him by said fiscal. And ordered that all contained in the auto be kept and obeyed.[21]

This ruling by the Audiencia represented a enormous triumph for Carvajal. Through it, all charges leveled against him by Salazar were dropped. More importantly, he was finally given the areas he had claimed as his. Thus, as described later, he apparently attempted to take over those areas soon after the 6 July 1584 ruling. However, realizing that Salazar would continue to pursue the issue and fearing that the ruling might be disregarded by the officers in Pánuco, Pedro de Vega requested that an Ejecutoria be issued to force those officers to comply with the Audiencia's order. Furthermore, he also requested that the document should explicitly list the names of the towns that belonged to Carvajal. The request was forwarded to oidor Garcia Sánchez Paredes for consideration.

A week later, Salazar requested that the case be re opened, a request that was apparently declined, although a separate document shows that request was being considered as late as mid September of 1584.[22] In the mean time Sánchez Paredes had reviewed Vega's request to issue an Ejecutoria, and on 18 July he approved the request. Not surprisingly, Salazar objected to the decision "arguing certain points by which, in effect, he pretended that before giving our Ejecutoria be given to said governor, he should pay the bonds stipulated by our law of the Indies, until the Real Consejo decides the amount."

Confrontation in Valles

Although the next entry in the Ejecutoria refers to events that took place in 1585, when the Audiencia issued its final ruling, other documents show that Salazar continued to oppose Carvajal despite the Audiencia's order of 6 July of 1584. These documents show that soon after that ruling Carvajal went to the areas that had been declared his and attempted, once more, to replace existing officers with his own, as he had done more than a year earlier. But as Pedro de Vega had anticipated, Carvajal found that the Crown officers in Valles refused, again, to obey the Audiencia. Thus, Francisco Guerrero, the alcalde mayor of Valles, issued some strong threats against Carvajal.[23] In the opening statement accompanying the Información he prepared he said that Carvajal had written to him telling him he was coming to Valles with 30 soldiers, with the intention of taking the town, and that he, Guerrero, was warning Carvajal not to do so, and that if he did he would have to pay 1000 ducats in fines and face death. It is unlikely that Carvajal had written to him, for if he had a copy of the letter would have been included in Guerrero's Información. Also, it is interesting to see an alcalde threatening a governor with death. Obviously, some powerful force was behind him.

After the opening statement by Guerrero, his Información contained Carvajal's signed response, in which he repeated the usual arguments based on the capitulación and cédulas, adding that the Crown had twice ruled that Valles was one of his towns. After this response, there is a statement by Guerrero, where he said that in spite of Carvajal's answer, his previous fines and threats remained. The Información then continued on August 29, when Guerrero obtained affidavits from three resident of Valles, all of whom stated that Valles did not fall in Carvajal's jurisdiction. Guerrero's Información was then sent to Salazar on that date, which means that the documents arrived in Mexico City a few days later.

The Audiencia's response, written at Salazar's request, was issued only two weeks later. The date was 14 September 1584, ten days before Archbishop-Inquisitor Pedro Moya de Contreras become viceroy, that is, when Salazar still had the extended responsibilities that he had acquired at the time of the death of the Conde de Coruña. The response was in the form of a royal order that says, in part:

> D. Phelipe, etc., etc. To you Luis de Carvajal, our Governor and General Captain of Nuevo Reino de León. *Salud y gracia*. Be informed that Licentiate Eugenio de Salazar, our fiscal in our Audiencia . . . begged us to give him our letter and order so that you should not use said Ejecutoria until it would be determined if we should admit his second supplication, and . . . he asked we order you not to enter in said village of Valles and towns in its jurisdiction. . . . And having seen his petition we agreed that we should send said letter, by which we order you that in what pertains the jurisdiction of Santiago de los Valles you should not do anything new until we order differently. Given in Mexico City on 14 September of 1584.[24]

Thus, the order repeated the arguments made earlier by Salazar when he requested that the issuing of the Ejecutoria be delayed. In the mean time,

Carvajal was ordered not to "do anything new" in Valles, which meant that he should not take possession of that town.

Also remarkable is the fact that while the document was supposedly intended for Carvajal, it was instead sent to Guerrero. It was not until December that the order was shown to him for a note that added below the document says: "In Santiago de los Valles, on 19 December of 1584 . . . I, Luis de Herrera Salazar, notified the order contained above to Governor Luis de Carvajal de la Cueva, in person." After the Herrera's signature, the document has the following inscription signed by Carvajal and by Guerrero's lieutenant:

> Governor Luis de Carvajal de la Cueva said that he obeyed said royal letter. . . . And about it he said that he has not made, nor is making anything new, and that he is only obeying his obligations as governor . . . exercising his office in his government, which includes this village of Valles and other towns around it, which are from the river Pánuco towards the north, in accordance with the sentence that in degree of Vista and Revista was given and pronounced by the president and oidores of the Audiencia. . . . And that if the sense of the order is, or could be, against his title and the sentences of Vista and Revista given about his limits . . . he begs H.M. in his royal Audiencia to order him whatever is most convenient to his royal service and he will obey and keep what is ordered.

Thus, although Carvajal knew that the order was against the two Audiencia sentences in his favor he realized that before he could take Valles he would have to wait until the Audiencia made a final ruling about issuing the Ejecutoria. In the mean time he was forced to leave the area without accomplishing anything. And so, soon after these events, Carvajal left the Pánuco area and went to the northern regions of Nuevo Reino de León, where another Indian uprising had taken place in his absence.

Conclusion of the pleito

The Ejecutoria is silent about the events that took place there between July of 1584 and May of 1585, when the Audiencia ended the pleito between Salazar and Carvajal and issued their final decree:

> In Mexico City on 20 May 1585, the president and oidores. . . having seen this pleito . . . about the fiscal's petition that before said Ejecutoria be given to Governor Luis de Carvajal he should pay bonds to pay what the Consejo de Indias would decide in this cause, they said that despite of what the fiscal asks, they confirmed the ruling made . . . on 18 July of 1584, in which it was ordered to give said governor the royal Ejecutoria of what has been determined in this cause in degree of Revista, in the towns about which there has been litigation. . . . And they so determined and ordered. And so that said autos be obeyed . . . . we order all and each of you that after said Ejecutoria is shown to you, you

should see what is stated in it and keep and make keep and execute said statements. . . . Given in Mexico City on 7 June 1585. Doctor Pedro Farfán, Doctor Sánchez Paredes, Doctor Francisco de Sande, Doctor Robles, Doctor Palacio. I, Cristóbal Osorio, chamber scribe of the Audiencia Real of New Spain by H.M. had it written by order and agreement of its presidente and oidores. Registered by Joan Serrano, Chancellor.[25]

And so, two years after Carvajal first decided to assert his authority in the Pánuco region, the Audiencia closed the pleito with a strongly worded decision in his favor. Not only had the October 1583 order been re-affirmed on July of 1584, but also, a Royal Ejecutoria had been issued that stated these facts and listed the areas belonging to him. Carvajal probably thought that he could finally get control over the territory granted to him by the king. However, when the final ruling was made, he was in León and could not take the towns that had been contested in Pánuco. Thus, even though the Audiencia had ruled in his favor several times, Valles and the Indian towns in its vicinity had remained in the hands of Francisco Guerrero. However, after spending a year or so in San Luis and León, Carvajal went to Tampico in the spring of 1586. One purpose of the journey was to open a road that could be traveled with wagons. These actions were briefly described at the end of the previous chapter.

The record shows that Carvajal stayed in Tampico to work on some of the tasks that he was required to fulfill, such as the construction of a fort at the mouth of the river Pánuco. He also intended to take over the villages and towns in the Pánuco region that had been given to him, thinking that the jurisdictional problems that had plagued him were over, and that he could now freely govern his Nuevo Reino de León. Instead, while working on he construction of the fort, news arrived that brought far more serious problems, as described in the next chapter.

Carvajal's Downfall

I had him come here and ordered him to have whatever soldiers he had to leave that province.

Álvaro Manrique de Zúñiga, November 15, 1586.[1]

As described in the previous chapter, the Salazar-Carvajal pleito was decided in favor of the latter several times. Those rulings represented a serious blow to Salazar, accustomed as he was to win. Perhaps another fiscal would have let go, but he was a zealous prosecutor who had a very high opinion of himself. These traits, coupled with a rather low opinion of the oidores, made his defeat difficult to accept. In this he was not alone. Other Crown officers and some encomenderos had, as a result of the rulings, lost some lands and did not want to accept the loss. However, Salazar's petition to re-open the pleito did not succeed. This meant that jurisdictional complaints could no longer be used to gain those lands back. A different plan had to be devised that did not require the approval of the Audiencia, particularly since Pedro Moya de Contreras, the Archbishop-Inquisitor was now also the viceroy. As the reader may recall, Moya was acquainted with Carvajal and apparently had a good opinion of him. However, a viceregal change took place which brought unexpected support to Salazar and his accomplices.

1. ÁLVARO MANRIQUE DE ZÚÑIGA

On 18 October of 1585, four months after the final ruling by the Audiencia in favor of Carvajal, a new viceroy was inaugurated in New Spain. This was Álvaro Manrique de Zúñiga, Marqués de Villamanrique. His arrival, at this time, could not be more propitious to Salazar. As fiscal, he was the intermediary between the oidores and the viceroy and was well acquainted with the inner workings of the Audiencia. It was therefore natural that the new viceroy would turn to him for advise and information. Apparently, the viceroy regarded Salazar as one of his most trustworthy officers, for as Salazar's own list of accomplishments shows, the viceroy let him decide many cases brought before the Audiencia, a questionable decision given the obvious conflict of interest. It also appears that the viceroy's interests and personal traits made him receptive to Salazar's views, particularly with regard to his cause against Carvajal. In fact, the viceroy took the lead in that cause, allowing Salazar to remove himself from front stage, although his mark can be clearly seen behind the viceroy's actions.

Because of the decisive role that Viceroy Manrique played in Carvajal's downfall, it is useful to briefly review some known facts about him. First, it should be noted that because of the vague similarity of their names, he has often been confused with Viceroy Enríquez, although their personalities and their administrative capabilities differed enormously. Enríquez is considered one of the best viceroys of New Spain, whereas the record of the Marqués de Villamanrique was, at best, a mixed one.[2] To avoid confusion between these two viceroys, the latter will in what follows be referred to as Villamanrique. Second, for the reasons presented below, the king decided to terminate Villamanrique's tenure as viceroy four years after he was appointed, doing so with some urgency and ordering that he be held in house arrest while Bishop Diego Romano, his *visitador*, examined his deeds.[3] Romano had no difficulty in finding many reasons to accuse Villamanrique. The charges he leveled against him appear in several

Fig. 10.1. Viceroy Álvaro Manrique

documents that include Villamanrique's self-defense as well as the bishop's comments about it.[4] In total, there were 341 charges listed, including one that refers to Villamanrique's unfair treatment of Carvajal.

Examination of the charges against Villamanrique shows that many were trivial, and that many others were related to his treatment of Archbishop Moya de Contreras. However, a significant number of them were serious and caused considerable aggravation to Villamanrique, including his dying a poor man and in disgrace before the king. Taken as a whole the charges show him as a high-handed ruler who would often disregard orders from the king; imprison people for no reason; release prisoners convicted by the Audiencia; practice nepotism on a grand scale; help himself to money and other valuables from the royal treasury; and borrow money from many individuals in New Spain—some of whom were being considered for Crown appointments—but never paying back. Also troublesome was his censoring letters that prominent individuals and official bodies sent to, or received from Spain.[5]

Several other important points emerge from the long list of charges against Villamanrique. One was that he wanted to be have absolute authority in New Spain, when in fact Nueva Galicia, Nueva Vizcaya, and Nuevo León were, by royal order, largely autonomous entities, deferring to the viceroy only in military matters. No less important was Villamanrique's quarrelsome personality. According to many reports, he was prone to fits of anger for both important and trivial reasons.[6] These traits would affect his performance as viceroy, as can be seen from the following excerpt from a letter by the Audiencia de Nueva Galicia to the king. The letter, written on January of 1588, anticipated the great confrontation between that Audiencia and Villamanrique, which occurred a year later, and says, in part

> Even though this Audiencia has tried, and tries, to avoid differences and to remove competitions with the Marqués de Villamanrique, he, on the contrary, seeks them and is pleased by them. Therefore, each day he disturbs things, taking advantage of whatever occasion is presented to disturb the peace and tranquility in the whole kingdom.[7]

This states, in no uncertain terms, that Villamanrique was a contentious man. And the events that occurred the following year show that he was willing to attack Guadalajara with a large force simply to arrest the fiscal of its Audiencia who had apparently disregarded a trivial order of his. There is little doubt that this event, together with the opinions of the Archbishop and of Carvajal, prompted the king to remove Villamanrique from power in 1589.[8]

Of course, the viceroy had his admirers, and among them was Eugenio de Salazar. In a letter that he wrote to the king on 20 May 1586, Salazar stated that "the marquis shows good intentions and is willing to change his mind when good reasons are presented to him." It is not unreasonable to assume that those good reasons were often presented to him by his persuasive fiscal, who understood human nature better than most, and who saw in Villamanrique's desire for absolute control of New Spain a good avenue for his own wishes.

Now, as stated earlier, Carvajal's enemies were considerably upset at the loss implied by the Audiencia's rulings and wanted to recover the territories they had lost, but could no longer hide behind jurisdictional issues to achieve their goals. Instead a new ploy was used to convince the viceroy to help their cause. The plan had a most laudable basis: the pacification of the frontier. But the connection between that goal and the viceroy's reasons for his actions against Carvajal, while clear in purpose, was based on lies.

Although the pacification problem has been touched on several occasions, it is useful to briefly review the basic issues that were involved in it. As noted before, the Crown had for a long time tried to eliminate the damages that the Chichimeca had been inflicting on the Spaniards. Fueling the Chichimeca attacks were the Spanish soldiers who, in order to augment their meager salary, would continue to take Indians and sell them. Viceroy Enríquez knew this and had always insisted that the Indians should not be taken prisoner unless it could be proven they had committed a serious crime. He had also ordered that certain procedures be strictly followed when Spanish soldiers would enter Chichimeca territory to explore the land or to punish Indians who had committed some crime. In this context it is recalled that Enríquez had advised the Conde de Coruña to make use of Carvajal in the pacification, as he himself had done, because Carvajal, was "less inclined to drink their blood" than other Spaniards.

Villamanrique was made aware of the problem by Eugenio de Salazar, who, as fiscal of the Audiencia, was also responsible for the well being of the Indians. In fact, Villamanrique issued a general order to try to alleviate the problem. Unfortunately, he also issued other orders that would have severe consequences for the future of Nuevo Reino de León.

2. VILLAMANRIQUE'S ORDERS

On August of 1586, less than a month after Moya left New Spain, Villamanrique issued an order that included a set of rules that prescribed how the captains and soldiers should pacify the Chichimeca Indians. The rules largely followed those of Viceroy Enríquez. This is not the place to examine the effectiveness or consequences of the new rules. Suffice to say that the problem in the frontier subsisted for at least 150 years after they were issued.[9] But the pacification did play an important role in Carvajal's downfall because it gave the viceroy an excuse to persecute him, using as a basis the fabrications against the governor that were initiated in Valles after Villamanrique arrived in New Spain. Thus, two weeks after signing that order, the viceroy, no longer restrained by the archbishop, took the first steps against Carvajal. Those steps appear in two royal orders that he, alone, issued in the name of the king on September 4, 1586; one directed to Carvajal; the other to Francisco Guerrero, who two years earlier, as alcalde of Valles, had threatened Carvajal with death.[10] The order to Carvajal reads, in part:

D. Felipe, etc., etc. To you Luis de Carvajal de la Cueva, my governor in Nuevo Reino de León. Be informed that for my royal service it is convenient that you come to this court, to discuss and communicate some businesses of importance and consideration to the conservation and increase of this kingdom, with D. Álvaro Manrique de Zúñiga, Marqués de Villamanrique, my viceroy. . . . And I order you that within 30 days, to be counted from the day that this letter reaches you, you should appear in this court before my viceroy. And you should make sure that all captains and soldiers that serve in your government leave it, provided they are not settlers there. . . . And I warn you that if you do not arrive here within that period, I will send a person to bring you here at your expense. Given in Mexico City on 4 September of 1586. I the Marquis.

As this shows, the order did not specify the issues that the viceroy wanted to discuss with Carvajal, although the reference to the soldiers in Nuevo Reino de León might have been a hint. Carvajal received the order in Tampico, where he was working on the construction of a fort at the mouth of the river Pánuco. Believing that the viceroy's business was important, he left Tampico immediately, reaching México City a few days later. Accompanying him was Felipe Núñez.[11]

The order sent to Francisco Guerrero included a very important development. After the salutation, he was informed that Carvajal had been ordered to go to México City and had been told to order his soldiers to leave Nuevo Reino de León, which if they did not, "they would be punished with death and confiscation of assets." The rest of the order includes a point not mentioned in the order to Carvajal, but which must have pleased Guerrero:

And because of this it is convenient that . . . I provide justices [there] in the manner that used to administer, and should administer, my alcalde mayor, before that Ejecutoria was issued in favor of said Luis de Carvajal by my Royal Audiencia about said jurisdiction. . . . In view of this I order you to take jurisdiction . . . as you had before my Ejecutoria was issued. And do not permit said Luis de Carvajal de la Cueva, or his lieutenants, interfere in it in any manner. . . . I the Marquis.

Both orders were highly irregular because they were written in the voice of the king, but were issued by the viceroy alone, without approval of the oidores of the Audiencia, a procedure that went against Crown rules. This fact was pointed out in a letter that Carvajal sent to the king a year later. But irregular or not, the order invalidated the Ejecutoria that the Audiencia had issued the year before in favor of Carvajal. More harmful, however, was Villamanrique's order about the soldiers in Nuevo Reino de León. By ordering that they should leave that province, he put in grave danger the Spanish settlements that had been founded there as they were inside Chichimeca territory, a fact that should have been known to Villamanrique and to those advising him.

Although the viceroy gave Carvajal no reason for his actions, he and his accomplices knew that sooner or later he would be required to explain them. For this purpose Villamanrique included in his 15 November 1586 letter to the king a section that contained strongly worded charges against Carvajal. In addition to stating that Carvajal had not founded any settlements or fulfilled any of the requirements imposed by the capitulación. The evidence presented in earlier chapters shows that this was another lie. Villamanrique also said that he was forced to issue a certain order because of Carvajal's excessive abuses of the Indians. It appears that the evidence presented for this accusation was the false testimony obtained in Valles by Guerrero, as described at the end of Chapter 4. These accusations were to be repeated many more times, both by Villamanrique and by his successor and will be discussed later in more detail.

In the same report, Villamanrique also informed the king of the steps he had taken to solve the problems that, according to him, Carvajal had created:

> And so that Luis de Carvajal would not succeed in destroying that land . . . and to learn from him what was happening in it and to end *the infinite number of complaints and suits from the fiscal* (emphasis added). . . . I commanded him to order all the people of war he has there to leave. . . . And he came here and the situation is being examined to see if he has fulfilled what he had promised Y.M. And in the mean time I have ordered that certain towns which this royal Audiencia had adjudicated to him be given back to the alcaldes mayores of Tampico, Pánuco and Valles, as they had them before, so that the region is not left without justices, until it has been decided what to do.

By this action those areas that the Audiencia had repeatedly ruled belonged to Carvajal were given to others, as Salazar had wanted. But the prize to the Crown was high. Soon after the order was issued, the Indians in the northern parts of Nuevo Reino de León, seeing that the soldiers had left the area, attacked and destroyed the towns that had been built there. This would cost many Spanish lives and a ten year delay in the colonization of the northern provinces of New Spain.

Carvajal's version of the viceroy's order is described in a letter dated 30 January of 1587 in which he requested the king to order the viceroy not to interfere in his task. The letter states, in part, that:

> When I was occupied building the fort at the mouth of the river of Tampico . . . the Marqués de Villamanrique sent for me, and without any just cause has kept me in this City of Mexico, preventing me to serve Y.M. without any cause other than his wish. And to do this he issued an order, signed by him alone, without

a person from the Audiencia, in which he ordered me to appear in this court within 30 days.[12]

And in the same manner, he alone and with the same name issued two other orders. In one he orders that the alcaldes mayores of Pánuco and Valles enter in my jurisdiction, in the towns which by the Ejecutoria have been adjudicated to me . . . and administer justice there. . . . And the other to proclaim in every place of my jurisdiction that all captains and soldiers that are there and in my government should leave under the penalty of death. And although by reason of my title of governor I am not subject to him . . . I came to this court, where I have been four months without any cause or blame . . . and I suspect he does this because he does not want any other governor and captain general but himself.

And he has done so without thinking about the harm that can happen . . . or to the events that have taken place in my absence and that of the soldiers that he ordered leave said government, because, since I arrived in this city, the Indians around the village of San Luis in the valley of Extremadura, seeing that the settlers were alone, raised and rebelled against the obedience to Y.M., in which I left them, and burnt the houses and took the cattle and killed those they could. And the burghers who live in the other settlements fear the same if my absence last longer, because of which it is necessary for my to depart for said government, to avoid the anticipated damage. I will try first to have an audience with him even though I suspect it will not succeed.

Fig. 10.2. Carvajal's signature in 1587. (*Courtesy Ministerio de Cultura, Archivo General de Indias.*)

The letter makes several important points, namely that Carvajal did not have to obey the viceroy's order; that even though the viceroy had ordered him to go to see him to discuss important issues four months had passed after his arrival in Mexico City and the viceroy had not yet received him, although Carvajal had often tried to see him.[13] This meant that he had not been told of any charges against him. However, the strongest point was that because of the viceroy's order his soldiers had abandoned Nuevo Reino de León, leaving the province without protection. Because of this, Carvajal said, he had to leave Mexico City.

3. The destruction of San Luis and León

And so, some time in February of 1587, Carvajal left México City without permission from the viceroy. It is not difficult to imagine the viceroy's reaction when he learned this. It is likely that he wanted to send, immediately, soldiers to capture the governor and to bring him back to Mexico City as a common criminal, as Salazar had wanted to do three years earlier. However, Carvajal had left without stating his destination, although, as seen in his letter to the king, he had gone to the northern parts of Nuevo Reino de León, more than 600 miles away. The route he took was through Tampico, where he had been before being ordered to go to México City.

Although Carvajal's letter makes reference to the destruction of the village of San Luis, the city of Leon had also been destroyed by the Indians while he was in Mexico City. The chain of events that resulted in their destruction began with the orders Villamanrique sent regarding Carvajal's soldiers. The viceroy had also instructed Guerrero that his order regarding those soldiers should be proclaimed in all the settlements where Carvajal soldiers lived, and that if the they did not obey it, the punishment would be death.[14] Of course, after hearing the order from the viceroy, Carvajal's soldiers obeyed it, leaving the settlements without defense:

> And the soldiers, after seeing the rigorous command that the viceroy had issued, went out of said kingdom and left the settlements without defense, with only the burghers and their wives, who did not want to leave their haciendas alone.[15]

This had severe consequences, as reported by an eye witness:

> And when the Indians saw that only some people remained, and understanding from some servant Indians and soldiers what the viceroy had ordered, they rose and rebelled against the Spaniards and killed Lucas de Linares, lieutenant of governor, and eight other Spanish soldiers, and attempted to kill the treasurer Diego de Montemayor and this witness and others . . . and killed many horses, mules and cattle . . . so that the people had to leave on foot, leaving the town desolate . . . which was a great disservice to our Lord and to H.M.[16]

The attacks seem to have lasted a few days, for as Felipe Núñez stated:

> And the burghers, seeing that every day said Indians, having gathered more than 6,000 of them, would attack the city and do much harm . . . they went to the village of Saltillo, where they are now. . . . And they abandoned said city [León] and the villages of La Cueva and San Luis.[17]

Even if the number of attackers was exaggerated, it is evident that it must have been large because the Spaniards were not able to repel it.

While Villamanrique's order was ultimately responsible for these events, it is believed that El Mozo had incited the Indians to attack because in a note added to his self defense before the Inquisition, Carvajal wrote that the reason San Luis was destroyed was that his nephew had condemned certain Indians to death.[18] Whether this happened is uncertain. The note was intended to discredit El Mozo's testimony before the inquisitors and seems to contradict what Carvajal had stated in his letter of January 30, 1587. Furthermore, it is also in conflict with El Mozo's claim that he left León before Linares was killed.[19]

In any event, by the time Carvajal reached San Luis and León, these settlements had been destroyed. His reaction was described by Pedro Hernandez de Almanza:

> And being informed of this, the governor entered said kingdom to remedy the situation, and this witness went with him and arrived in the village of San Luis and other parts and found that the Indians had destroyed and burnt the houses, and burnt a great quantity of wheat, all of which was a great sadness to those who saw it. And seeing that he had no people or order to fight the Indians and to rebuild the houses, and being fearful of the Indians, he went to the village of Saltillo.[20]

In Saltillo, Carvajal was reunited with some of the settlers of San Luis and León who had survived the attacks. Among them were Gaspar Castaño de Sosa, the alcalde mayor of San Luis, and Diego de Montemayor, the treasurer of Nuevo Reino de León, both of whom appear later in this work; the first as the leader of the first attempt to colonize Nuevo México; the second as the founder, years later, of the city of Monterrey, in the same site where the village of San Luis had been.

It is not known how long did Carvajal stayed in Saltillo, or what he did there. While he considered Saltillo to be his, the village now formally belonged to Nueva Vizcaya. It is true that many of its settlers had been associated with him at one time or another, but they could not help him in his quarrel with the viceroy.

4. IN NUEVA GALICIA

The only place where Carvajal could get some support was in Guadalajara, the seat of the Real Audiencia de Nueva Galicia. Not only was that body independent of the viceroy but, also, its oidores were at odds with him, as their letter of January of 1588 shows.[21] Thus, around mid 1587 Carvajal left Saltillo together with some of the soldiers he still had, and headed for that city, passing through Mazapil. There, the events of the last few months were well known. These included Carvajal's departure from Mexico City without permission from the viceroy and the destruction of San Luis and León. Also, Mazapil was periodically visited by Rodrigo del Río Loysa, the viceroy's military lieutenant in Nueva Galicia. It is thus likely that Carvajal's passage through that town and his destination were noted and conveyed to the viceroy.

In any event, Carvajal and some of his soldiers arrived in Guadalajara in the summer of 1587. What he wanted from the Audiencia there was some kind of support that could add weight to his pleas to the king. In this he succeeded because, by the end of August, that Audiencia had agreed to receive an Información de Oficio about his deeds, which, when completed would be transmitted the king.

After receiving permission to present that Información, Carvajal prepared the required *Interrogatorio* for the witnesses. Careful reading of the thirty three questions appearing in it shows that Carvajal had learned the allegations that the viceroy had made against him, that is, the questions were selected to prove that the viceroy's allegations were false. As required, the oidores selected some witnesses from a list provided by Carvajal, to which others, independently selected by them, were added. Among the latter group were Matheo del Río and Francisco de Leyva Bonilla. As stated earlier, Matheo del Río was an important officer in Nueva Galicia, and Francisco Leyva Bonilla, was a captain under Rodrigo del Río Loysa.

With the list of witnesses and the *Interrogatorio* completed, the oidores began to obtain the Información on the first day of September, but the process was interrupted two weeks later, resuming on 20 October when the last two witnesses appeared. The interruptions were caused by two unexpected events. One was the arrival of captain Juan de Zayas, who, as the reader may remember, was one of the captains in Nuevo Reino de León who had raised against Carvajal because of the governor's leniency towards the Indians. On this occasion, however, Zayas was a captain in the viceroy's army. His arrival in Guadalajara, his purpose, and what happened after he arrived are described in a letter from the Audiencia in Guadalajara to the king. That letter included several complaints against the viceroy. The one involving Carvajal stated that:

> While the governor was in this Audiencia asking and soliciting commissions related to your royal service and presenting some information to be sent to your Real Consejo, the Marqués de Villamanrique, having learnt that he was here, sent soldiers to arrest him. . . . And one morning, at sunrise, when the governor and his soldiers were resting in the Casas Reales, there arrived a captain with twelve soldiers with an order from the marquis, and apprehended him in his room without first notifying this Audiencia. But after taking him prisoner and seeing the commotion that had begun, the captain alerted us, and we sent an oidor to put the governor in the jail of the court until the reasons for his arrest were learnt, which he did. And if he had delayed his arrival, there might have been many deaths and disturbances in this city because the governor's soldiers

were already armed, and together with many of his friends—of which he has many because he his a prudent and well mannered man who treats others very well—were trying to release the governor by force, all of which was prevented. And because the causes *did not justify his imprisonment* (emphasis added), and to avoid the harm that would result if the governor were given to the soldiers of the marquis, this Audiencia ordered that he be freed so that he could go to his government of [Nuevo Reino de] León, as he did after he finished the businesses he had with this Audiencia.[21]

Obviously, the oidores in Guadalajara regarded the viceroy as a difficult and contentious man who was willing to resort to arms for trivial reasons. Indeed, the following year they would have even stronger arguments which, very likely, weighed heavily in the king's decision to remove Villamanrique.[22]

The second unexpected event that took place when Carvajal was in Guadalajara is also interesting. Since July of 1587, the English corsair Thomas Cavendish had been marauding the Pacific coast of New Spain, and in early September he anchored in Barra de Navidad, where he and his men caused some damages.[23] The news reached Guadalajara a few days later. Although all military matters in New Spain were the viceroy's responsibility, the oidores in Guadalajara felt they had to take some action on their own. As luck would have it, Gov. Luis de Carvajal, who reportedly had some experience with English pirates, was at hand. Therefore the oidores commissioned him to go after Cavendish:[24]

On 16 September 1587, the royal treasury in Guadalajara paid Juan de Montaña 500 pesos... to purchase provisions and other necessary things for the journey of Luis de Carvajal, governor of [Nuevo] Reino de León, who with commission of this royal Audiencia went after the Lutheran Englishmen, corsairs who were in the Mar del Sur searching and waiting for the ships from China.[25]

Carvajal left Guadalajara with his men after the 16th, for on that date day, Pedro Hernandez de Almanza, one of the witnesses, appeared before the Audiencia. In any event, Carvajal and his men arrived in Barra de Navidad seven days after Cavendish departed.[26] Thinking that the corsairs might be nearby, Carvajal spent some time looking for them along the coast north of that port. Failing to find them he returned to Guadalajara.

A few days after his return, the Audiencia resumed the gathering of Carvajal's Información. The last witness, Juan de Ochoa, appeared on October 20. It seems that the document was completed before November 14, for on that day the Audiencia granted Carvajal's request that he be given two sealed copies of it. The Información was then reviewed by the oidores, who transmitted it to the king together with their opinion of Carvajal. The transmittal letter is shown in figure 10.3 and says:

> By the Información that accompanies this, it will be certified for Y.M. of what Governor Luis de Carvajal has worked in your royal service, fulfilling the capitulaciones that with Y.M. he has made, and of the expenses and use of his hacienda and of the condition of the affairs assigned to him, and of impediments that he has experienced which have prevented him from finishing his tasks. This Audiencia can inform Y.M. that said *Luis de Carvajal is regarded as a very honest man, good Christian, judicious, and of good understanding and determination, and very much loved everywhere* (emphasis added), and that he has not ceased to work wishing to serve H.M. and to complete that which has been given to him.[27]

In spite of these very positive remarks by the Audiencia, and of the evidence presented in the *Información*, Carvajal's outlook was bleak. True, he still had a few soldiers, but because of the Indian rebellion in the north, he had lost a considerable part of his assets. Furthermore, his assets in Pánuco were not available to him because of Villamanrique's arbitrary action regarding the jurisdiction of that region. Also, the incarceration he suffered in Guadalajara at the hands of Juan de Zayas had made him aware of the real intentions of the viceroy. Furthermore he realized that the rebuke by the Guadalajara oidores would only increase the viceroy's determination of imprison him. The only hope he had was for the king to rule in his favor, although a long time would pass before his request could be answered. In the mean time, Carvajal had to find a place where he could hide from Villamanrique and yet find some activity that was profitable.

One place that seemed to meet those requirements was Almadén, the only settlement in Nuevo Reino de León that had been spared from the Indian attacks that destroyed San Luis and León. Thus, Carvajal went to that village soon after receiving the copies of the Información he had requested. His path crossed Mazapil and Saltillo, where many of his people lived at the time, including Gaspar Castaño de Sosa who, among others, joined Carvajal. It also appears that the decision had been made to make Almadén the center of Nuevo Reino de León, for in May of 1588 the treasurer Diego de Montemayor brought there the *Caja de Tres Llaves*, which until then had been in León.

Probably thinking that the viceroy might be able to find where he was and send soldiers to arrest him, the governor decided to divide his territory into three separate areas, appointing in each a lieutenant. Those appointed were Gaspar Castaño de Sosa, in the Almadén area; Diego de Montemayor,

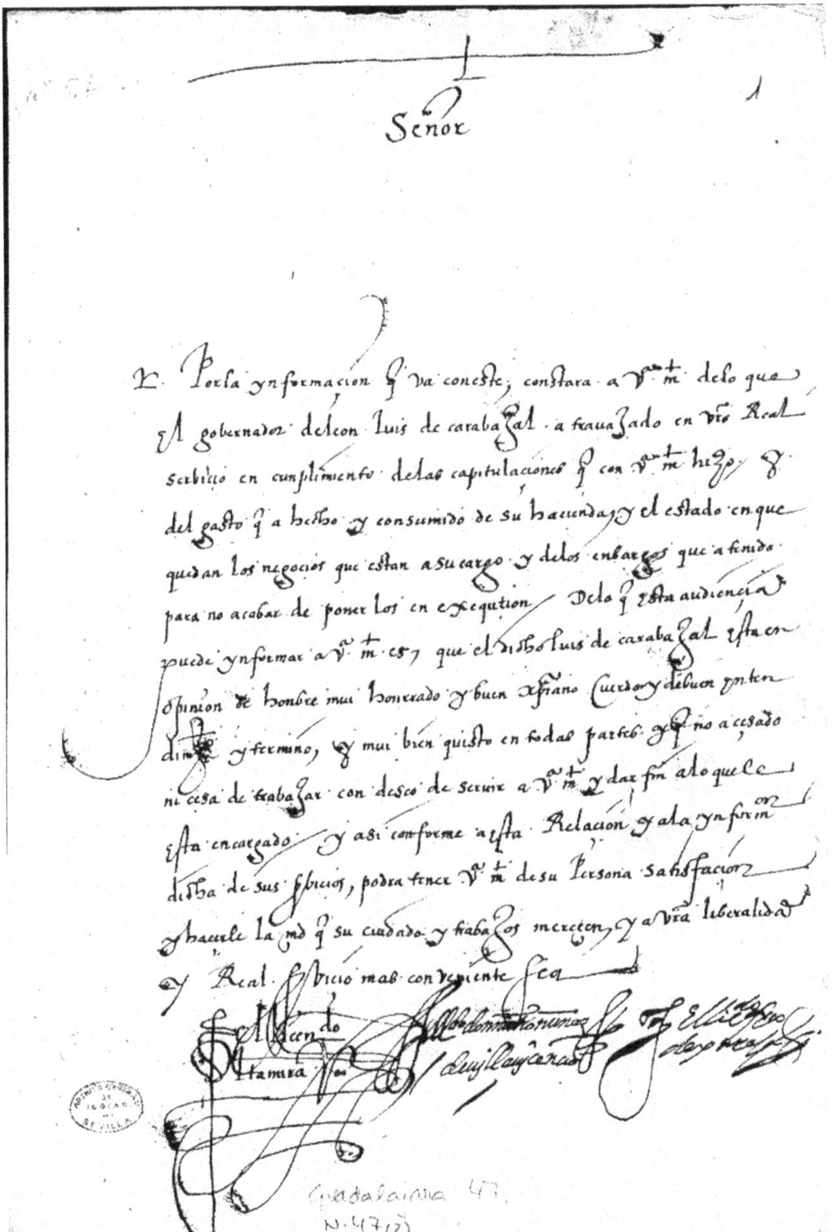

Señor

Por la ynformacion q̃ va con este, constara a V. m. de lo que
el gobernador de Leon luis de carabajal a trabajado en V. Real
serbicio en cumplimiento de las capitulaciones q̃ con V. m. hizo, y
del gasto q̃ a hecho y consumido de su hacienda, y el estado en que
quedan los negocios que estan a su cargo y de los enbargos que a tenido
para no acabar de poner los en execution. De lo q̃ esta audiencia
puede ynformar a V. m. es, que el dicho luis de carabajal esta en
opinion de hombre mui honrrado y buen cristiano (cuerdo y de buen yngen—
dio y termino, y mui bien quisto en todas partes, y q̃ no a cesado
ni cesa de trabajar con deseo de servir a V. m. y dar fin a lo que le
esta encargado, y asi conforme a esta Relacion y a la ynformacion de sus oficios, podra tener V. m. de su Persona satisfacion,
y hacerle la m. q̃ su cuidado y trabajos merecen, y a V. liberalidad
y Real servicio mas conveniente sea

[signatures]

Guadalajara 47.
N. 47 (2)

Fig. 10.3. Letter from the Audiencia de Nueva Galicia about Carvajal. (*Courtesy
Ministerio de Cultura, Archivo General de Indias.*)

in the area around San Luis and León; and Felipe Núñez, in the area around Tamaholipa.[28] A brief description of what these men did after Carvajal's death is given in the next chapter.

By early in 1588, Carvajal's plea to the king about Villamanrique's interference in Nuevo Reino de León had been communicated to the Consejo de Indias by his emissary, Gonzalo Rodríguez. The plea included certified copies of the Royal Ejecutoria and of the orders issued in the king's name by Villamanrique alone. In his petition, Rodríguez repeated some of Carvajal's complaints against Villamanrique. Apparently this was not the first time such complaints had been made for the king seems to have paid attention. Thus, at the end of Rodriguez' petition, the king wrote:

> Gather all the chapters from before and all the other documents and bring them to me to answer. And in the meantime I order that no rumors be circulated and that no documents be issued.[29]

It is not known whether the king answered Carvajal, but it is likely that this complaint alerted him to the problems that Villamanrique was causing in New Spain. Less than a year later, he received a much stronger complaint against the viceroy, this time from the Audiencia de Nueva Galicia. These complaints, as well as the rather negative opinion that Archbishop Pedro Moya de Contreras had of Villamanrique, induced the king to replace the viceroy with Luis de Velasco II. But that replacement took place too late to be of any help to Carvajal.

II

The Final Years

And ten days ago died Luis de Carvajal.

Luis de Velasco II, February 23, 1591.[1]

Although Carvajal had found a remote place in which to wait for the king's response, his movements were known to the viceroy. The long distance between Mexico City and Almadén was not going to deter him from taking Carvajal prisoner, particularly since the Audiencia de Nueva Galicia had frustrated his previous attempt. And so, in late 1588, he sent another captain with soldiers to arrest Carvajal and to take him to México City. This chapter considers these actions as well as the event that decisively ended his quest for justice: his trial by the Inquisition.

1. PRISONER OF THE VICEROY

In his 1649 history of Nuevo Reino de León, Alonso de León wrote the following account of Carvajal's arrest:

[Ordered by the viceroy], a judge left [México City] with soldiers to apprehend him. He first went to Tampico, and following the trail arrived in León, from where the lieutenant Diego de Montemayor, seeing the viceroy's commission, went with them to Saltillo, and from there, guiding Captain Morlete, went to Almadén, where [Carvajal] . . . let himself be taken prisoner, naming captain Gaspar Castaño as his lieutenant in the province.[2]

Although incorrect in certain details, this account is important because it states that one of Carvajal's lieutenants guided the viceroy's soldiers to Almadén. The statement has been interpreted by some authors to mean that Montemayor betrayed Carvajal.[3] Indeed, the contemporary evidence indicates that Carvajal was betrayed, but not by Montemayor. Before the main suspect is named, it is useful to review all available evidence. So far as the capture of Carvajal is concerned, the best sources is Villamanrique himself. In his instructions to his successor, written in 1590 he repeated his accusations against Carvajal, adding that:

I ordered Captain Alonso López to go with 20 soldiers to apprehend him and to visit that land and report to me about the settlements that had been made. . . . And he went everywhere, from Tamaholipa until Mazapil, where his government is, and found none. . . . And with this Alonso López followed him and found him 50 leagues from Mazapil, in a province called Caula (sic for Coahuila), where he had founded four houses made of sticks, naming it Almadén.[4]

Thus, the name of the captain sent by Villamanrique to capture Carvajal was Alonso López, not Juan Morlete as implied by León's narrative. That information was confirmed years later by several members of Carvajal's group who had gone to Nuevo México with Gaspar Castaño de Sosa.[5] One of them stated that "And this witness saw that Captain Alonso López went to the village of Almadén by order of the Marqués de Villamanrique and apprehended Governor Luis de Carvajal . . . and this witness does not know the reason."[6]

It also appears that López first went to Tampico, but it is doubtful that from there he went to Mazapil, as Villamanrique stated, because that path would have required him to cross the high sierras. More likely, from Tampico López went to Tamaholipa, which was still part of Nuevo Reino de León. There he probably met Felipe Núñez, Carvajal's lieutenant in that area. It is also likely that after seeing López's orders Núñez told him where Carvajal was and agreed to show him the way, but to avoid the areas controlled by the Chichimeca they went to Saltillo, where Diego de Montemayor joined them. The remaining events seem clear. Villamanrique's captain arrived in Almadén, where he found Carvajal and arrested him, as León stated.

This is where León's narrative seems to fail, for according to him Carvajal offered no resistance, which is unlikely. Carvajal knew what would happen to him if he were taken prisoner. Furthermore, it will be recalled that when Juan de Zayas arrested Carvajal in Guadalajara, the governor's soldiers wanted to free him by force. How, then, could it be that no resistance was offered in Almadén? Although the available evidence does not provide an unequivocal answer, it is likely that López arrived in Almadén accompanied by one or more persons that Carvajal trusted, making him drop his guard. Alonso de León mentioned that Diego de Montemayor was among those who went with the viceroy's captain to arrest Carvajal. If so, his presence and that of Felipe Núñez in López's party would be sufficient to convince Carvajal that there was nothing to fear from the incoming group.

And so it was that Carvajal was taken prisoner and brought to México City, where he was put in the Crown jail, probably in early 1589.[7] Given that the viceroy had ordered the arrest, no formal charges were needed, although in the instructions he wrote the following year for the next viceroy he accused Carvajal of two crimes. One was that Carvajal had sent one of his captains to take over Valles. Indeed, as discussed in the previous chapter, Carvajal had attempted to take over that village, but that occurred five years earlier, after the Audiencia decided that Valles and other towns in the province of Pánuco belonged to him. The second accusation was that Carvajal mistreated the Indians. Although never substantiated, this accusation was repeated so often that it become accepted as the truth. It is therefore important to consider it in some detail.

2. Villamanrique's main accusation

In a letter to the king dated November of 1586, Villamanrique stated that:

> One of the things that forced me to give said order . . . was the excess that in this Luis de Carvajal de la Cueva had made and was making. . . . [He] would send [soldiers] to Río de Palmas and to Río Bravo to hunt and take barbarous Indians who had never seen Spaniards or made harm to them. And he would make reports of the [supposed] resistance or other damages, and would condemn them as slaves, sending them to be sold to this city and other towns.[8]

This was the main accusation against Carvajal. Both Villamanrique and his successor repeated it, again and again, but no credible evidence was ever presented. The reason, in short, is that there was none.

First of all, the statement about the Indians who supposedly were taken by orders of Carvajal and, also supposedly, had never seen a Spaniard or had done any harm against them, is strongly contradicted by many contemporary documents that show that the Indians living in the areas mentioned by Villamanrique were well acquainted with the Spaniards and had for many years harmed them.[9] In fact, Carvajal had punished some of those Indians because of this, but that had occurred in 1573, when Viceroy Enríquez ordered him to do so.

As for Carvajal's abuse of the Indians, many other documents show that this accusation was also false. That charge was made nearly 20 years after Carvajal arrived in New Spain. During that long period he had performed many tasks related to the pacifications of Indian rebellions and to the Crown's efforts to expand the frontier. Not once *before* Villamanrique's arrival in New Spain had Carvajal been accused of wrong doing against the Indians. Quite the contrary, all reliable records show him to be concerned with their well being. This is why viceroy Enríquez trusted him with many delicate tasks that related to the

Indians. And this is why, he, Enríquez, advised the Conde de Coruña that he should use Carvajal to pacify the Indians.[10]

As governor, Carvajal continued his good treatment of the Indians and was more able to prevent soldiers and others from abusing them. This is shown by the many times he released Indians that had been taken prisoner on the basis of hearsay or because of insignificant reasons. He did this with Indians made captive by both his soldiers and those from other jurisdictions. These incidents were confirmed by either the culprits, as was the case of Francisco Leyva Bonilla, or by officers of other jurisdictions, such as Matheo del Río, the inspector of the presidios and soldiers for Nueva Galicia. This external verification added considerable support to the testimonies of many others who described Carvajal's good treatment of the Indians.

Incidentally, after describing how Carvajal had released the Indians that had been taken by captains Francisco de Leyva Bonilla and Cristóbal Caldera Matheo del Río added that:

> He saw that Captain Gaspar Castaño de Sosa who . . . was complaining against said governor . . . because the governor had freed some Indians he had taken prisoner. . . . And this witness, as a visitador in Galicia, has seen many titles of Indians that captains of said governor had taken, in which titles are the commissions of the governor, which are very limited and justified.[11]

The evidence presented in this book, consisting of records that span more than twenty years, is overwhelming proof that Carvajal was one among a very small group of Spaniards who treated the Indians well. Of course, he was a man of his times, and as such there is no doubt that he profited from the sale of the service of Indians. However, if he did, it was sparingly and only when their offenses warranted it. Time and again he released Indians that others had taken prisoner. He also forgave many Indians who had rebelled, and, on many occasions, fed and clothed Indians who crossed his path. Because of that, he was loved and respected by them, as he stated in his self-defense, and as the following incident shows.

Fifty three years after Carvajal's death, Martín de Zavala, then governor of Nuevo Reino de León, went to Almadén to try to prove that the area was in his jurisdiction. To support his case, he obtained an Información that included the testimonies of several Indians who had lived there for a long time.[12] Among them there were two who were in their twenties when Carvajal was in Almadén. The first to give testimony was named D. Diego who said that:

> They always saw, a long time ago, that *Tatuane* (meaning Benefactor father.[13]) Carvajal was in this village with many Spaniards . . . and that he had known

Carvajal and Castaño, and that Carvajal always treated them as a Tatuane. And that when said Tatuane Carvajal left Almadén, he left Castaño, and after a while he saw Castaño leave with many wagons, towards the place where the sun sets, and that he had crossed the big water.[14]

The second Indian, named D. Justo, stated that:

> He was not scared when the Spaniards came because he, being old, remembers that a long time ago there was in this village one Tatuane named Carvajal . . . who came from San Luis, and they (the Spaniards) extracted silver from the mines and cultivated corn, and this witness helped them. . . . And even if some Indians believed that those [Spaniards] who came now would punish them, he and D. Diego and other old men told them not to be afraid because *those who came from San Luis had never done them any harm* (emphasis added).[15]

These statements by old Indians from Almadén who had personally known Carvajal are clear evidence of his good treatment of them. Taken together with the evidence presented above and in the previous chapters, it does away with Villamanrique's accusations.

Incidentally, one of the charges leveled against Villamanrique by Bishop Diego Romano had to do with his unfair treatment of Carvajal. Villamanrique defense to the charges includes a lengthy chapter, numbered 29, in which he repeated the accusations against Carvajal that he had mentioned in his letter to his successor in 1590.[16] In his report to the king Romano commented on Villamanrique's defense, saying in part:

> I [Iow] little substance is contained in chapter 29 of the marquis' [defense], which is only a report of an imprisonment he made of Luis de Carvajal and the pleito that the fiscal had against the exercise of his office. . . . And he relates this as being a notable service, although it was not, because to punish the excesses, *if there were any* (emphasis added), it was not the business of the marquis but of the Alcalde del Crimen, which dealt with the case. And since *no serious offense was found* (emphasis added), he was given a light sentence. And he died begging satisfaction of many aggravations.[17]

This makes it clear that Bishop Romano doubted Villamanrique's accusations and that, in any case, the charges were insignificant.

The reader may have wondered why Pedro de Vega, who had represented Carvajal before, did not defend him from Villamanrique. The simple and ironic answer is that he had been engaged by Villamanrique to defend him from Romano's charges.[18] Whether this means that Pedro de Vega betrayed Carvajal is not known, but that possibility cannot be disregarded.

3. Before the Inquisition

The final and decisive action against Carvajal occurred in early 1589, after he had been incarcerated in the jail of the Crown. Although according to Bishop Romano the sentence that Carvajal had received for his supposed crime was minor, he was kept in jail. That was why Romano charged Villamanrique with mistreating the governor. In any event, the lack of evidence supporting any serious accusation against Carvajal was not going to deter his enemies from attempting to destroy him. The final tool used to achieve their goals was the iron hand of the Inquisition.[19] For the reasons described below, the Inquisition was brought on board, though not in an obvious or direct manner. On 14 April 1589, a few months after Carvajal was put in the Crown's jail, the inquisitors asked the viceroy to release Carvajal into their custody, a request that was granted the same day. The transfer to he secret jails of the Inquisition also took place the same day. Both of these events were remarkable, given the normally strained relations between the inquisitors and the viceroys. In any event, that transfer was to become the event that allowed his enemies to have the final say.

Much has been written about the Inquisition trials of Carvajal and of several members of his family. The concern here is with the governor, but given the exposure that his trial has had, there is no need to describe it in detail. There remain, however, certain questions that deserve closer examination, including perhaps the most important among them: Why was he brought before the Inquisition? To answer this, it is necessary to review the origins of his trial.

Religious accusations

The inquisitorial records show that on 7 March of 1589 Felipe Núñez, then 28 years old, appeared before the inquisitors and stated that a niece of Gov. Carvajal had told him certain things against Catholic doctrine.[20] That statement was sufficient to have her arrested by the Inquisition. A few days later, she told the inquisitors that she was a good Catholic and that she had not said anything against the Church. However, after being tortured, the thirty year-old widow declared that she and her parents were Jewish and that she had promised his uncle's wife that she would tell both him and Felipe Núñez that they should obey the law of Moses.[21] She also confirmed what Felipe Núñez had said, adding that she had told the same anti-Christian statements to her uncle, the governor of Nuevo Reino de León. The consequences of this were unavoidable. On April 13 the Inquisition's fiscal stated that:

> From the confessions of Doña Isabel Rodríguez de Carvajal, his niece . . . it is verified and appears that said Governor Luis de Carvajal is guilty . . . [for] not

having denounced her, as he was obligated. . . . And he must be brought to one of the jails of the Inquisition, to be punished and so that he declares what he knows about her niece.[22]

These remarks seem to indicate that the reasons for taking Carvajal to the Inquisition were strictly religious; that is, that the governor knew that his niece was a heretic and had not denounced her, as required. So far as the Inquisition was concerned this was a crime. But, in addition, Isabel had told the inquisitors that her mother—Carvajal's sister—was Jewish, and so was Carvajal's wife. That made the inquisitors suspect that Carvajal himself was also a heretic. This seems to show that Carvajal was brought before the inquisition because of religious matters. However, other evidence shows that the reasons were political.

Political maneuvering

The clearest evidence for a political motivation is provided by the appearance of Felipe Núñez before the inquisitors. Apparently, he had been in Mexico City for some time, having come with the party that arrested Carvajal. After stating his name and giving other personal information, Núñez told the inquisitors that:

He came to discharge his conscience and to say that the Christmas before last, two or more years earlier, a widow whose name or that of her husband he cannot remember, but that she is the niece of said Governor Luis de Carvajal, and daughter of Doña Francisca de Carvajal, sister of said governor . . . told him . . . 'in what law does thou live.' And he said, in Christ's . . . to which she responded 'that is not a good law.'[23]

This short paragraph raises many questions. The first relates to Núñez' long delay in clearing his conscience. He could have done so earlier for he had been in Mexico City many times since that conversation but had felt no need to do it until now. It is clear that another reason existed on this occasion. In the next sentence Núñez said that he did not remember the name of Carvajal's niece. There is no doubt that this claimed forgetfulness was a lie. By his own account, he had met Isabel ten years earlier, when he accompanied Carvajal in his recruitment journey through Spain and Portugal. He remembered that she then lived in Astorga and was married to a merchant. And he was able to recall, with great accuracy, the names of every member of Carvajal's family, that is, his sister and her husband, nephews and nieces, and even the names of Isabel's two brothers in law, as well as their domiciles and occupation. Also, in addition to having met the Carvajal family in Spain, he had traveled with them to

New Spain, and had stayed in their houses in Tampico and Pánuco on several occasions since arriving in New Spain. No, Felipe Núñez knew Isabel's name very well and had not forgotten it as he claimed. Why, then, did he claim he did not remember it? The reason was simply to bring up the governor's name before the inquisitors and make them aware that he, the governor, was a close relative of a heretic. Making that association known to them was a sure way of getting the Inquisition to participate in the downfall of Carvajal.

Involving the Inquisition

The action by Felipe Núñez was not motivated by a guilty conscience, as the inquisitorial narrative implies. Rather, it was the result of a plan, conceived by the enemies of Carvajal, that would insure his elimination while allowing them to remain in the background. It has already been established that the viceroy and some of his close aids wanted to eliminate Carvajal. And while it is true that Carvajal was in jail and could not do anything to defend himself, it is also true that he could not be kept there unless the Audiencia would rule against him on the basis of some demonstrable charge. But the viceroy had none to offer. Therefore, a different means had to be found.

This is where the idea to involve the Inquisition was born. The reader may recall that in 1580, when Carvajal went to the Mexico City to present his credentials to the viceroy, the Audiencia had expressed some suspicions about his not being an Old Christian. Those suspicions did not go away as time passed since some officers in the Audiencia were resentful because of the territories they had lost to Carvajal. And after the arrival of Eugenio de Salazar in Mexico City, the suspicions must have been reinforced because of his considerable experience with individuals who, like Carvajal, originated in La Raya de Portugal. Salazar must have realized that Carvajal was a Portuguese New Christian, and probably suspected him of being a Jew. After all, well before 1580, it was known that many like him shad came to the New World to escape the Portuguese Inquisition.

Salazar also knew that Carvajal would be completely defeated if he were sentenced by the Inquisition of any charge. However, the viceroy could not openly ask the inquisitors to look into the governor's background. That would reveal the political goals of the viceroy and required a much better collaboration between him and the inquisitors than existed at the time. On the other hand, the suspicions about Carvajal, and by inference about his family, were real. Therefore all that was needed was to find somebody close to him or to his family, who might know some incriminating fact that could brought to the attention of the Inquisition.

Finding a suitable candidate was not difficult. Although there were several individuals that could help serve that purpose, one of Villamanrique's men had been a captain under Carvajal and probably could offer some useful information. This was Juan de Zayas, who has twice appeared in this narrative, first as the captain who had raised against the governor because of his lenient treatment of Indians, and, second, as the captain who, on orders of the viceroy, had gone to Guadalajara to take Carvajal prisoner. Although Zayas was not sufficiently close to Carvajal to know family secrets, he knew some who were, namely El Mozo and Felipe Núñez, both of whom were relatives of Carvajal. However, the whereabouts of El Mozo were not known. On the other hand, Núñez was in Mexico City, having gone there with the party that took the governor prisoner. And Núñez knew considerably more than was needed to incriminate Carvajal's family. All that remained was to convince him to collaborate with the viceroy. Although a bribe may have been offered, it is likely that a threat to punish him may have been used instead. After all Núñez was one of Carvajal's lieutenants and could also be accused of the same wrongdoings as Carvajal. And so it is not surprising to see that on that day in March of 1589, Núñez appeared before the inquisitors to denounce the oldest niece of Carvajal, whose name he did not know, although, he said: "In his life he had not met anybody else whom he loved more."

4. CARVAJAL'S TRIAL

Carvajal's trial proceeded in the usual manner. Three days after being transferred to the secret jails of the Inquisition he appeared before the inquisitors, gave his name and birth place, listed his genealogy, and declared that he was an Old Christian from an hidalgo family. He also gave a brief account of his life. When asked if he knew why was he was arrested, he said he did not know, but later told them what his niece had said to him some years earlier. His excuse for not having previously informed the Inquisition about that incident was that at that time he had been occupied in a pacification in Nuevo Reino de León, and that afterwards he had forgotten it. Having found that Carvajal had not fulfilled the obligation of denouncing her, the inquisitors proceeded to try to find something else that might further incriminate him. In particular, they did their best to try to establish that Carvajal, like all other members of his family, was a heretic. But Carvajal insisted time and again that he was a sincere Catholic.

However, Licentiate Lobo Guerrero, the Inquisition's fiscal, was not convinced. On July 24, three months after the trial started, he presented his case

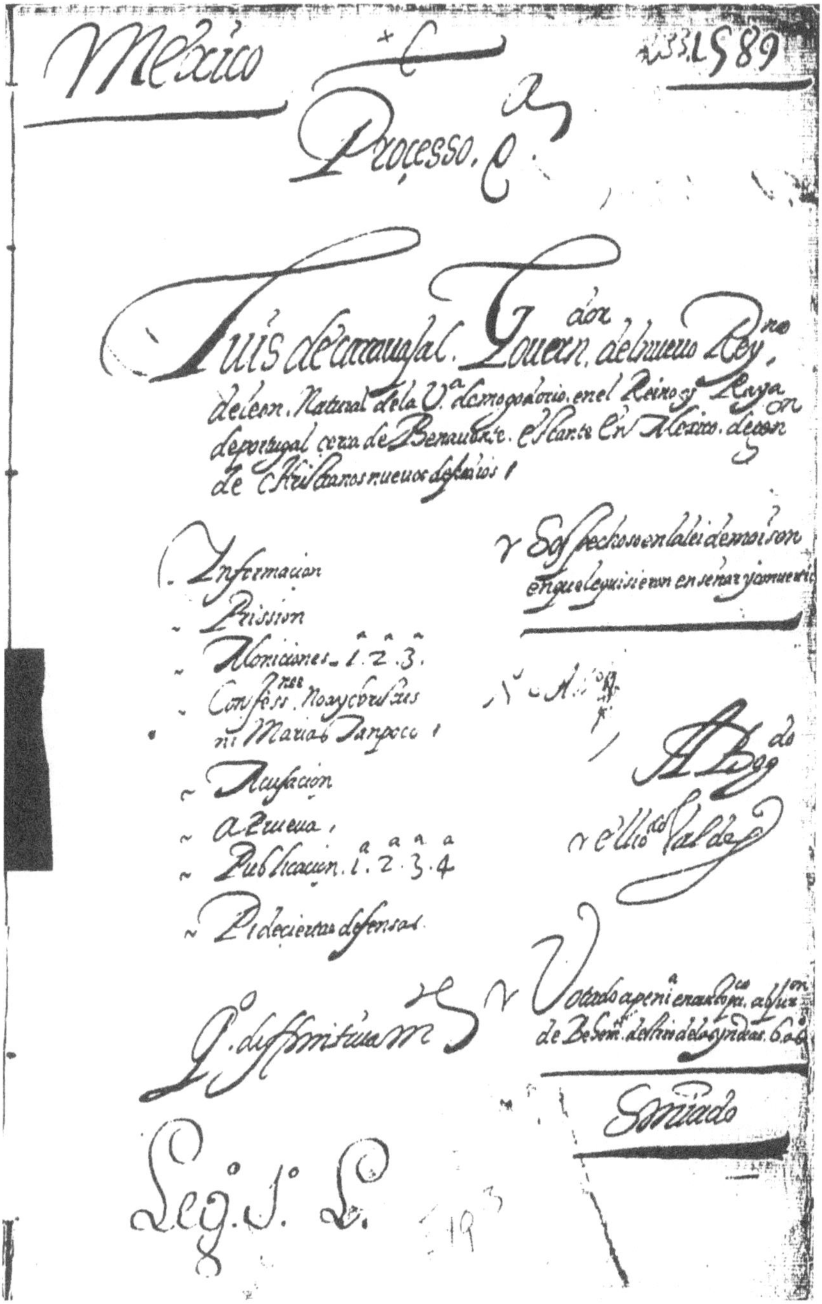

Fig. 11.1. Cover page of the Inquisition trial against Carvajal. (*Courtesy of the Archivo General de la Nación, Mexico City.*)

to the inquisitors and made his first accusations, asking that Carvajal be given
a strict sentence

> for being an agent and concealer of Jews, apostates of our Holy Faith, and of
> dogmatic teachers of said law of Moses, accomplice and guilty with them of
> said crimes and having incurred in sentence of major excommunication. . . .
> And as such they should condemn him in the most grave penalties. . . . And in
> case that the inquisitors did not think his intentions are well proved . . . let him
> be tortured . . . until he confesses the whole truth.[24]

Probably because of Carvajal's high position the inquisitors did not go along
with Lobo Guerrero's proposal to torture him, but his other recommendations was accepted.

For his part, Carvajal attempted to rebut each of the charges made against
him, insisting time and again that he and his ancestors were Old Christians.
Later, he asked that he be given paper in which he could write some notes that
might be helpful to his defense lawyer. The first part of this material contains
a self-defense against those charges, which makes sense, given that they were
of a religious nature. But the second part is a narrative of some of the services
he had performed on behalf of the Crown and had nothing to do with the
charges. The reasons for including that information in his self-defense are unclear. Surely, he and his lawyer must have known that those services would not
help his cause in the Inquisition, no matter how great they might have been.
Of course, it could be that Carvajal wanted the king or his representatives
know about his deeds, but the Información de Oficio prepared in Guadalajara
already listed his services since 1580, and previous services were known in the
Consejo de Indias. A possible explanation is that the self-defense was written
in October of 1589, shortly after the arrival in New Spain of the new viceroy,
Luis de Velasco II.[25] This fact must have been known to Carvajal. It is therefore
possible that the narrative of his accomplishments was written with the new
viceroy in mind.

On November 8 of 1589, after the fiscal concluded his case against the
governor, inquisitors Bonilla and García agreed that Carvajal be declared
guilty of having committed major sins against the church, and that he should
be exiled from the Spanish New World for a period of six years. On the other
hand, the consultants, doctors Pedro de Farfán and Saavedra Valderrama, both
oidores of the Audiencia, and Santiago del Riego, alcalde of the Audiencia,
were in agreement that Carvajal should abjure in the degree of *Levi*, and
that he be exiled for only four years. A second vote was taken on Tuesday 13
February with the identical result. Obviously, the inquisitors' views carried

the day, for the final sentence was exactly what they had initially proposed. That sentence reads:

> We declare that said Luis de Carvajal has fallen and incurred in sentence of major excommunication for being an agent and concealer [of heretics] . . . and that if we had followed him more closely, we could condemn him for greater and more severe punishments. But wishing to show mercy . . . we condemn him that today . . . he comes out [of his jail] to hear the sentence in the habit of a penitent, with a wax candle in his hands. . . . We order him to abjure publicly, in degree of *Vehemente*, the mistakes that by the trial have been verified, of which he remains gravely suspect of other types of heresy. And after said repentance, we absolve him of said excommunication, and condemn him to exile from the Indies of H.M. for precisely six years, which he should begin in the first fleet going to Castile, or in other occasion that we might order, all of which he should keep and obey. . . . And in this manner we pronounce and order these writings. Licentiate Bonilla. Licentiate Santos García.

Thus, the inquisitors believed that Carvajal was guilty of "more serious charges" and remained suspicious of his being a heretic.

The public-repentance ordered by the Inquisition was carried out in an *Auto-da-fe* held in Mexico City's cathedral. On that occasion the governor and nineteen other penitents—two of them in effigy, were read their sentences. In the opinion of inquisitor Santos Garcia the ceremony was a great success. Writing to his superior in Spain the following May he stated that:

> In the summary that accompanies this letter, Your Lordship will see the cases that on Saturday, 24 February, day of S. Mathias of this year, were dealt with in a public auto inside the Iglesia Mayor of this city, to which so many people assisted that we would have been happy to have held it outside, in the plaza, because the quality of the transgressions deserved it.[26]

To accommodate the dignitaries participating in the ceremony, a stand was built on the cathedral's altar. Sitting high on that stand, on a velvet chair, was the viceroy. Others sat on plain chairs placed in an order that depended on their status. Among those dignitaries were the inquisitors, the fiscal of the Inquisition, the oidores and fiscal of the Audiencia, the alcaldes of the court, as well as some invited guests. The penitents stood in front of the platform, waiting for their sentences to be read, an act that concluded the ceremony. Those sentenced to be burnt at the stake would be *relaxados*, that is, released to the secular arm of the Crown to be taken to *El Quemadero*, or burning place, where they would later be burnt. On this occasion, there were two individuals who received that sentence, but one had died years before and the other was absent, which meant that they were burnt in effigy.

Immediately after the sentences were read, Carvajal, appeared with a candle in his hands and abjured his transgressions and errors. Probably reading from a previously written document, he made a long statement, the first words of which are as follows:

> I, Luis de Carvajal, born in the village of Mogadouro, in the Raya y Reino of Portugal, near Benavente, descendent of Jewish New Christians, governor of Nuevo Reino de León, *which at present I am* (emphasis added), of my own free will abjure and renounce any heresy, in particular this one about which I have been informed.[27]

Among the guests who heard this were D. Diego de Ibarra, the brother-in-law of the viceroy and brother of the governor of Nueva Vizcaya, and Rodrigo del Río Loysa, the lieutenant of the viceroy's army in Nueva Galicia, whose name has appeared several times in this work. Although both had reasons to be pleased by the events, more so must have been Eugenio de Salazar, recently installed as an oidor of the Audiencia.[28]

The following Monday, the inquisitors stated that since Carvajal had been brought from the jail of the Crown by order of the Marqués de Villamanrique, that he should be sent back to that jail. However, at that time the viceroy was no longer Villamanrique but Luis Velasco II. The new viceroy had learned about Carvajal's Inquisition trial from Villamanrique's instructions which stated that "Having him prisoner in Mexico City, to conclude his cause . . . the Inquisition asked me to give him to them saying that he had committed heresy. And because of the Cédula of the Concordia, I agreed." However, probably before reading Villamanrique's instructions, Velasco had learned about the sentence from oidor Farfán, who was one of those who voted to sentence Carvajal. That sentence meant that Velasco would not raise a finger to help Carvajal, even if he had any intentions of doing so prior to his arrival in New Spain. In fact, Velasco's fiscal, Luis de Villanueva Zapata, was approached by the inquisitors who told him that Carvajal should not be put in jail and that he should be allowed to leave New Spain because it did not seem fair to grieve him more. However, Villanueva Zapata felt, probably after consulting with Eugenio de

Fig. 11.2. Viceroy Luis de Velasco II

Salazar, that it was better to leave things as they were.[29] Thus, Carvajal was thrown back in his cell where he would remain until his death on 13 February of 1591, not yet fifty five years old.[30]

5. CARVAJAL'S SISTER AND HER FAMILY

The political persecution of Gov. Luis de Carvajal had, as is well known, serious consequences for his sister, her sons and daughters and some other members of his family. On 24 February of 1590, in the same Auto-da-Fe where Carvajal abjured his sins, there were sentenced his first cousin, Catalina de León, age 29; his sister Francisca Núñez de Carvajal, her husband, Francisco Rodriguez de Matos, their daughters Isabel Rodriguez de Andrade, age 30; Catalina de León, age 24; Mariana Núñez, age 17; and Leonor de Andrade, age 16; their sons Luis de Carvajal (El Mozo), age 22; and Baltazar Rodriguez. Also sentenced was their oldest son, Fray Gaspar de Carvajal, age 33, who did not appear in the ceremony and received only minor admonitions. Francisca's husband, Francisco Rodriguez de Matos, who had died before that date, and son Baltazar, who had left New Spain, were burnt in effigy.[31] All others were sentenced to wear penitent's habits and to be jailed in perpetuity. However, because the Inquisition lacked suitable jail cells in which to put them, they were sent to other places to serve their sentence. For example, Doña Francisca and her daughters were placed in a house adjacent to a church. In any event, none of them served their sentence in full. Three years later their sentences were commuted on the recommendation of the Bishop of Guadalajara, because of their good Christian behavior.

That good behavior did not last. In 1595, the Inquisition apprehended Doña Francisca, her daughters Isabel, Catalina, and Leonor, and her son Luis, and subjected them to new trials which showed they had reverted to

doña isabel

Fig. 11.3. Signature of Carvajal's niece Isabel in her second trial.[32] (*Courtesy of the Bancroft Library, University of California, Berkeely.*)

Judaism, an action that meant death. The sentences were read at the *Auto-da-fe* celebrated on Sunday December 8, day of Advent, of 1596. Francisca de Carvajal, daughters Isabel, Catalina and Leonor, and son Luis were sentenced to be burnt alive, but were told that if they repented sincerely they would be garroted before, an offer that was accepted.

Absent in the *Auto-da-fe* of 1596 were Francisca's daughters Mariana and Ana. However, they both appeared in the Auto-da-Fe celebrated in 1601. Mariana was sentenced to be burned at the stake, and Ana, or Anica as she appears in the Inquisition records, was sentenced to two years in jail but in 1649, she was also burnt at the stake. Ana was the last surviving relative of Carvajal who came from Spain with him and carried his surname. In essence, the family was exterminated by the Inquisition, but the force behind that action was Villamanrique. Of course, other relatives of the governor remained in New Spain, although their surnames were not Carvajal, but León, Márquez, Núñez, López, Pimentel, Rodríguez, Herrera, and others, some of which were adopted to avoid persecution.

12

The Man and his Legacy

It is not convenient that somebody should go there who had been named by Luis de Carvajal; only the viceroy can name who should be the governor.

Philip II, 1591.[1]

The narrative in the preceding chapters has followed the life of Luis de Carvajal, from birth to death, by means of official and legal documents that were written in his days. Although these documents give a fair description of his accomplishments, failures, and defeats, they do not say much about him as a person. Nevertheless, the same documentation does offers a glimpse of some of his personal traits. This is presented in this chapter together with a brief discussion of what his followers did during the immediate years after his arrest in Almadén.

1. Carvajal, the Man

Luis de Carvajal was born in Portugal, into crypto-Jewish families that had their roots in Spain. His paternal family was not wealthy, nor highly educated, as indicated by the professions of his brothers; one was a soldier, the other a monk. On the other hand, several members of the maternal side of the family seem to have had some wealth. Thus, Antonio de León, Carvajal's maternal grandfather, was one of the most successful merchants in Mogadouro; his son Duarte was a wealthy businessman in Lisbon and a Crown contractor in Guinea and Cape Verde. Also, it would appear that Antonio's sons received a good education, particularly Francisco, who was educated in Salamanca and become the senior military leader in Guinea.

Although his ancestors practiced Judaism, Carvajal was raised as a Christian and must have been confirmed as such at the age of seven. His first language was obviously Portuguese, in which he learned to read and write. His birthplace was in Tras-os-Montes, also the birth place of Magellan. Nearby was Belmonte, the birthplace of Pedro Álvarez de Cabral, the discoverer of Brazil. It is likely that young Carvajal's imagination was influenced by their stories, for throughout his mature life he showed a desire to discover new places.

Although Portuguese by birth, Carvajal's character was molded in Spain. From the ages of eight to fourteen, he lived in Benavente, in the castle of the Conde de Benavente, one of Spanish Grandees and a friend of both Charles V and Philip II.[2] There, he received the same basic education as the son and daughters of the count, and as the sons of other noblemen who also served the count as pages. Thus, not only did Carvajal learn the speech and manners of a Spanish nobleman, but also received a strong Christian upbringing.

Of course, the very fact that a royal capitulación was awarded to him is clear evidence of that demeanor. It is nevertheless useful to quote the comments made by some highly respected individuals who knew him personally. For example, Dr. Luis de Villanueva, an oidor of the Audiencia de Mexico, said that he has "known Captain Luis de Carvajal for about twelve years and he regards him to be a nobleman, an hidalgo, because he shows it in his behavior and treatment of his person."[3] Another highly respected individual was D. Francisco de Puga, the viceroy's lieutenant in the northern frontier of New Spain, who stated that he regarded "Captain Luis de Carvajal as a nobleman and well-born and that he is a man of courage and strength."[4] In addition, we have the opinions expressed by the Audiencias in Mexico City and in Guadalajara. In the eyes of the latter, Carvajal was "regarded as a very honest man, good Christian, judicious, and of good understanding and determination, and very much loved everywhere." Many similar opinions can be added to these, including those of Viceroy Enríquez, Archbishop Moya de Contreras, and Father Pedro de San Luis.

The personal traits attributed to Carvajal by these individuals were based on their personal knowledge of him as well of his actions and accomplishments. Unlike Nueva Vizcaya's first governor, Francisco de Ibarra, who was an in-law of the viceroy who appointed him, Carvajal received his appointment from the king even though he had no close connections to the Crown. This does not minimize the achievements of Ibarra in any way. Rather, the difference emphasizes the caliber of Carvajal's accomplishments. These were the result of his hard work in the interest of the Crown as an administrator, pacifier of rebellions, discoverer, conqueror and settler of vast regions that were under the control of the Chichimeca. These and other endeavors were instrumental in his obtaining a type of royal award that was coveted by many, but rarely granted. True, it took him ten long years to obtain it, but it should be remembered that when he arrived in New Spain in 1567, he was not even a minor officer of the Spanish Crown.

The contemporary record also indicates that Carvajal was a cut above many other Europeans who lived in New Spain during the same period. Although he had not received a university education, he had many skills, including accounting, trading, navigation, building, urban planning—though not in the modern sense—and administration. He also was a tenacious and brave military leader of men who personally confronted dangerous situations on various occasions, whether as admiral of a merchant fleet, alcalde in Tampico, corregidor in Tamaholipa and in Guejutla, captain of soldiers in New Spain, or as the Governor of Nuevo Reino de León. However, he was not a man eager to use force to resolve differences when other means were available, as shown by the quarrels in Tampico with Diego Ramírez in 1568, with Gonzalo Jorge (or Gaspar Jorge, as the Ejecutoria states) in 1580; with Juan de Villaseñor and with Francisco Guerrero between 1583 and 1585; and, most importantly, by the way he pacified many Indian uprisings. In this regard, Carvajal was one of a few Spaniards who regarded the Indians as human beings. His treatment of them shows that he was a compassionate man who often came to their defense from the abuses of the soldiers, captains, and encomenderos. It was this treatment that earned him the love of the Indians and the respect and trust of Viceroy Enríquez and of other clerical and secular leaders.

Carvajal's actions also show that he was a proud man who would not accept anything from those he felt had betrayed him, such as El Mozo and his siblings who had brought him food while he was in jail. However, he was a trusting man who was betrayed by some of those he trusted, and a naïve man who thought that his royal appointment would shield him from the persecutions of an egomaniacal viceroy.

Of course, Carvajal was not without shortcomings. Perhaps most visible was his inability to compromise when settling differences with others, as shown by his jurisdictional fights, where he displayed a fair amount of intransigence. For example, relative to the size of his territory, the contested areas in the province of Pánuco represented a miniscule part, and yet, he would not give them up. Also, at least to modern eyes, it would appear he was an authoritarian ruler in the sense that he sometimes disregarded the economic needs of his soldiers. This made him unpopular with some of them, although the reason for his disregard was his unwillingness to let them take innocent Indians for the purpose of selling their service.

Carvajal also seems to have failed to understand that loyalty, honesty, reason, and good treatment of the Indians were not the means by which power and wealth were acquired in sixteenth century New Spain. That was a world in which some people seemed eager to bring down those who had achieved success through personal effort. True, he was not the only one to be affected by these practices, but his fall illustrates better than most the methods used at the time to bring down men of his caliber.

Before leaving this section, it is pertinent to repeat that Carvajal, the man, was held in high esteem by his contemporaries. Perhaps the best expression of this was the support that Viceroy Enríquez gave to Carvajal, without which he would not have received a capitulación from Philip II. That view was strongly backed by many other important individuals whose opinions of Carvajal appear in many sixteenth century documents including the *Méritos de Carvajal*, the *Ejecutoria*, and the letters written by the Real Consejo de Indias and by other authorities in New Spain.

Religion

Consider now Carvajal's religion. In his Inquisition trial he claimed he was a sincere Christian. However, as his sentence shows, the inquisitors suspected he was a Jew. Modern historians have been divided about this issue. Those who believe he was a good Christian base their views on what his niece, Isabel Rodríguez, and her brother, El Mozo, stated before the Inquisition. Others simply assume that, since some of his relatives practiced Judaism, he did also. Fortunately, there exist contemporary records that are more reliable than those of the Inquisition. Those records show that Carvajal was a sincere Christian, and that he was also very sincere in his desire to convert the Indians to Christianity.

Although several anecdotal stories exist that add weight to his being a good Christian, one, cited below, shows both his sincerity and his special interest in the conversion of the Indians. This story stems from an eye-witness account of something that Carvajal did in 1576, many years before he was brought before the Inquisition, that is, when he had no need to prove anything regarding his religious beliefs. At that time he had been asked by Viceroy Enríquez to suppress an Indian rebellion in Xalpa. After accomplishing that task, he built a fort there in order to provide some protection from future Chichimeca attacks. The fort had a monastery and a chapel where, as an eye witness stated:

> To insure that the Indians be properly indoctrinated in the Catholic faith, Captain Luis de Carvajal ordered that the prayers of Our Lady should be sung every day and on holidays in a small chapel that he made. . . . And he made the rebelling Indians gather there so that they would learn the Christian doctrine. . . . And said captain, *with his person, would bring the little ones to the chapel* (emphasis added).[5]

On the other hand, there is the question of his marriage to Guiomar Núñez who, according to Carvajal's niece, Isabel, and nephew, El Mozo, was a devout Jew. However, this information was, at best, hearsay, because they learned about the Jewish practices of the family only *after* their arrival in New Spain. This means that in 1580, when they stayed a few days in Seville, in the house of Miguel Núñez, they did not witness any Jewish activities. This does not mean that Guiomar did not practice Judaism; it only means that if she did, Isabel and her brother had no way of knowing about it first hand. It is, of course, possible that Guiomar practiced Judaism. After all, her father had been tried by the Portuguese Inquisition when he was young.[6] However, there seems to be no credible evidence confirming that she was. Evidence to the contrary is also lacking. The only first-hand information that touches on that point stems from a document written on February of 1580, soon after Guiomar's father died. In that document she and her siblings appeared together with Carvajal before a notary public in Seville to name Blanca Rodríguez, Miguel Núñez's widow, as the administrator of his estate. For that purpose, Guiomar had to swear to obey the terms of the contract, which she did by saying:[7]

> I swear and promise this for God and for Saint Mary, and for the sign of the Cross, which I make with the fingers of my hand.

Of course, this does not prove she was a sincere Catholic. Nevertheless, her statement is the only first-hard evidence available at present that points in either direction. As such, it carries far more weight than the hearsay evidence provided, either under torture or threat of it, by the children of Francisca Nuñez de Carvajal. But even if Guiomar practiced Judaism, it is unlikely that Carvajal knew about it. Although they had their residence in Seville, he was a merchant who spent most of his time at sea.

Connections

In their 1588 letter to the king, the oidores of the Audiencia in Guadalajara said that Carvajal "had many friends." While this may have been true, the contemporary documents say very little about his personal relations to others, including his family. It is true that inquisitorial records of his trial and those of some members of his family contain some information along these lines. Unfortunately, that information is distorted by the conditions in which it was obtained. Nevertheless, it would appear that before the governor was brought before the Inquisition, he was as close to his sister and her family as he could be, given that he was occupied elsewhere with government matters. It also appears that he maintained a rapport with other family members such as Jorge de León, a cousin who had come with him from Spain and who lived in Nuevo Reino de León. This man was a brother of Diego Márquez, whom Carvajal came to regard as an enemy. The records also mention a Jorge de León Andrada, possibly one of Carvajal's maternal uncles, who lived in Mexico City and represented Carvajal in financial matters. Although he and Carvajal had been business associates, it is unlikely that they were close. Thus, from this very limited evidence it appears that Carvajal was not close to any relative in New Spain. Perhaps this is not surprising, given that he did not grow up near them and that he left Spain at a young age.

It is also known that Carvajal was not close to his wife. Several facts attest to this. For example, in the two years after his wedding, he was engaged in the transportation of wheat around the Mediterranean, which meant he spent little time with her. And after Carvajal was named governor she did not go to New Spain with him. Even niece Isabel retorted that her uncle "never had much of a life" with his wife. Also, the relationship between Carvajal and Guiomar's siblings must have been quite distant. Evidence for this is provided by the fact that when she died her brother did not notify. Instead he added that information in a letter he sent to his brother-in-law Francisco Rodríguez.[8]

Even less is known about Carvajal's relationships outside of his family. It is possible that he had many friends as the Audiencia in Guadalajara said but, if so, it is not known who they were. In 1589, when the inquisitors asked him: "Which of the persons who came in said ship were closest and known to you and with whom did you have particular friendship," he listed the names of his relatives and of a few others persons. Later on he mentioned many other names, but these were mostly religious leaders or officers of the Crown. Of course, as governor he must have been relatively close to the three lieutenants who had helped him govern. However, these were associates, not friends, at least in the sense the term is now understood.

It should be also mentioned that Carvajal had no sons or daughters, for when the Inquisitors asked him if he and Guiomar had any, he responded that he had none with her or "with any other woman." This posed some problems for him, as discussed below.

2. Carvajal's legacy

Alonso de León said that the governor died in sorrow, which undoubtedly was the truth. But while in the jail of the Crown, Carvajal was not, at least in his own mind, completely impotent. After all, as he said in the Auto-da-Fe where he appeared as a penitent, he was, even then, the governor of Nuevo

Reino de León. This position had been given to him by the king and nobody else could take it away. The same also applied to the many royal prerogatives given to him, including the right to name a successor. Apparently he took advantage of that right, for Villamanrique reported that "and I have been informed that he has transferred the government to somebody else; this is a matter that requires remedy."[9]

What Villamanrique wanted to do was to put an end to Nuevo Reino de León and to rid New Spain from the people left behind by Carvajal. But since he was no longer the viceroy, that task belonged to Velasco II, who tried to carry it out, no doubt under the influence of Eugenio de Salazar, now a permanent oidor in the Audiencia de México.

Of course, Carvajal knew that there was no hope of regaining his freedom, much less his governorship. Even if the king had sided with him in his fight against Villamanrique, he would not allow a person tried and sentenced by the Inquisition to occupy a high position in his empire. On the other hand, Carvajal did not want to abandon his dreams about Nuevo Reino de León. Thus, he did the only thing he could to insure continuity, namely, transfer his governorship to somebody else. Unfortunately, the name of the successor is unknown. The closest blood relatives he had in New Spain whom he might have named as successors were his nephew, El Mozo, and Jorge de León, a second cousin. El Mozo had been named successor years earlier but Carvajal had changed his mind about him and had broken all connections with him. Further, although Jorge de León was a blood relative, he was only a minor officer in Nuevo Reino de León. It is also possible that Felipe Núñez, one of Carvajal's three lieutenants was considered. However, Núñez was only a distant in-law relative and, furthermore, Carvajal knew what Núñez had told the inquisitors and would not, therefore, name him as his successor.

Almadén

Villamanrique's statement also makes it clear that he regarded Carvajal's transfer of power as a serious problem. Indeed, he felt that there was no reason for the continuation of Nuevo Reino de León as a separate political entity. The same view was expressed by Viceroy Velasco II in a letter he wrote to the king on 8 October 1590, although he was only thinking of the people that Carvajal left in Almadén under the command of Gaspar Castaño de Sosa.[10] According to both Velasco II and Villamanrique, those people were of the worst kind, *forájidos,* or outlaws, without religion, who lived from the illicit Indian-slave trade. True or not, the viceroy believed that it would be desirable to rid New Spain of them. In the same letter Velasco described two plans that he and his advisors had devised that could achieve that goal.[11] The first was to invite Castaño to come to Mexico City, supposedly to discuss his wishes to go to Nuevo México. However, the real purpose was to imprison him, so as to deprive the Almadén people from its leader. Velasco's alternate plan was to send Castaño and his people to Nuevo México, where, as he put it in that letter to the king, "the mines, the Indians and the conditions would finish them."

As it happened, the first plan had been put into effect months before Velasco wrote to the king. Soon after Carvajal was sentenced by the Inquisition, Velasco sent Castaño an invitation to go to Mexico City to meet him and to discuss his plans about Nuevo México. The invitation was delivered by Domingo Martínez de Cearreta, the first treasurer of Nuevo Reino de León. However, Castaño and his people were not naïve. They knew what had happened to Carvajal and had sufficient reason to suspect the viceroy's intentions. Therefore, when Castaño received the viceroy's invitation, he declined it, offering many excuses. To that effect he sent a letter to the viceroy with a soldier of Capt. Juan Morlete, explaining why he could not go to see him at that time.

But less than a month later, instead of going to Mexico City, as he had promised in his letter, he and all of the people of Almadén, more than 160 men, women, and children left that settlement. They took with them their cattle, all the provisions they could get, seed for planting purposes, and the *Caja de Tres Llaves.*[12] Obviously, they meant to settle permanently in Nuevo México. The historical details of the events that preceded and followed the departure are both interesting and important, but relate more to Castaño de Sosa's journey to that province than to Carvajal. Suffice to say that the departure of Castaño and his people was reported, years later, by D. Diego, one of the old Indians from Almadén, who said that they had left "towards the place where the sun sets, with many wagons, reaching the big water which they crossed."[13]

From the crossing point they first followed a river, which they called Río Salado, and then another, now called Pecos, reaching five months later Pecos Pueblo, an Indian town to the east of Santa Fe. They then explored several other pueblos in the area. However, in March of 1591, Juan Morlete and a large number of soldiers arrived in Santo Domingo, an Indian pueblo south of Santa Fe now called Kewa, where Castaño's camp was. He had an order to arrest Castaño and his group, and to take them to México City to respond to the accusations of the viceroy. Castaño surrendered without offering any resistance, and was taken in shackles to Mexico City.[14]

Although no record of his trial has been found, it appears that one took place in which Castaño was sentenced to exile and service in the Philippines.[15] The Audiencia had ruled that his sentence could not be appealed in Mexico City, but an appeal was apparently sent to Spain, where, according to Alonso de León, the Consejo de Indias commuted the sentence. However, by the time the pardon arrived in New Spain, Castaño had been killed by rebelling Chinese rowers in a Spanish galleon, where he and the then governor of the Philippines, Gomez Pérez das Mariñas, were traveling.[16] Alonso de León summed up Castaño de Sosa's life saying that he "was Portuguese, of valiant effort, pleasant to all and liberal, which was the reason that the hearts of his people were so much on his side." In this he agreed with D. Justo, another old Indian in Almadén who knew both Carvajal and Castaño and told Governor Zavala that "when Carvajal was leaving he left a very good man [in charge] whose name was Castaño, whom they saw leaving with all the people . . . and never returned."

While Castaño's attempt to colonize Nuevo México is well known thanks to his *Memoria*, very little is known about the more than 160 individuals who left Almadén with him and who, supposedly, were taken back to Mexico City by Capt. Juan Morlete. Of course some were taken there and others went to other places in New Spain. It is however unlikely that everybody else in the group left Nuevo México. The distances to population centers in New Spain were long and the road difficult. Also, feeding such a large number of people would have presented serious problems, particularly since the group included women and children. Furthermore, although everybody in the group had experienced the rigors of the journey from Almadén to Nuevo México, it is likely that few were willing to accept the challenges of a return journey.

As it turns out, there is some evidence that some of Castaño's people stayed behind. Thus, when Oñate's colonizing expedition reached Santo Domingo in 1598, he found there two Indians who had been in Castaño's group. On the other hand, Oñate did not report having encountered in Nuevo México any European member of that group. However, during the course of this work a document was found in the Spanish archives that shows that one of Castaño's captains remained in Nuevo México. This was Andrés Martínez Palomo, whose name appears in a trial against Oñate and some of his officers. One of the charges against Oñate accuses him of ordering a death "in the settlement that belongs to the *zarco* (blue-eyed) Andrés Martínez Palomo."[17] Of course, if Martínez Palomo remained in Nuevo México it is at least probable that other European members of Castaño's group did the same.

San Luis

As described earlier, the city of León and the village of San Luis had been destroyed by the Indians in 1586 as a result of the irresponsible orders issued by Villamanrique. The European colonizers who had been living in those places and who had survived the Indian attacks had gone to Saltillo after the Indian attacks. Although some among them later went to Almadén, many remained in Saltillo and were later joined by some of Castaño's people after his arrest. There they lived for several years wishing to return to those areas they had been forced to abandon. This they could not do because the political conditions would not allow it.

But in 1595 Viceroy Velasco II was replaced by Gaspar de Zúñiga y Azevedo, Conde de Monterrey. This change may have induced some of the earlier settlers to return to their lands to attempt to re-settle them. Thus, sometime in 1596 Diego de Montemayor and many of those who had been in Saltillo went back to San Luis, where on the first day of September of that year they founded a city with the name of *Ciudad Metropolitana de Nuestra Señora de Monterrey*, obviously in honor of the viceroy. That this was a *ciudad metropolitana* meant it was to be the capital of what was left of Nuevo Reino de León. Present at the foundation were some of those who accompanied Castaño to Nuevo México, including Pedro Iñigo, Juan Pérez de los Ríos, and Diego Días de Berlanga. Others members of Castaño's group may have also been present, but the deed of the foundation mentions only those who were appointed to official positions or those who served as witnesses in the foundation.

The continuation of Nuevo Reino de León implied by the foundation of Monterrey is interesting because Viceroys Villamanrique and Velasco had separately told to the king that they thought Nuevo Reino de León should be eliminated as a separate entity, a view that was not rejected by the king as the epigraph at the head of the chapter indicates. In principle that view should have prevented Montemayor from leading the re-settlement of San Luis. And yet the name given to the city founded by him clearly indicates that the viceroy had given his consent. Realizing that he had ignored the king's order, the viceroy attempted, to explain what had happened in two letters he sent to the king. The first of these, dated June 8, 1599, reads, in part:

> For about two years, or more, I have received news that a certain Montemayor had entered that government with a title of Lieutenant of Governor that had been given to him by a son of Carvajal, who had succeeded his father in the government. It was my intention then to bring that man here to punish him, but afterwards there started arriving here reports that the effort was beginning to

be fruitful. Therefore, consulting with the Audiencia it was decided to pretend nothing had taken place, ordering him, on one hand, to come here as a prisoner, and on the other, giving him a certain commission, in the interim, to rule a small town that he had made. This last path was chosen because if he were not there he would be missed, and because during his absence everything would be ruined by a captain Morlete, who in name of Nueva Vizcaya was pretending to exclude Montemayor and his companions. And I understand that he continues that which he started and it seems that there are several Spanish haciendas, and other Spaniards want to settle there.[18]

This makes it clear that the viceroy had given Montemayor permission to settle a town in Nuevo Reino de León. In 1601 the viceroy wrote again about Diego de Montemayor in which he repeated some of what he had said in the first letter, adding that he had named Montemayor as Governor in the interim while he waited for the king to order something else.[19] Incidentally, the reference to Juan Morlete in the viceroy's letter of 1599 shows that Morlete had been an impediment to the re-settlement of Nuevo Reino de León. This probably explains Alonso de León's view that Morlete was "a contentious man of bad intentions."[20]

Tamaholipa

In addition to the groups of Castaño and Montemayor, there was another group associated with Carvajal. This group inhabited the northeast part of the Guasteca region, that is, the southern region of the modern Mexican state of Tamaulipas. As the reader will recall, this was the region Carvajal left under the command of Felipe Núñez. However, he and those who may have been with him seem to have left no record of their activities.

Other settlements

Other villages and towns were later settled in Tamaulipas, Nuevo León, Coahuila, and, perhaps San Luis Potosí. However, no other foundation seems to have taken place during Carvajal's time or soon after. Rather, it appears that people simply settled wherever they wanted in what once was Nuevo Reino de León, without marking the event in any way. But by the mid seventeenth century many other settlement appeared. It is likely that some of these may have been founded by the descendants of Carvajal's colonizers.

By 1596, sixteen years had passed since the arrival of Carvajal and his colonizers, certainly a sufficiently long time for most of the minors in their company to have children of their own. The question at hand is, therefore, whether these people had a significant impact in the development of Nuevo Reino de León, that is, in the area covered by the four Mexican states mentioned above, plus certain regions of New Mexico and Texas. A definite answer requires a knowledge of the number of them who remained in that area but that information is lacking. Nevertheless, a rough estimate indicates that the number was high. It is likely that most of them remained in the vast territories that were then part of Nuevo Reino de León. In some of those places they, and those who later joined them, continued the work that Carvajal had started, founding other settlements and growing in number while preserving many customs, words, traditions, and favorite foods. Even today, in spite of the considerable influx of people from other parts of modern Mexico, some of these customs and traditions are still noticeable. And even though Spanish is the language used in northeast Mexico as well as the language still used by many who live in the American Southwest, there is little doubt that a good number of them descended from people who long ago were born in Portugal.

.

Appendix A

The Capitulación of Luis de Carvajal

THE KING

Because you, Captain Luis de Carvajal de la Cueva, have informed us that by commission and order of our viceroy of New Spain you went to discover, and discovered, with soldiers and at your expense, a way from the province of Pánuco to the mines of Mazapil and kingdom of the Nueva Galicia, and had also discovered certain provinces and territories inhabited by many natives that are to the north of said mines of Mazapil, and which, by latitude, extend to both North and South Seas; and that with the zeal that you have to serve Our Lord and our wish that our Catholic faith be glorified and that our crown and rents and assets increase, you are determined to go in our name and at your expense, to colonize and pacify said territories and those adjacent to them in those lands, and to try to bring their natives to the knowledge of God our Lord, and to our obedience, and you have supplicated us to give you license and ability to do so, and that about it we should order take with you agreement and capitulación. And having our Consejo de Indias seen your request, and because of our great desire to convert the natives of those provinces, and that in those provinces our Holy Evangelical Law be obeyed—because through its knowledge the souls of said natives can be saved—we have deemed this to be good and have ordered make and take with you, about said discovery, colonization and pacification, an agreement and capitulación in the following manner:

1. In the first place, you, said captain Luis de Carvajal de la Cueva, promise that from the river of Pánuco and port of Tampico until the mines of Mazapil and their surroundings, until the end of pacified land and the Nueva Galicia and the provinces of the New Vizcaya, will make the necessary settlements for the tranquility of those frontiers. And that the first town will have fifty burghers, and the other towns will be in the parts that the viceroy of New Spain will order you.

2. Within five years, starting from the date of this agreement, you will have discovered 200 leagues Tierra Adentro and will attempt to pacify and to bring the Indians native to those provinces to the knowledge of our Holy Catholic Faith and to our obedience

3. You will make settlements in every place convenient to the security of the coast, in the ports that exist in it, from that of Tampico to the Bay of Saint Joseph, which you say is the limit of the territory of La Florida.

4. You commit yourself to go Tierra Adentro, to continue to make settlements wherever is more convenient until reaching the limits of said territory of La Florida, on that side, and on the other –north and north west, so that from La Florida it will be possible to go to yours and to the provinces of New Spain and New Galicia, so that from them it will be possible to take provisions, cattle, and other necessary things.

5. And because the town of Tamaholipa is in the frontier of the province of Pánuco is six leagues inside the Tierra de Guerra and the Spaniards and the peaceful Indians go there at considerable risk because of the Chichimeca Indians who live around, from whom they receive many damages, deaths and robberies, and the same do to the Indians of the town of Tamaholipa when they leave it, you promise that in order that said deaths and damages that they do in those parts, you will make a village between said town of Tamaholipa and the last lands of peace.

6. And because when you entered said land you found eight leagues of *tunales* where cochineal grows, you promise to settle another village of Spaniards where it is more convenient to benefit and take said cochineal.

7. You promise that at the mouth of said Pánuco river, at the beginning of your territory, you will make a fort for the security of the port of Tampico and for the defense of the land, and to hamper the damages that could happen there if corsairs came for that purpose.

8. And because in said province of Pánuco, in the limits of your territory, near the village of Valles, there are the towns of Tampasquín, Tamotela, Sant Miguel, and from there to the town of Xalpa and Sechu, all of which had been Christian, but five years ago rebelled against our royal service destroying churches and making other insults, because of which our viceroy has sent captains and soldiers, and even if they had tried [to quell the rebellion] with great care and intention, it has not been possible to do so, you promise that within eight years, which also start from the date of this agreement, you will return to peace those towns and will bring them to the knowledge of our sacred Catholic Faith.

9. You promise to take to that province, at your expense, up to 100 men, sixty of whom married farmers with their wives and sons, and the rest soldiers and officers for said population, without taking from them anything, and without playing drums or raising a flag to gather or house them in any town in these kingdoms of ours, except in form of settlement, preparing them so that they can come to Seville to the time that you should depart.

10. You commit yourself to take to your territories major and minor cattle to work the land and to sustain the neighbors, within the necessary time.

11. For the discovery, the good government of said province, and the indoctrination, teaching, and to keep the Indians in peace, you commit yourself to keep the laws described in the Instruction about Discoveries, Pacification and New Settlements, which will be given to you.

12. In order to fulfill the requirements stated above, you promise that as son as you arrive in New Spain, you will give plain bonds to the satisfaction of our viceroy and of

our Audiencia that resides in Mexico city, in an amount of up to eight thousand ducats, so that you will keep and obey the contents of this agreement, and that if you do not you will have to pay said eight thousand ducats for our treasury, and that the written bonds be given to our officers of said city, so that they can keep it in the Caja de las tres llaves, which they have, and so that they can use it when and if becomes necessary.

13. And because this agreement and capitulación that we have ordered take with you pre-supposes that it has to be executed so that our lord will be served, and our treasury and royal holdings increased, as it has been said, in such a manner that no inconvenience follow from it, as soon as you arrive to said New Spain, and before you start said settlement, you have to be compelled to show the capitulación before our viceroy of New Spain, to whom we order that in that part of it that he does not find inconvenient, he should order you to put it into effect, and that part which he does, to suspend it until he informs us of it, so that after we see it we will provide whatever is convenient to our service.

And so that with more desire, spirit and comfort of yourself and of the people that go with you can make, and make, said discovery, colonization and pacification and your sustenance in those lands we give you, and offer give, privilege in the following things:

1. We confer on you the title of our Governor and Captain General of the provinces and lands that are from the port of Tampico, river of Pánuco, and in the mines of Mazapil, to the limits of Nueva Galicia and Nueva Vizcaya, and from there to the north what is to be discovered, from one ocean to the other, provided it should not exceed 200 leagues of latitude, and another 200 of longitude, to be called and titled the Nuevo Reino de Leon, for all of the days of your life and, afterward, for those of a son or your heir that you will name, with two thousand pesos of mines in salary from the products of the land, if they exist, and if not, we shall not be compelled to give you anything in said salary.

2. We allow you to take for yourself the places that you decide in your provinces, up to two distributions of Indians, so that you can profit from them according to the law of succession.

3. We shall give you our cédula to grant you power and sufficient faculty so that you can distribute Indians of the province that you will discover, pacify and colonize among the persons who might have served us in said discovery, and among the first settlers so that they profit from its fruits and from the tributes of said Indians according to the law of succession. However, you are forewarned that the principal towns, military strongholds, seats of administration, and sea ports will be incorporated in our real crown.

4. We shall grant you the position of *alguacil* mayor of said provinces for the duration of your life and that of an heir son of that of your successor, that you might name, with the faculty that you and said successor can put and take the alguaciles in the towns that will be settled, or are already settled, in said government.

5. We grant you license so that, from these our kingdoms, you can take to said province, and not other part of our Indies, forty black slaves, one-third of

whom females, free of all tax rights that might be ours, for your personal service, and for the work and benefit of the mines that might exist in your territory, and everything else that might be convenient to do in it, provided they are registered in the usual manner, for which license we will order give you our cédula.

6. We give you license and faculty so that for six years, one ship each year can go form these our kingdoms to New Spain with provisions, arms and other necessary things for the people that might live in your government, and for the work of its mines and to work the lands, without paying us any taxes, provided that said ship leave these kingdoms on its way to your province with the fleet that in each of those six years leaves our kingdoms to go to said New Spain, and provided that your ships are inspected by one of our officers in the House of Trade in the city of Seville.

7. We shall grant you our cédula so that said our viceroy of New Spain indicates a site and hacienda for you at the mouth of the river of Tampico, in land of peace, from which your territory has to begin, so that you can bring to it whatever mayor cattle you have for that purpose, provided no harm is done to anybody else.

8. We shall grant you, and to said your son or your successor, the lieutenancy of the fort that, as it has been said, you have to build at the mouth of the river of Pánuco, for which we will order give you our title of said holding, and we offer that after the fort is finished, you shall be given commensurate salary from the fruits of the land, and with the agreement of our viceroy of said New Spain.

9. We will order to give you our cédula so that said our viceroy order that Indians are made available to you to build said fort, from those Indians that might live in the towns near that mouth of the river Pánuco, where you have offered yourself, and are compelled to build such fort.

10. We grant you, said Captain Luis de Carvajal and to your heir son, or to a person that will follow you in your government, and to the persons that would administer it, that of the gold, silver and gems that were obtained in your land, we be paid only the twelfth instead of the fifth that belongs to us, for period of ten years.

11. We will order that our cédulas be given to you so that our viceroy in New Spain and the president and oidores of the royal audiencia of Nueva Galicia, and the government of the Nueva Vizcaya favor and help you in every necessary manner so that you can make said discovery, pacification and colonization, and so that they order others to give you horses, sustenance and other things that you might need at fair and moderate prices.

12. We order that from this moment be of your jurisdiction the towns of Tampasquín, Tamotela, Sanct Miguel and from there, the others that, as has been said, have rebelled against our service, until Xalpa and Sechu, provided that all of them be kept in peace and brought to our obedience within said eight years, as has been said before.

Therefore, if you, said Captain Luis de Carvajal de la Cueva, obey the stipulations contained in this capitulación in the manner that you have offered, we will order that in consideration to your services and in regard to their quality you will receive our privileges. By means of this we commit yourself and assure you, because of our

Faith and Royal word, that what from our part is offered to you, we will order be obeyed and fulfilled. And that against it nothing happens or done in any manner. But if you do not fulfill what you have offered we shall not be compelled to keep anything that was stated above; instead, we shall order that you be punished as a person who does not keep and obey the commandments of his king and natural lord. And for your security we order that this be given to you. Dated in Aranjuez on the last day of May of one thousand five hundred and seventy nine years. I, The King. Verified by Antonio de Erasso and signed by the members of the Consejo.

Appendix B

Summaries of Carvajal's Cédulas

1. That the officers in Seville allow Captain Luis de Carvajal to return to New Spain, and that he can take with him one hundred men, sixty of whom married farmers with their wives and sons, and the rest soldiers and officer for the discovery and colonization of Nuevo Reino de León.

2. That the Officers of justice of these kingdoms favor Captain Luis de Carvajal so that he can gather and take from them to the city of Seville and port of San Lucar de Barrameda, in the manner of colonizers, one hundred men that he has to take to the Indies for the colonization of Nuevo Reino de León.

3. So that Captain Carvajal can take with him 40 black slaves, one third female, free of all taxes.

4. So that Captain Carvajal can take each year, for a total of six years, a ship with provisions, arms and other necessary things to Nuevo Reino de León without paying taxes.

5. Title of Governor of Nuevo Reino de León given to Captain Luis de Carvajal.

6. So that starting now the government of Nuevo Reino de León include the towns of Tampasquín, Tamotela and S. Miguel, and from there all others that have rebelled until the towns of Xalpa and Sechu.

7. So that Captain Luis de Carvajal can take for himself two distributions of Indians for two lives in Nuevo Reino de León, to which he is going to discover and colonize.

8. That the viceroy of New Spain inform about the cost, labor, and danger of what Captain Luis de Carvajal does, and that his colonizing and pacifying activities should be followed, and that if it is possible to pay him in some way other than from the royal treasury.

9. That the viceroy of New Spain and the Audiencia of Nueva Galicia and the governor of Nueva Vizcaya favor Captain Luis de Carvajal in the discovery and colonization of Nuevo Reino de León and order give him provisions and other necessities at fair prices.

10. That the viceroy of New Spain order give Indians to Captain Luis de Carvajal to build the fort that has to be built at the mouth of the river Pánuco of Nuevo Reino de León, provided the Indians go to work voluntarily and that they are treated well and are paid for their work.

11. That the viceroy of New Spain indicates for Captain Luis de Carvajal a site and hacienda at the beginning of his government where he can put cattle.

12. That the viceroy of New Spain decide if, as Captain Luis de Carvajal says, it would be desirable to bring to Nuevo Reino de León some Indians of the principal towns of New Spain, so that those living there can see the good treatment and given to those, and the good that could come if these could voluntarily come to be baptized.

13. That for a period of ten years the colonizers of Nuevo Reino de León not pay more than the twelfth, instead of the fifth, of the gold, silver and gems that are found in Nuevo Reino de León.

14. Title of *Alguazil Mayor* of Nuevo Reino de León for Captain Luis de Carvajal de la Cueva for his life and that of a successor.

15. That Captain Luis de Carvajal may divide his territory in villages and towns and appoint in them alcaldes mayores and ordinarios that were elected in those towns.

16. That Captain Luis de Carvajal may give and distribute to the colonizers of Nuevo Reino de León, lands and haciendas for horses, mills, and ingenios de sugar.

17. That Captain Luis de Carvajal may provide and name officers for the royal treasury in Nuevo Reino de León.

18. That the viceroy of New Spain order make tools to mark the gold, silver and other metals that are extracted in the provinces of Nuevo Reino de León.

19. That Captain Luis de Carvajal may compel those who with him will go to said provinces to reside and persevere in them.

20. Title of Alcalde for the fort that Captain Luis de Carvajal will make at the mouth of the river of Pánuco, for him and his successor.

21. So that Captain Luis de Carvajal de la Cueva can distribute the Indians of Nuevo Reino de León.

Appendix C

Carvajal's Colonizers

Name	Birth Place	Father	Mother	Spouse	Minor
Águila, Andrés del	Almaden de los Azoguez	Bernabe Martín	María Sánchez	Francisca Núñez	
Alcega, Antonio de	Nra. S. de Aranda en Viscaya	Juan de Alcega	D. Mayora de Alcega		
Aronte, Gonzalo de	Lerguerias en la Montaña	Garcia de Aronte	Elvira García		
Ballestero, Gabriel	Toro	Blas Ballestero	María Trabazos		
Bardales, Bernardino de	V. del Barco de Avila	Macías de Bardales	Francisca Hernández	Isabel Rodríguez	3m, 1f
Barrera, María de la	Olivares	Ascencio Hernández	Florentina Díaz	Andrés de Herrera	
Bea, Bartolomé de	Sayas de Bascones	Bartolomé de Bea	María de Tapia		
Beltrán, Elvira	S. Juan del Puerto	Melchor Martín	Catalina Martín	Andrés Velasco	
Beltrán, Juan	S. Juan del Puerto	Melchor Martín	Catalina Martín	Francisca Hernández	2m
Beltrán de Guevara, Pedro	Vitoria	Juan Beltrán	Elvira de Avendaño		
Burbano, Andrés	Hornachuelos	Nicolás Ruiz			
Carrión, Pedro de	Placencia	Pedro Carrión	Catalina Ximénez	Juliana de Hermosilla	
Carvajal, D. Francisca de	Benavente	Gaspar de Carvajal	Catalina de León	Francisco Rodríguez de Matos	

Name	Birth Place	Father	Mother	Spouse	Minors
Copete, Alonso	Alcántara	Alonso Copete	Francisca Durana		
Delgado, Gaspar	Córdoba	Francisco Delgado	Isabel Rodríguez		
Díaz, Catalina	Almares	Francisco López	Catalina Díaz	Pedro Rodríguez	
Díaz, Juan	Sevilla	Pedro Díaz	Francisca Xuárez	Catalina Rodríguez	
Duarte de Figueroa, Andrés	Xerez de la Frontera	Duarte Rodríguez	D. Isabel González		
Enríquez, Pedro Alonso	Fuente del Maestre	Alonso Guerrero	Catalina Enríquez	Ana de Porras	1m
Espinosa, Isabel de		Diego Hernández	Juana de Espinosa	Agustin Rodríguez	
Espinosa, Catalina de	Guadalupe	Barolome Garcia de Suero	Pasquela Martínez	Juan de Saucedo	
Estevan, Benito	Mallorca	Nicolás	María	Leonor de Mota	1m, 1f
Estevan, María	V. del Almendralejo	Gonzalo Hidalgo	Olalla Rangela	Francisco Ortiz	
Fernández Salgado, Gómez	S. Martín de Noguera en Galicia	Alonso Hernández	Aestanza Rodríguez		
García, Alonso	Laredo	Alonso García Mendoza	Teresa Hernández		
García, Olalla	V. del Lobón	Miguel Sánchez de la Vara	Isabel Rodríguez	Bartolomé Martín	
García del Corro, Alonso	Sevilla	Nuño González	María López	Francisca de Guzmán	3m, 1f
Gil, Roque	Torrija	Juan Gil	Isabel de Cuevas		
Gómez, Maríana	Alcalá de Henares	Cristóbal Gómez		Melchor de Serdeño	
Gómez, Martín	Sta. Cruz de la Zarza	Juan Gómez	Catalina Sánchez		
Gómez, Mateo	Ocaña	Alonso Martínez de Noblejas	Mari Gómez	Gerónima López	1m

Name	Birth Place	Father	Mother	Spouse	Minor
Gonzáles de Paredes, Pedro	Amusco tierra de Campos	Pedro González	Marta Álvarez		
González, Luis	Sevilla	Diego Martín	María Hernández	Ana Rodríguez	
Gutierrez, Francisco	Alcalá de Guadaira	Diego de Torres	Juana Pérez		
Gutierrez, Gabriel	Valladolid				
Guzmán, Francisca de	Frejenal	Geronimo de Guzmán	Mayor de Bustos	Alonso García del Corro	
Heredia, Ana de	Sevilla	Hernando de Aguilar	Leonor de Eslava	Pedro de Salas	
Heredia, Nicolás de	Adamuz	Bartolome Gómez	María González		
Hermosilla, Juliana de	Burgos	Pedro de Hermosilla	Inés de Cavías	Pedro de Carrión	
Hernández, Diego	Benavente	Gerome Hernández	María Rodríguez		
Hernández, Francisca	V. de S. Juan del Puerto	Juanes de Arteaga	Catalina de Ramírez	Juan Beltrán	
Hernández, Francisco	Jerez de los Caballeros	Pedro Hernández	Inés González	María de Tuesta	2m, 2f
Hernández, Inés	Arjona	Diego Hernández	Isabel de Morales	Juan de Piedrola	
Hernández, María	Ecija	Pedro Hernández	Catalina Pérez	Francisco Ximénez	
Hernández, Pedro	V. de Zafra	Juan Fernández	Leonor Díaz	Elvira Sánchez	5m, 6f
Herrera, Andrés de	Medina del Campo	Antonio de Herrera	María de Ortega	María de la Barrera	1m, 3f
Hoyo, Juan del	Llerena	Alonso Martín	Catalina Alonso		
Izquierdo, Juan	V. de Cariñeno en Aragón	Juan Izquierdo	Isabel Cegarra	Rufina Rodríguez	
León, Catalina de		Antonio Márquez	Isabel de León	Gonzalo Pérez Ferro	

Name	Birth Place	Father	Mother	Spouse	Minors
León, Jorge de	Medina del Campo	Gonzalo Rodríguez		Ginebra Márquez	
López, Antonio	Sta. Cruz (de la Zarza)	Juan Gómez	Catalina Sánchez		
López, Gerónima	Ocaña	Alonso Robledo	María López	Mateo Gómez	
López, Juan	Sta. Cruz de la Zarza	Hernan López Gómez	Catalina Alonso		
López de Mendoza, Pedro	Laredo	(Gíllén?) de Mendoza	Teresa Rodríguez		
López Urbano, Juan	Hornachuelos	Nicolás Ruiz	Isabel Gutierrez		
Madrid, Diego de	Sevilla	Alonso de Madrid	Isabel González	Ana de los Reyes	1m
Madrid, Francisco de	Córdoba	Gerónimo Ruiz	María de Madrid		
Márquez, Ginebra	Medina del Campo	Antonio Márquez	Isabel de León	Jorge de León	
Martín, Bartolomé	V. del Lobón	Alonso Martín	María Andrés	Olalla García	3m, 2f
Martínez, Domingo	Guernica	Pedro Martínez de Cearreta	Juana Gómez		
Mazo, Francisco	Carrion de los Condes	Francisco Mazo	Felipa de Escobar		
Medina, Hernando de		Luis Ardillones	Isabel de Medina		
Mexía, Hernando	Sevilla	Melchor Ortiz	Ambrosia Suárez		
Morales, Andrés de	Arjona	Diego Hernández	Isabel de Morales		
Morales, Bartolomé de	Arjona	Francisco Morales	Catalina Díaz		
Morales, Manuel de	Arjona	Diego Hernández	Isabel de Morales	Isabel Pérez	2m, 2f
Mota, Leonor de	Sevilla	Hernán Núñez	Margarita de Mota	Benito Estevan	

Name	Birth Place	Father	Mother	Spouse	Minors
Muñoz, Ana	Sevilla	Pedro Muñoz	Ana Garcia	Juan de Nava	
Nava, Juan de	Sevilla	Diego Hernández de Nava	Catalina de Espinosa	Ana Muñoz	1m
Núñez Francisca	Cd. Rodrigo	Pedro Vicioso	Inés Pacheco	Andrés del Aguila	
Núñez, Vicente	Sevilla	Gerónimo Núñez	Leonor Méndez		
Núñez de Ribera, Felipe	Sevilla	Andrés Núñez	Gracia Núñez		
O, María de la	Morón	Juan Rodríguez	Leonisa de Cervantes	Pedro de Rojas	
Ortiz, Francisco	Torrecilla del Duque de Najera	Juan Ortiz	María Tejada		
Ortiz, Francisco	V. del Almendralejo	Alonso Hernández	Leonor Ortiz	María Estevan	3m, 2f
Pérez, Isabel	Arjona	Andrés Pérez	María de Mesquita	Manuel de Morales	
Pérez Ferro, Gonzalo	Medina del Campo	Juan Rodríguez	Felipa Rodríguez	D. Catalina de León	
Piedrola, Juan de	Arjona	Francisco de Piedrola	Barbola de Bormas	Inés Hernández	
Pimentel, Luis	Villada (Burgos)	Enrique Pimentel	Isabel Carvajal		
Porras, Ana de	V. de Zafra	Francisco de Porras	Leonor Mexia	Pedro Alonso Enríquez	
Porras, Francisco de	Medina del Campo	Francisco Rayas de Porras	Ana de Porras		
Portugal, D. Juan de	México	D. Hernando de Portugal	D. Madalena Pinelo de Villegas		
Prado, Pedro de	Peñafiel	Jusepe de Villanueva	Antonia de Prado		
Reyes, Ana de los	Sevilla	Juan Rodríguez	Ana Pérez	Diego de Madrid	

Name	Birth Place	Father	Mother	Spouse	Minors
Rodríguez, Agustin	Sevilla	Juan Rodríguez	Catalina Rodríguez	Isabel de Espinosa	
Rodríguez, Ana	Sevilla	Diego López	Ana López	Luis González	
Rodríguez, Catalina	Sevilla	Diego López	Ana Rodríguez	Juan Díaz	
Rodríguez, Domingo	Sevilla	Simón Rodríguez	Blanca Rodríguez		
Rodríguez, Francisco	Santiago de Sotorde	Pedro González	Inés Rodríguez	María Rodríguez	2m
Rodríguez, Isabel	Fuente de Cantos	Rodrigo Sánchez	Elvira Sánchez	Bernardino de Bardales	
Rodríguez, Juan	S. Juan del Puerto	Juanes de Unceta	Catalina García		
Rodríguez, María	Santiago de Sotorde	Diego Rodríguez	María González	Francisco Rodríguez	
Rodríguez, Miguel	Sevilla	Juan Rodríguez	Catalina Pérez	Violante Rodríguez	
Rodríguez, Pedro	Pasarón en la vera de Plasencia	Pedro Rodríguez	Mari Gómez	Catalina Díaz	2m, 3f
Rodríguez, Rufina	V. de Ferce en Galicia	Alonso Rodríguez	Francisca González	Juan Izquierdo	
Rodríguez, Violante	Sevilla	Antonio Rodríguez	Margarida Hernández	Miguel Rodríguez	
Rodríguez de Jaque, Alonso	Cd. Rodrigo	Juan de Paz	D. Madalena Rodríguez		
Rodríguez de Matos, Francisco	Benavente	Baltazar Rodríguez		D. Francisca de Carvajal	5m, 5f
Rodríguez Matalobos, Joan	Frejenal	Lorenzo Hernández	Elvira García	Catalina Sánchez	1m, 1f
Rojas, Gaspar de	Guadalajara	Pedro el Rojo	Leonor Pérez		
Rojas, Pedro de	Sevilla	Pedro de Vergara	María de los Angeles	María de la O	1m, 2f
Sagasti, Martín de	Guernica	Juan de Sagasti	María Ochoa		

Name	Birth Place	Father	Mother	Spouse	Minor
Salas, Pedro de	Salamanca	Martín de Salas	María Pérez	Ana de Heredia	
Salvador, Pedro	Alcalá de Guadaira	Pedro Sánchez	Estevanía Hernández		
Sánchez, Catalina	Frejenal	Hernán Vázquez	Inés Garcia	Joan Rodríguez Matalobos	
Sánchez, Elvira	Zafra	Pedro Sánchez	María Estevez	Pedro Hernández	
Sánchez, Rafael	Pazarón	Alonso Sánchez	Catalina de Arroyo		
Saucedo, Juan de	Guadalupe	Pedro de Saucedo	María Núñez	Catalina de Espinoza	3m, 2f
Serdeño, Melchor de	Medina del Campo	Jácome Serdeño	Luisa del Aguila	Mariana Gómez	1f
Tascón, Luis	Villalpando	Alvaro Tascón	Catalina Hernámdez		
Tuesta, María de	Granada	Pedro Martínez	María de Tuesta	Francisco Hernández	
Valdés, Pedro de	Burgos	Juan de Valdés	Madalena Ortiz		
Valladar, Diego de	Ysla, Junto a Laredo	Juan Martínez de Valladar	Mari Sánchez		
Velasco Andrés	S. Juan del Puerto	Andrés Garcia	Elvira Ximénez	Elvira Beltrán	1m
Ximénez, Francisco	Granada	Gonzalo de Aguilar	Ana Ximénez	María Hernández	1f
Ximénez, Juan	Laredo	Gonzalo de Mendoza	María Sánchez		
Yñiguez, Pedro	Pazaron	Alonso Yñiguez	Juana Yñiguez		

Appendix D

The 1580 Fleet

NEW SPAIN

Francisco de Santiago, maestre of the nao *Santa María de Begonia*. Capitana.
Hernán García, maestre of the nao *La Trinidad*.
Alonso Rodríguez de Noriega, maestre of the nao *San Miguel*.
Francisco Bernal, maestre of the nao *Santa María de Arratia*.
Juan de Atibar, maestre of the nao *San Miguel*.
Manuel Díaz, maestre of the nao *San Cristóbal*.
Antón Sánchez de Armas, maestre of the nao *Santa Catalina*.
Pedro de Esco, maestre of the nao *Nuestra Señora de Guía*.
Andrés Felipe, maestre of the nao *Santiago*.
Lope Machorro, maestre of the nao *San Salvador*.
Rodrigo Rico, maestre of the nao *Santa María de Jesús*.
Juan Bautista Machorro, maestre of the nao *La Trinidad*
Esteban de Zubieta, maestre of the nao *La Concepción*.

HONDURAS

Juan de Micina, maestre of the nao *La Concepción*.
Ñufio Rodríguez, maestre of the nao *San Vicente*.

SANTO DOMINGO

Juan Quintero, maestre of the nao *San Marcos*.
Manuel Alonso, maestre of the nao *Nuestra Señora de la Misericordia*.

CAMPECHE

Nicolás de Rodas, maestre of the nao *Nuestra Señora de la Victoria*.

HABANA

Antón Conquerro, maestre of the nao *Nuestra Señora La Bella*.
Martín Rodríguez, maestre of the nao *Los Tres Reyes*, to La Florida.
Francisco del Tejo, maestre of a frigat to La Florida.
Hernando de Miranda, maestre of a frigat to La Florida.
Lope Hernández, maestre of the nao *San Antonio*, to Puerto Rico

Glossary

Alcalde	Magistrate of a town, village, or province
Alguacil	Constable
Arroba	Unit of weight equivalent to 25 lbs
Asentamiento	Temporary camp
Asiento	Agreement; contract
Audiencia	Highest court in a major province or colony
Auto	Decree or sentence made by an Audiencia
Auto-da-fe	Inquisition ceremony where sentences were read to the accused
Caja de Tres Llaves	Royal Chest that required three different keys to be opened
Capitulación	Contract issued by the Crown
Cédula	Royal order or decree
Converso	Person who had changed his religion to Catholicism
Criado de	Servant of; raised by
Ducado	Currency unit equivalent to 375 maravedíes
Encomendero	Spaniard who had an encomienda.
Encomienda	A system whereby Indians were distributed among Spaniards, ostensibly to be indoctrinated in the Catholic faith.
Entrada	Incursion into unconquered territory

Fiscal	Prosecutor in an Audienca or in the Inquisition
Hidalgo	Lowest ranked member of the Spanish nobility.
Información de Oficio	Information obtained before an Audiencia
Juez comisario	Person commissioned to act as a judge for some special task
Letrado	University-educated person
Limpieza de sangre	Not having a non-Christian ancestor for at least three generations
Maestre	Officer below the captain in a ship, charged with governing the ship.
Maravedí	Currency unit, equivalent to 1/375 of a ducado
Oidor	Judge in an Audiencia
Peso, oro común	Coin, equivalent to 300 maravedíes
Peso, oro de minas	Coin, equivalent to 450 maravedíes
Pleito	Legal dispute before an audiencia
Procurador	Advocate before an audiencia
Provisión	Document issued by a magistrate or court
Quintal	Unit of weight equivalent to 100 lbs
Quinto	Royal tax amounting to 20% of proceeds
Relator	Person in an audiencia in charge of recording affidavits
Tierra Adentro	Unconquered or unexplored territory
Visita	Examination of the deeds of a Crown official
Visitador	Person charged by the king to carry out a visita

Abbreviations

AGI	Archivo General de Indias, Seville
AGN	Archivo General de la Nación, Mexico City
AGS	Archivo General de Simancas, Valladolid
AHN	Archivo Historico Nacional, Madrid
AHP	Archivo Histórico de Protocolos, Seville
ANTT	Archivo Nacional Torre de Tombo, Lisbon
CLAHR	Colonial Latin American Historical Review
CDII	*Colección de documentos inéditos relativos al descubrimiento, conquista y organización de las antiguas posesiones españolas de América y Oceanía.* Madrid: 1864–1888
HAHR	*Hispanic American Historical Review*
INAH	Instituto Nacional de Antropología e Historia, México City
MDC	*Información de Oficio recibida en la Real Audiencia de México sobre la que dio el capitán Luis de Carvajal sobre sus Méritos y Servicios*
NGI	*Información de Oficio recibida en la Audiencia Real del Nuevo Reino de Galicia contra la que hizo de parte de Luis de Carvajal de la Cueva, gobernador y capitán general del Nuevo Reino de León.*
NMHR	*New Mexico Historical Review*

Notes

INTRODUCTION

1. Vicente Riva Palacios, *Mexico a Través de sus Siglos,* Vol. 2, *El Virreinato.* Mexico City: Ballesca y Compañía, 1870, 443.
2. Martin A. Cohen, *The Martyr: Luis de Carvajal, a Secret Jew in Sixteenth-Century Mexico.* Albuquerque: University of New Mexico, 2001.
3. Vito Alessio Robles, *Coahuila y Tejas en la Época Colonial.* Mexico: Cultura, 1938.
4. Mariano Cuevas, *Historia de la Nación Mexicana.* Mexico City: Modelo, 1940
5. Primo Feliciano Velázquez, *Historia de San Luis Potosí,* 3 vols. Mexico City: Sociedad de Geografía y Estadística, 1946.
6. Lesslie Byrd Simpson, *Many Mexicos, Revised edition.* New York: G. P. Putnam's Sons, 1946, 168).
7. Eugenio del Hoyo, *Historia del Nuevo Reino de León (1577–1723),* segunda edición. Mexico City: Libros de México, 1979, 110.
8. *Ibid.,* 105.
9. Robert S. Weddle, *Spanish Sea, The Gulf of Mexico in North American Discovery, 1500–1685.* College Station: Texas A&M University Press, 1985, Chapter 18; Peter Gerhard, *A Guide to the Historical Geography of New Spain.* Revised edition. Norman: University of Oklahoma Press, 1993, 213; Abraham Nuncio, *Vision de Monterrey.* Mexico City: Fondo de Cultura Económica, 1997, 52–53.

CHAPTER ONE

1. Alonso de León, "Relaciones y Discursos del Descubrimiento, Población y Pacificación de este Nuevo Reino de León, 1649," in 'Historia de Nuevo León, con noticias sobre Coahuila, Tejas y Nuevo Mexico por el Capitán Alonso de León, un autor Anónimo y el General Fernando Sánchez de Zamora,' in *Documentos inéditos para la historia de México,* Genaro García, ed., Mexico City: Librería de la viuda de Ch. Bouret, 1909, 25:89.
2. Alfonso Toro, compilador, "Proceso integro de Luis de Carvajal, el Viejo, Gobernador del Nuevo Reino de León, por Judaizante," in *Los Judíos en la Nueva España,* segunda edición facsimilar. Mexico City: Fondo de Cultura Económica, 1993, 209–372.
3. Isabel Vaz de Freitas, *Mercadores entre Portugal e Castela na Idade Media.* Gijón: Ediciones Trea, 2006, 169.
4. José Ledo del Pozo, *Historia de la Nobilísima villa de Benavente,* facsimile edition.

Benavente: Centro de Estudios Benaventanos, 2000, 25.

5. Processo de Catarina de Carvajal, novembro 2, 1558. ANTT. Lisboa, no. 6740, folio 11.

6. Although Carvajal named uncle Joan as Juan de Carvajal, his sister said his name was Joan Núñez, the same name with which he appears in the Portuguese documents. See Proceso contra Doña Francisca de Carvajal. 1589. AGN, Inquisición lote Riva Palacio, Vol. 1488, exp.1, folio 101v.

7. Processo de Belchior Vaz, janeiro 30, 1546. ANTT, Lisboa, no. 5165, folio 1.

8. Since both Gaspar de Carvajal and Catalina de León were born in Mogadouro, it would appear that the marriage took place there.

9. The change of surname occurred in 1580, when Francisca and her family left Spain.

10. Toro, *Judíos en Nueva España*, 268.

11. *Procesos de Luis de Carvajal (El Mozo)*, Gonzáles Obregón, Luis, and Rodolfo Gómez, eds. Mexico City: AGN, 1935, 211.

12. Isabel Beceiro Pita, *El Condado de Benavente en el Siglo XV.* Benavente: Centro de Estudios Benaventanos, 1998, 85.

13. The contemporary documents make a distinction between *vecino, morador,* and *estante.* Vecinos were men who owned property in a town. A morador was a person who had lived in a given place four or more years but did not own substantial property, and an estante was a temporary town dweller.

14. Vaz de Freitas, *Mercadores*, 77.

15. Processo de Álvaro de Leão, dezembro 2, 1544. ANTT, Évora, no. 8779, folio 67v.

16. In Toro's transcription of Carvajal's trial Afonso (or Alonso in Spanish) appears as Antonio, but in the original records of the trials of Carvajal and his sister his name appears as al⁰. By comparison, the same scribe abbreviated Antonio as ant⁰.

17. Initially, the jurisdiction of the Évora Inquisition seems to have included most regions of Portugal, including Mogadouro. A listing of the cities and towns from which some of the accused originated or lived is given by António Borges Coelho, *Inquisiçao de Évora, 1533–1668*. Lisboa: Editorial Caminho, 2002, 191–192.

18. Processo de Jorge de Leão, janeiro 10, 1545. ANTT, Évora, no. 11267, folio 47v.

19. *Procesos de Luis de Carvajal (El Mozo)*, 364.

20. Payment of 400 ducats to Jorge de León and Francisco de Soria. Archivo de la Real Chancillería de Valladolid, Pleitos Civiles. Alonso Pérez, fiscal. Caja 195, 1.

21. *Memorial sobre la pacificación de 1581*, enero 26–febrero 9, 1581. AGI, Patronato, Legajo 183, no. 1, ramo 2, 9. This document shows that Jorge de León de Andrade was given power of attorney to represent Carvajal in Mexico City.

22. Processo de Álvaro de Leão, dezembro 2, 1544. ANTT, Évora, no. 8779, 1.

23. Proceso contra Francisca de Carvajal, folio 102.

24. Perdão para Duarte de Leão, agosto 4, 1552. ANTT, Chancellery of D. Joan III, Perdoes e Legitimaçaos, Liv. 20, folio 168.

25. Maria Manuel Ferraz Torrão, "Rotas Comerciais, Agentes Economicos, Meios de Pagamento" in *Historia Geral de Cabo Verde*, II:29. Coordenação de Maria Emilia Madeira Santos, Praia, Cabo Verde: Instituto Nacional de Investigação Cultural, 2001.

26. *Procesos de Luis de Carvajal (El Mozo)*, 364.

27. Among them was a distinguished Jewish physician by the name of Rodrigo de Castro who was married to a Catarina Rodriguez.

28. Ferraz Torrão, "Rotas Comerciais, Agentes Economicos, Meios de Pagamento" in *Historia Geral de Cabo Verde*, II:64.

29. Zelinda Cohen, "Administração das Ilhas de Cabo Verde e seu Distrito no Segundo Século de Colonização (1560–1640)," in *Historia Geral de Cabo Verde*, II:193. In the same volume, pages 515–547, there is a compilation, by Iva Cabral, of the vecinos of Ribeira Grande in which Francisco de Andrade is mentioned. His report, dated 26 January 1582, is reprinted as the "Relação de Francisco de Andrade sobre as ilhas de Cabo Verde," in Antonio Brassio, *Monumenta Missionaria Africana*, 2ª serie, III:96–107. A translation into English of one of its sections appears in *The Discovery of the River Gambia by Richard Johnson (1623)*, David P. Gamble and P. E. H. Hair, eds. London, The Hakluyt Society, Series III, vol 2, 1999, 273–274.

30. Several examples of the Hispanicisms written by Francisco de Andrade are pointed out in the notes of the reprint. Thus, the first note points out that the word "diezmo," appearing in the first paragraph of the report is an "Espanholismo."

31. Pilar Huerga Criado, "La Familia," in *En La Raya de Portugal: Solaridad y Tensiones en la Comunidad Judeoconversa*. Salamanca: Universidad de Salamanca, 1993, 51–94.

32. The literature on the Spanish Jews and the Spanish Inquisition is rather extensive. An important earlier work, published in 1817, is Juan Antonio Llorente, *Historia crítica de la Inquisición en España*. Madrid: Hiperión, 1980. Early works in English include Henry Charles Lea, History of the Inquisition in Spain, 4 vols., New York: 1908; and Cecil Roth, The Spanish Inquisition, 1937. Recent works include B. Netanyahu, *The Origins of the Inquisition in Fifteenth Century Spain*. New York: Random House, 1995; Henry Kamen, *The Spanish Inquisition: A historical revision*, New Haven: Yale University Press, 1997.

33. Jose Ramón Ónega, *Los Judíos en el Reino de Galicia*. Madrid: Editora Nacional, 1999.

34. Jaime Contreras, *El Santo Oficio de la Inquisición de Galicia (poder, sociedad y cultura)*. Madrid: Akal/Universitaria, 1982.

35. Haim Beinart, "Return and Conversion," in *The Expulsion of the Jews from Spain*. Portland, Oregon, Littman, 2002, 329–412.

36. Joan II gave permission so that up to 600 families could enter Portugal through Zamora and Badajoz. In reality many more Jews entered that kingdom through the long and porous border (see, for example, Elias Lipner, *Os Baptizados em Pé: Estudos acerca da Origin e da Luta dos Cristãos-Novos em Portugal*. Lisboa: Vega, 1998).

37. Maria José Pimenta Ferro Tavaris, *Os Judeos em Portugal no Século XV*, Lisboa: Universidad Nova de Lisboa, 1982, 74.

38. The oldest known account of the forced conversion of the Jews in Portugal in 1497 is included in the sixteenth century work of Samuel Usque entitled *Consolaçam as Tribulaçoens de Israel*. The work has been translated and edited by Martin A. Cohen, under the title *Samuel Usque's Consolation for the Tribulations of Israel*. Philadelphia: The Jewish Publication Society of America, 1965, 201–208.

39. Standard works on the Portuguese Inquisition include Alexandre Herculano, *History da Origem e estabelecimento da Inquisição em Portugal*, 3 vols., Lisbon: 1855–1859 and J. Lucio de Azevedo, *Historia dos Christãos Novos Portugueses*, Lisboa: Libraria Clássica Editora, 1921, 43. A shorter discussion appears in Amador de los Ríos, *Historia social, Politica y Religiosa de los Judíos de España y Portugal*. Buenos Aires: editorial Bajel, 1943, II:297–326.

40. The tribunal of the Spanish Inquisition was officially installed in Mexico City in 1571 by order of Philip II, although an Ecclesiastical Inquisition had existed previously (see, Richard E. Greenleaf, *Zumárraga and The Mexican Inquisition, 1536–153*. Washington: Academy

of Franciscan History, 1961. An early discussion of the Inquisition in Mexico is included in Henry Charles Lea, *The Inquisition in the Spanish Dependencies*. London: Macmillan, 1908, 191–299. More recent works are those of Yolanda Mariel de Ibañez, *El Tribunal de la Inquisición en México (siglo XVI)*, segunda edición. Mexico City: Universidad Nacional Autónoma de México, 1979; and Solange Alberro, Inquisición y Sociedad en México 1571–1700. The most complete catalogue of those tried in Mexico City as Judaizers is *Judaizantes en la Nueva España. Catálogo de documentos en el Archivo General de la Nación* by Alicia Gojman de Bacal (Mexico City: Universidad Nacional Autónoma de México, 2006).

41. During his 1546 arraignment before the Portuguese Inquisition, Melchor stated that he was 30 or 31 years old.

42. Processo de Luis de Carvajal, janeiro 8, 1546. ANTT, Évora, no. 8976.

43. Beceiro Pita, *Condado de Benavente*, 319.

44. See Azevedo, *Historia dos Christãos Novos*, 66–111.

45. Processo de Jorge de Leão, 1.

46. Processo de Álvaro de Leão, 1.

47. Elias Lipiner, "Homens à Procura de Nome," in *Os Baptizados em Pé: Estudos acerca da Origin e da Luta dos Cristãos-Novos em Portugal*. Lisboa: Vega, 1998, 53–104.

48. Among the men named Luis de Carvajal who were known to the Crown were the Admiral of the Spanish Armada in Flanders, who is sometimes confused with Governor Carvajal, and a Crown painter whose work can be seen in the Escorial.

49. In both Portuguese and Spanish naming traditions, it is the father's surname that is transmitted to the following generation.

50. This speculation can not be confirmed because the archives in Mogadouro were burnt in 1855.

51. Toro, *Judíos en Nueva España*, 322.

52. Pleito entre Miguel Núñez y el fiscal de la Casa de la Contratación sobre que se le de licencia para tratar y comerciar en Indias (herein after referred to as *Expediente de Miguel Núñez*), 1571–1575. AGI, Indiferente, legajo 925. no. 8, 1–112.

53. *Expediente de Miguel Núñez*, 20.

54. *Diccionario de la Lengua Española, 22nd ed.* Madrid: Real Academia Española, 2001.

55. In 1589 Carvajal stated that Miguel Núñez was a Crown contractor in the slave trade in Santo Domingo. However, in 1575 Núñez insisted that his business in Santo Domingo was limited to the trading of goods with such contractors (*Expediente de Miguel Núñez*, 24).

56. Gutierre's brother was surnamed Núñez, as were three of his children. Thus, it is likely that a familial connection existed between the Carvajal and Núñez families.

57. Peter Russell, *Prince Henry 'the Navigator': A Life*. New Haven: Yale University Press, 2000, 106.

58. Toro, *Judíos en Nueva España*, 281

59. Oficio para Luis de Carvalhal. Tesoreiro das fazendas dos difuntos no islas de Santiago e Fogo no Cabo Verde, dezembro 3, 1559. ANTT, Chancellery D. Sebastião e D. Henrique. Liv. 4, folios 130r–130v, doc. 2.

60. Licencia para Luis de Carvalhal para que possa ir a Corte a negociar seus negócios por tempo de dois anos, agosto 7, 1563. ANTT, Chanceleria D. Sebastião e D. Henrique, Doações, Livro 12, folios 58r–58v, doc. 2. Cited by Iva Cabral in "Vizinhos da cidade da Ribeira Grande de 1560 a 1648," in *Historia Geral de Cabo Verde*, II:522.

61. Carvajal's statement before the Inquisition seems to imply that he got married in 1565. However, it is likely that the wedding took place in 1564 for in November of 1575 several individuals stated that the wedding took place "eleven years ago . . . and that they lived in the Magdalena Quarter." *Expediente de Miguel Núñez*, 74.

62. Miguel's parents were Nuño Alvarez and Isabel Núñez. *Expediente de Miguel Núñez*, 68.

63. Fernando Braudel, *The Mediterranean in the Age of Philip II*, second revised edition, 2 vols. New York: Harper Colophon Books, 1976, 570–604.

CHAPTER TWO

1. Toro, *Judíos en Nueva España*, 338. Carvajal's choice of words seems to indicate that he had traveled to New Spain before 1567, for it was on that year that he first *entered* that colony.

2. After a long litigation, the judges of the House of Trade denied Núñez petition. However, the Consejo de Indias approved it three years later. *Expediente de Miguel Núñez*, 12–60, 61–108.

3. The Royal Cédula says: "To the royal officers in Seville I order you not to let go to our Indies any passenger with or without a license from the Crown, unless they show you information made in their lands, by which it can be verified if they are single or married, their age and appearance, and that they are not new converts to our Holy Catholic Faith, from that of the Moors, or Jews, or son of such or of those tried (by the Inquisition) and reconciled (with the church), or sons or grandsons of those who publicly wore the Sanbenito, or sons or grandsons of those burnt at the stake, or condemned as heretics, either on the masculine or feminine line." Diego de Encinas, *Cedulario Indiano*, vols. I–IV. Reproducción facsímile de la edición única de 1596. Madrid: Ediciones Cultura Hispánica, 1945, I:397.

4. Encinas, *Cedulario*, I:440–448.

5. Nombramiento de Francisco de Vera, enero 13, 1564. AGI, Contratación, 5784, legajo 1, folios 145v–146r. An abridged version of this appointment appears in Encinas, *Cedulario*, III:223.

6. *Información de Oficio recibida en la Real Audiencia de México sobre la que dio el capitán Luis de Carvajal sobre sus Méritos y Servicios* (Herein after referred to as *Méritos de Carvajal* and abbreviated as *MDC*), enero to marzo de 1578). AGI, México, Legajo 103, S/N.

7. Testimonio de Juan de Urribari, febrero 15, 1578. *MDC*, folio 100v. Urriabrri was one of the passengers who traveled to New Spain with Carvajal. Some years later Urriabarri become *alcalde ordinario* of Tampico.

8. Testimonio de Bartolomé Pérez, enero 16, 1578. *MDC*, folio 55r.

9. In June of 1567 Francisco de Vera was in Spain trying to collect part of his salary. For this he had to initiate a legal suit, or *pleito*, against the House of Trade in Seville. The pleito document (AGI, Justicia, legajo 1182, no. 1, ramo. 3) shows that a Pedro de Estopiñán Cabeza de Vaca had represented him in Tenerife in June of 1564. There is little doubt that this was the man who dispatched Carvajal's fleet in La Palma.

10. The name of the governor is unknown. D. Pedro de Arellano was the brother in-law of D. Martín Cortés, the son of the conqueror of the Aztecs, Hernán Cortés.

11 Testimonio de Bartolomé Pérez, enero 16, 1578. *MDC*, folio 55r.

12. Testimonio de Matéo Hernán, enero 22, 1578. *MDC*, folio 13v,

13. For a short and accessible account of the Spanish conquest of the Aztecs see The Oxford History of Mexico, edited by Michael C. Meyer and William H. Beezley (New York: Oxford, 2000).

14. Salvador de Madariaga, *Hernán Cortés*, sexta edición. Mexico City: Hermes, 1955.

15. Philip W. Powell, *Soldiers, Indians & Silver*. Berkeley: University of California Press, 1969.

16. J. Lloyd Mecham, *Francisco de Ibarra and Nueva Vizcaya*. New York: Greenwood, 1968.

17. Silvio Zavala, *La Encomienda Indiana*, tercera edición. Mexico City: Porrúa, 1992; Lesley Byrd Simpson, *The Encomienda in New Spain: The Beginning of Spanish Mexico*. Berkeley: University of California Press, 1982.

18. Silvio Zavala, *El Servicio personal de los indios en la Nueva España*, 3 vols. Mexico City: El Colegio de México, 1985.

19. Alvar Núñez Cabeza de Vaca, "Naufragios," in *Historiadores Primitivos de Indias*, Enrique de Vedia, ed., Madrid: Biblioteca de Autores Españoles, 1946, I:517–518.

20. Herbert Bolton, "Coronado on the Turquoise Trail, Knight of Pueblos and Plains," in *Coronado Cuarto Centennial Publications, 1540–1949*, vol. I, G. P. Hammond, ed. Albuquerque: University of New Mexico Press, 1949.

21. Luis Gonzalez Obregón, "México Bajo el Terror," in *Los Precursors de la Independencia Mexicana en el Siglo XVI*, Mexico City: Librería de la viuda de Bouret, 1906, 337–361.

22. Antonio F. Garcia-Abasolo, *Martín Enríquez y la Reforma de 1568 en Nueva España*. Sevilla: Artes Graficas Padura, 1983.

23. Among the affidavits confirming that Carvajal bought a hacienda with cattle was the somewhat hostile statement of Diego Ramírez who said that Carvajal "came to this province and bought in it some haciendas with cows and mares." Testimonio de Diego Ramírez, febrero 25, 1578. *MDC*, folio 130v.

24. Hernán Cortés, "Second letter to Charles V," in MacNutt, *Letters of Cortés*, 2 vols. New York: Putnam, 1908, I:308.

25. Pedro de San Luis al Presidente del Consejo de Indias, diciembre 7, 1572. AGI, Patronato 29, r. 27 (1).

26. *Petición de los regidores de Tampico y de Pánuco*, enero 30, 1567. AGI, México, legajo 94, S/N, 1–31. The officers from Tampico were Diego Ramírez, Cristobal de Frías, and Antonio de Villadiego; those form San Esteban include Juan de Navarrete, Pedro de la Calle, and Francisco Martín.

27. Testimonio de Juan Lorenzo, enero 30, 1567. In *Petición de los regidores de Tampico y de Pánuco*, folio 17.

28. Testimonio de Juan Muñóz, enero 30, 1567. In *Petición de los regidores de Tampico y de Pánuco*, folio 6.

29. Marqués de Altamira, *Pacificación de los Chichimecas de la Sierra Gorda, 1755*. Facsimile reprint. Mexico: Biblioteca Aportación Histórica, 1944, 22.

30. Testimonio de Juan Lorenzo, febrero 15, 1578. *MDC*, folio 107r.

31. Testimonio de Diego Ramírez, febrero 25, 1578. *MDC*, folio 130v.

32. Testimonio des Alonso Ortiz de Zúñiga, febrero 25, 1578. *MDC*, folio 135r.

33. Martín Enríquez al rey Felipe II, in *Cartas de Indias*, I:LV.

34. Enríquez was attempting to convince the king to revoke a suspension of Villanueva as oidor. Thus, after the quoted paragraph, the viceroy wrote that "After so many unfortunate events and travails, the only thing that remains is H.M.'s mercy."

35. Petición de Luis de Carvajal before the Audiencia de México, enero 13, 1578. *MDC*, folio 25r.
36. Testimonio de Luis de Villanueva, enero 29, 1578. *MDC*, folio 62v.
37. Testimonio de Juan de Urribarri, febrero 15, 1578. *MDC*, folio 100r.

CHAPTER THREE

1. Toro, *Judíos en Nueva España*, 338.
2. For a more detailed description of this voyage see Raynor Unwin, *The Defeat of John Hawkins: A Biography of his Third Slaving Voyage*. London: Readers Union, 1921. A work of broader scope and depth is Antonio Rumeu de Armas, *Viajes de John Hawkins*. Sevilla: Escuela de Estudios Hispano-Americanos de Sevilla, 1947.
3. John Hawkins, "The unfortunate voyage made with the Jesus, the Minion, and four other ships to the parts of Guinea and the West Indies in the years 1567 and 1568," in *The Principal Navigations* by Richard Haklyut, vol. 6.
4. Eugenio de Salazar is best-known as the author of several long letters that he wrote to some of his friends. For a translation of one of those letters see John Frye, *Seafaring in the sixteenth century: The Letter of Eugenio de Salazar, 1573*. San Francisco: Mellen, 1991.
5. Eugenio de Salazar al rey, noviembre 15, 1596. The reactions of other Spaniards in Tenerife are described in several depositions made there on May of 1567. See Romeu, *Viajes de Hawkins*, Documento 19, 429–435.
6. Testimonio de Robert Barrett, octubre 8, 1568. In Romeu, *Viajes de John Hawkins*, Documento 25. For an English translation see Irene A. Wright, *Spanish Documents*. Document 28.
7. Miguel de Castellanos al rey, septiembre 26, 1568. In Romeu, *Viajes de John Hawkins*, Documento 21. For an English translation see Wright, *Spanish Documents*, Document 23.
8. Testimonio de Robert Barrett.
9. Testimonio de Antonio Delgadillo, septiembre 27–30, 1568. In Romeu, *Viajes de John Hawkins*, Documento 28. For an English translation see Wright, *Spanish Documents*, 138.
10. An analysis of the events leading to the battle appears in Wright, *Spanish Documents*, 1–26.
11. Miles Phillips, "A discourse written by one Miles Phillips, Englishman, on of the company put ashore in the West Indies by Master John Hawkins, in the year 1568," 1582, in *The Principal Navigations* by Richard Haklyut, vol. 6. Job Hortop, "The travails of Job Hortop, which Sir John Hawkins set on land within the Bay of Mexico after his departure from the Haven of S. John de Ullua in Nueva Espanna, the 8th of October, 1568," 1591, in *The Principal Navigations* by Richard Haklyut, vol. 6.
12. Testimonio de Antonio Goddard en Sevilla, noviembre 2, 1569. AGI, Indiferente, legajo 902, no. 1, no. 3, 5–10.
13. Phillips, "Discourse."
14. David Ingram, "The Relation of David Ingram of Barking," in *The Principal Navigations* by Richard Haklyut.
15. Phillips said that their journey to Tampico lasted 12 days, but Hortop's narrative as well as Spanish records show that the Englishmen arrived in Tampico seven days after they landed.
16. Phillips, "Discourse."
17. Testimonio de Antonio Goddard en Sevilla, 7.

18. Testimonio de Alonso Ortiz de Zuñiga, febrero 5, 1578. *MDC*, folio 135r.

19. In his testimony Ortiz de Zúñiga said that "he saw many scandals and passions that . . . occurred between Luis de Carvajal and Diego Ramírez . . . because this Diego Ramírez wanted take them (the prisoners), the cause not being his. And with the good attitude of Luis de Carvajal everything quieted down."

20. Luis Zegri to the Audiencia de México, septiembre 18, 1568. In Wright, *Spanish Documents*. Document 26.

21. *Diligencias hechas por el muy magnífico señor Luis de Caravajal, Alcalde Ordinario en esta villa por Su Majestad, sobre los ingleses*, octubre 8–18, 1568. AGI, Patronato, legajo 265, ramo 12, no. 3.

22. Carvajal's Diligencias states that the slaves reported seeing Englishmen, but it is unlikely that they knew that information when they saw the large group of men in the port.

23. Testimonio de Juan de Mejorada, febrero 20, 1578. *MDC*, folio 87r.

24. Testimonio de Pedro de Aguilera, enero 28, 1578. *MDC*, folio 58r.

25. According to Goddard the *Minion* carried about 90 men, and that in it there were about 40,000 ducats from the sale of slaves in Rio de Hacha and other Spanish ports.

26. This Hermandad, also referred as the *Maesta* by Ortiz de Zuñiga, was the place where cattle belonging to several owners was kept.

27. Testimonio de Pedro de Aguilera, enero 28, 1578. *MDC*, folio 58r.

28. Testimonio de Luis de Villanueva, enero 29, 1578. *MDC*, folio 62v.

29. The royal cédula establishing the Holy Office of the Inquisition in the New Spain was issued on August 16, 1570 (see Encinas, *Cedulario*, I:45) but it was not until November 4 of the following year that the decree was put into effect.

30. The inquisitional trials of two of these men, David Alexandro (Alexander) and Guillermo Calens (William Collins) appear in Julio Jimenez Rueda, ed., *Corsarios Franceses e Ingleses en la Inquisición de la Nueva España (Siglo XVI)*. Mexico City: AGN, 1945. Collins' proceso contains the names and descriptions of many others members of the group left behind by Hawkins. A complete list of those sentenced in Mexico City can be found in Yolanda Mariel's *Tribunal de la Inquisición*.

Chapter Four

1. *Comisión Título de Capitán para Luis de Carvajal*, abril 11, 1572. AGI, México, legajo 103, S/N, folios 87v–88v.

2. Samuel Temkin, "El Descubrimiento Europeo del Valle de Monterrey," *Revista de Humanidades*, no. 19, (2005): 117–143.

3. Sherburne F. Cook and Woodrow Borah, *The Indian Population of Central México, 1531–1600*. Berkeley: University of California, 1960.

4. Martín Enríquez a Carvajal, abril 17, 1572. AGI, México legajo 103, no. 4.

5. Testimonio de Nicolas Hernán, enero 24, 1578. *MDC*, folio 19v.

6. Testimonio de Juan Lorenzo, febrero 15, 1578. *MDC*, folio 107v.

7. *Ibid.*

8. Prior to the recent finding of the document about the merits of Carvajal (*MDC*), it was known that a discovery journey had taken place, but it was believed that the person charged with the task had been D. Francisco de Puga. The source of that belief was John

Chilton, a sixteenth century English traveler who wrote about his adventures in the New World many years after they took place. (Chilton, "Discourse." In *The Principal Navigations*.) While his account has several other factual errors, it is useful to repeat here some of its passages, starting mid way, after he arrived in New Spain. Referring to the discovery journey he said that: "After I came to Mexico [City], which was in the yere 1572 . . . [I came] to a towne where Christians inhabited, which was called S. Iago de los Valles. . . . In this towne I remained eighteene dayes . . . and in the meane space there came one Don Francisco de Pago, whom the viceroy Don Henrico Manriques had sent for captaine generall, to open and discover a certeine way from the sea side to the mines of Sacatecas. . . . So this captaine tooke me . . . with the rest of his soldiers, to the number of forty . . . and five hundred Indians, which we tooke out of two towns . . . called Tanchipa, and Tamaclipa . . . and went thence to the river de las Palmas. . . . Within thirty dayes after, travelling thorow woods, hilles, and mountaines, we came to the mines of Sacatecas." Leaving aside the obvious spelling errors, it noted that the narrative mentions some events that are corroborated by the Spanish documents. On the other hand, the narrative contains several erroneous statements. For example, the name of the person charged with the discovery of the road. Also the name of the viceroy ordering the discovery indicates some confusion between Martín Enríquez, the viceroy ordering the journey, and Álvaro Manrique, who was viceroy between 1585 and 1590, when Chilton wrote his narrative. More importantly, Chilton's statement that after gathering the Indians in Tanchipa and Tamaholipa, they went to the Río de las Palmas, and from there to Zacatecas. This is problematic because those two locations are in nearly opposite directions from Tanchipa.

9. Testimonio de Bartolomé Rodríguez, enero 25, 1578. *MDC*, folio 55v.

10. Testimonio de Juan Lorenzo, febrero. *MDC*, folio 107v.

11. Among the soldiers joining Carvajal in Mazapil were Gaspar de Vargas and Geronimo de Zarfate.

12. Vito Alessio Robles, Coahuila y Tejas, 61. Cano's narrative of his discovery appears in Valentina Garza Mertónez and Juan Manuel Pérez Zevallos, *El Real y Minas de San Gregorio de Mazapil 1568–1700*. Zacatecas: Municipio de Mazapil, 2004.

13. Testimonio de Juan Lorenzo. *MDC*, folio 108r,

14. Luis de Carvajal, enero 15, 1578. *MDC*, folio 79v.

15. Temkin, "Descubrimiento."

16. It seems that the canyon discovered by Carvajal was still used in 1739. In a description of the settlements in Nuevo Reino de León (Antonio Ladrón de Guevara, *Noticias de los Poblados*) it states that to go from Saltillo to Monterrey "it is necessary to pass through a port in a canyon, for about two or three leagues."

17. Joseph Goldsborough, *Sketch to correct the maps of the route of Genl. Wool's division, of Journey from Monclova to Monterrey, 1846*. US Library of Congress. G4450 1846 .B72 Vault.

18. Testimonio de Juan Lorenzo. *MDC*, folio 198r.

19. It is likely that the river Santa Catarina was so named in honor of Carvajal's own mother.

20. Testimonio de Geronimo de Zarfate, febrero 6, 1578. *MDC*, folio 84.

21. Testimonio de Juan de Urribarri, febrero 15, 1578. *MDC*, folio 105r.

22. In his testimony, Diego García stated that "he went to the Río de Palmas and close to Río Bravo which said captain passed." Enero 17, 1578, *MDC*, folio 9r.

23. In his testimony Pedro de Portes stated that "said captain returned to the pueblo of Tamaholipa, where this witness was waiting for him in the company of Antonio Pedraza,

who at that time was alcalde mayor of the province." febrero 12, 1578, *MDC*, folio 73r.

24. Escribanía de Pedro de Villalta, f.1, Libro del año 1574. This document appears to be lost. It is listed in *Catalogo de los Fondos Americanos del Archivo de Protocolos de Sevilla. Tomo 1, Siglo XVI*. Madrid: Compañía Iberoamericana, 1930, 435–436. Incidentally, the Francisca de Carvajal mentioned in the summary was not Carvajal's sister because, at that time, she was named Francisca Núñez.

25. The man who appeared before the public notary in Seville said he lived in the Magdalena quarter, which was the neighborhood where Carvajal and his wife lived. It is unlikely that two men by the same name lived in the same part of Seville at the same time. In addition, that man was the master of a ship that made the rounds between the New World and Spain, which Carvajal did. 26. The 1573 instructions about the new discoveries, pacifications, and settlements appear in Encinas, *Cedulario Indiano*, vol. IV, 232–246.

27. Howard F. Cline, "The Relaciones Geográficas of the Spanish Indies, 1577–1586." *HAHR*, Vol. 44, No. 3, (Aug., 1964), 341–374. For a discussion of the Meztitlán map see Barbara E. Mundy, *The Mapping of New Spain*. Chicago: University of Chicago Press, 1996, 38–44.

28. *Comisión para Luis de Carvajal*, abril 9, 1576. *MDC*, folios 89r–90r.

29. Martín Enríquez al rey D. Felipe II, enero 9, 1574, *Cartas de Indias*, I, LV.

30. The viceroy's order stated that the leaders of the uprising should be punished "in the manner of war." As for the others, it said that "if they are eighteen years or older, they should have their thumbs cut so that they cannot do harm with their arrows, and cut their feet so that they cannot spy nor return to such activities. And those from the ages of eleven to eighteen, whether men or women, their service is to be distributed among himself and his soldiers, so that said service can be sold and they can be sold for a period of twelve years. And those who are under eleven years old, he should send to this city, before me, so that I can send them to be indoctrinated and whatever is convenient in the salvation of their souls. . . . And in those cases that seem doubtful, they should rule in favor of the Indians."

31. Testimonio de Pedro de Portes, *MDC*, folios 70v–77v.

32. Testimonio de Juan Delgado, enero 24, 1578. *MDC*, folio 23. Delgado was the alguacil mayor in Puga's company and stated that "when they had gone to see the situation in Xalpa, they found Capt. Luis de Carvajal in the town of Xililta.

33. In his testimony Delgado added that "by order of Don Francisco de Puga, this witness carried the orders and letters from the viceroy to Capt. Luis de Carvajal, finding him in the town of Guejutla, in the province of Pánuco."

34. Martín Enríquez a Carvajal, junio 5, 1576, In this letter the viceroy stated that: "I now have to say is that in your letter of 26 May I see how you are getting ready to go to Xalpa."

35. Testimonio de Francisco de Aguilar, enero 25, 1578. *MDC*, folios 50v–54v.

36. *Idem.*, folio 52r.

37. Testimonio de Nicolás Pimentel, enero 24, 1578. *MDC*, folio 45r.

38. Testimonio de Francisco de Aguilar, *MDC*, folio 53r.

39. *Advertimientos del virrey Martín Enríquez al Conde de Coruña*, septiembre 25, 1580. AGI, México, legajo 20, no. 40.

40. Martín Enríquez a Carvaja, abril 22, 1576. AGI, México, legajo 103, folio 21.

41. In his testimony Portes declared that "even if by his Comisión he [Carvajal] had the power to proceed against said rebelling Indians and make them slaves and profit much from this . . . he procured to insure the safety of the Indians, and pacified them without doing them any harm."

42. Viceroy Enríquez' order about Xalpa, mayo 28, 1576. AGI, México, legajo 103, folio 22.

43. Martín Enríquez a Carvajal, octubre 26, 1576. AGI, México, legajo 103, S/N.
44. Martín Enríquez a Carvajal, junio 27, 1576. AGI, México, legajo 103, S/N.
45. Martín Enríquez a Carvajal, noviembre 10, 1576. AGI, México, legajo 103, S/N.
46. Bosquejo de un fuerte. Unidentified sketch. AGI, Mapas y Planos, México, 561.
47 Testimonio de Nicolás Pimentel, *MDC*, folio 45v.
48. Testimonio de Francisco de Aguilar, *MDC*, folio 53r.
49. Among the individuals who gave testimony about Xalpa was Nicolás Pimentel who said: "And so that the Indians of Xalpa remained without fear, he relocated the town to a safer part." *MDC*, folio 45r.
50. Testimonio de Francisco de Aguilar, *MDC*, folio 53r.
51. Orden del Viceroy Enríquez a sus captains en Chichimeca, julio 30, 1576. AGI, México, legajo 103, folio 90v.
52. Testimonio de Pedro de Herbiti, *MDC*, folios 64v–68v.
53. Testimonio de Diego García, enero 17, 1578. *MDC*, folios 8r–11v.
54. Primo Feliciano Velázquez, *Historia de San Luis Potosí*, 3 vols. Mexico City: Sociedad de Geografía y Estadística, 1946, I:314–320. Although Velázquez stated that the affidavits from the witnesses he presented were found by Joaquin Meade, he did not provide a citation for the original document. Meade himself appears to refer to the Valles Información in two separate works ("Luis de Carvajal y de la Cueva: Capitán en la Huasteca y Gobernador del Nuevo Reino de Leon", *Estilos*, 201–206, 1946; *Historia de Valles*. San Luis Potosí: Sociedad Potosina de Estudios Históricos, 1970), but neither one includes the quotations that appear in Velazquez's book.
55. Velázquez, *Historia de San Luis Potosí*, 320.
56. Idem., 317.
57. Idem., 330.
58. In a letter to Felipe II, the fiscal of the Audiencia, Eugenio de Salazar, mentioned that on August 8, 1587 the king ordered to "punish those found guilty of having taken as slaves certain Indians that Capt. Luis de Carvajal pacified in the Sierra de Xalpa." Salazar's response (diciembre 5, 1588, AGI, Mexico, legajo 71, ramo 2, no. 32, doc. 3, folio 2.), was that a decision had been made and that he was ordering that all documents be gathered so that the order be obeyed. However, the audiencia had absolved Francisco Guerrero on April 25, 1585. See Meade, *Historia de Valles*, 63.

CHAPTER FIVE

1. *Asiento y Capitulación con el Capitán Luis de Carvajal sobre el Descubrimiento y Población del Nuevo Reino de León*, mayo 31, 1579. AGI, Indiferente, 416, legajo 7, 1–31.
2. A more detailed description of these events appears, in Samuel Temkin "La Capitulación de Luis de Carvajal," *Revista de Humanidades*, no. 23, (2007): 105–140.
3. Encinas, *Cedulario*, 4:234–236.
4. At the time, the Crown officers in Tampico were the alcalde ordinario, Juan Navarrete, and the regidores Diego Ramírez, Sancho Frías, Francisco Nieto and Alvaro Pinto.
5. At the same time that Carvajal's Información was sent to the king, several other petitions were also transmitted. Of these, only Carvajal's resulted in a significant reward. (Martín Enríquez al rey, March 26, 1578. AGI, México, legajo 20, no. 6.)

6. In addition to goods and passengers from New Spain, the fleet carried many official documents, including Carvajal's Información de Oficio. (Martín Enríquez al rey, March 26, 1578. AGI, México, legajo 20, no. 6).

7. Schäfer, *El Consejo Real y Supremo de las Indias*. Sevilla: Universidad de. Sevilla, 1935.

8. Encinas, *Cedulario*, 1:1–24.

9. Stafford Poole, *Juan de Ovando*. Norman: Oklahoma, 2004.

10. Ordenanza 21 required that petitions for a royal privilege should not be considered unless all members were present in the discussion. After deliberation, the council would vote on it (Ordenanza 32), and, if approved, the petition would be elevated to the king.

11. Consejo de Indias al rey, febrero 26, 1579. AGI México, legajo 103, S/N.

12. The addition of "la Cueva" was necessary to distinguish him from two men namend Luis de Carvajal. One was the Admiral of the Spanish Armada in Flanders in the 1550s, when Carvajal lived in Cape Verde, and the other was an artist who at that time had been engaged to paint some frescoes in the basilica in El Escorial.

13. This was a reference to the capitulación of Pedro Menéndez. A complete transcription of that document appears in Milagro del Vaz Mingo, *Las capitulaciones de Indias en el siglo XVI*, Madrid: Instituto de Cooperación Interamericana, 1986, 405–412.

14. In general, once a ruling had been made by the Crown, no appeal existed, although they were allowed for meritorious petitions (Ordenanza 30). However, because of time limitations, no petition would be seen for a third time (Ordenanza 31).

15. La segunda suplicación de Carvajal, March 28, 1579. AGI, México, legajo 103, S/N.

16. Consejo de Indias al rey, abril 14, 1579. AGI, México, legajo 103, S/N.

17. The first transcription of the capitulación was made by Milagro del Vas Mingo in 1986. Since then it has been transcribed, independently, by several individuals, including the present author, whose translation appears in Appendix C.

18. Raymond L. Lee, "Cochineal production and trade in New Spain to 1600," *The Americas*, 4, (1948):449–473.

19. Instrucciones para Descubrimientos, Pacificaciones y Nuevas Poblaciones. Encinas, *Cedulario*, 4:232–246.

20. The terms legas, llanas y abonadas, stipulated, respectively, that Carvajal should not have an ecclesiastical position, that he not be a nobleman, and that he should have enough capital to pay the bonds should the need arise.

21. The original version of the granting paragraph appears in a 1585 document, where it was introduced as supporting evidence in a jurisdictional dispute.

22. Roland Chardon, "The Elusive Spanish League: A Problem of Measurement in Sixteenth-Century New Spain," *HAHR*, Vol. 60, no. 2. (1980): 294–302.

23. The first six cédulas of Carvajal contain the following statement: "I received this cédula in the original on 30 June of 1579. Luis de Carvajal." Thus, the AGI copy of the whole document was completed no later than one month after Carvajal received the capitulación.

CHAPTER SIX

1. Toro, *Judíos en Nueva España*, 291.

2. In Mirandela lived the descendants of Melchor Vázquez; Cortiços was the town where Álvaro and Jorge de León had lived.

3. AGI, Indiferente, legajo 416, Libro 7, folio 32. Although the king allowed many individuals to go to the New World without showing the required information, this seems to be the only time that he gave that dispensation to a large number of unnamed colonizers.

4. The process required that individuals wishing to emigrate to the New World should obtain both an official permit in Madrid, and, in the province of origin, an Información about their limpieza de sangre.

5. Peter Boyd-Bowman, "Patterns of Spanish Emigration to the Indies until 1600," *HAHR* 56, No. 4 (1976), 580–604. Boyd-Bowman's work shows that slightly more than 80% of those who went to the New World in the sixteenth century did so prior to 1580. More detailed information about the Spanish emigration can be found in José Luis Martínez, *Pasajeros de Indias–Viajes Trasatlánticos en el Siglo XVI*, tercera edición. Mexico City: Fondo de Cultura Económica, 1999, Chapter XIV.

6. *Relación de las personas nombradas por Luis de Carvajal en Sevilla*. 1580. AGI, Contratación, legajo 5538, Libro 1, folios 478r–483r. This important document, referred in this work as the *1580 List*, was found by Peter Boyd-Bowman in the early 1970s. For a transcription of this document that preserves its format see Israel Cavazos Garza, *Relación de las Personas*. Monterrey: Universidad Autónoma de Nuevo León, 1977.

7. Toro, *Judíos en Nueva España*, 291–292.

8. At least three of the individuals appearing in the 1580 List had permission from the Crown to go to New Spain. These were Alonso Rodríguez de Jaque, Pedro de Prado, and D. Juan de Portugal.

9. The colonizers mentioned in 1589 by Carvajal but not declared by him in 1580 were Pedro de Cearreta, Diego Márquez, Gregorio Pérez, Francisco López, and *Fulano* Lucero.

10. Boyd-Bowman, "Patterns of Spanish Emigration."

11. Poder a Diego Ruiz de Ribera, febrero 17, 1580. AHP, Escribanía de Juan Bernal de Heredia. Oficio 21, libro 1, folio 1019.

12. Contrato entre el Gobernador Luis de Carvajal y Diego de Madrid, enero 22, 1580. AHP 14288. Escribanía de Juan Bernal de Heredia. Oficio 21, Libro 1, folio 815; Contrato entre el Gobernador Luis de Carvajal y Juan de Saucedo, enero 25, 1580. AHP 14288. Escribanía de Juan Bernal de Heredia. Oficio 21, Libro 1, folio 819v.

13. Contrato entre el Gobernador Luis de Carvajal y Domingo Martínez de Cearreta, febrero 7, 1580. AHP 14288. Escribanía de Juan Bernal de Heredia. Oficio 21, Libro 1, folio 1001; Contrato entre el Gobernador Luis de Carvajal y ciertos hombres solteros, febrero 9, 1580. AHP 14288. Escribanía de Juan Bernal de Heredia. Oficio 21, Libro 1, folio 1005.

14. *Procesos de Luis de Carvajal (El Mozo)*, 50–55. In 1589 el Mozo said his father had taught him the Law of Moses five years earlier. Since he was born in 1567, it follows that he was 17 years old when he was told about his Jewish background.

15. On 13 February, 1580 Blanca Rodríguez, her three children—Nuño Álvarez de Ribera, Guiomar de Ribera, and Isabel de Ribera, appeared with Carvajal before a public notary to name her as the administrator of the estate of her recently deceased husband. AHP, Protocolos, 14288. Escribanía de Juan Bernal de Heredia, Oficio 21, Libro 1, folios 1073–1078.

16. Traspaso de poder sobre la nao *Nuestra Señora de la Luz*, enero 2, 1580. AHP, 14288. Escribanía de Juan Bernal de Heredia, Oficio 21, Libro 1, folio 804.

17. Cohen, *Martyr*, 63.

18. *Procesos de Luis de Carvajal (El Mozo)*, 80; Toro, *Judíos en Nueva España*, 264. An urca was a type of ship designed to hold a large quantity of cargo.

19. Luis de Carvajal al rey, octubre 15, 1580. AGI, México, legajo 104, ramo 3, S/N.

20. *Procesos de Luis de Carvajal (El Mozo)*, 80.

21. The date of departure of the fleet has been take to be June 1, 1580 because El Mozo stated (*Procesos de Luis de Carvajal*, 80) that the fleet left Seville on the day of the Santisima Trinidad (Pentecost). While that date is approximately correct, its deduction is not because, in 1580, the Julian calendar was in effect, which means that Pentecost fell on 22 May.

22. Letter from the Consejo de Indias to the authorities in Cádiz. June 10, 1580. AGI, Indiferente, legajo 1956, Libro 3, folio 98.

23. Lista de maestres y naos despachadas para la provincia de la Nueva España el año de 1580, junio 10, 1580. AGI, Contratación, legajo 2899, Libro 1, folio 2r.

24. Francisco de Luján al rey, noviembre 20, 1580. AGI, México, legajo 104, ramo 3.

25. Audiencia de México al rey, noviembre 13, 1580. AGI, México, legajo 70, ramo 3, no. 36.

26. Toro, *Judíos en Nueva España*, 292

27. Hoyo, *Historia de Nuevo León*, 221–225.

28. Toro, *Judíos en Nueva España*, 340.

29. Felipe II a Pedro Moya de Contreras, junio 17, 1580. Doc. no. 98 in the Hans P. Kraus Collection of Hispanic American Manuscripts, Library of Congress.

30. Felipe II a las autoridades en Sevilla, mayo 3, 1580. AGI, Indiferente, legajo 1969, Libro 3, folios 152v–153r.

31. Francisco de Luján al rey, noviembre 20, 1580.

32. Luis de Carvajal al rey, octubre 15, 1580. AGI, México, legajo 104, r.3, S/N.

CHAPTER SEVEN

1. Luis de Carvajal al rey, 15 octubre 15, 1580. AGI, México, legajo 104, ramo 3, S/N.

2. According to Carvajal the three villages "had no more than 22 or 23 burghers" before he arrived.

3. Testimonio de Felipe Núñez, septiembre 1, 1587. *NGI*, 44.

4. *Advertimientos de D. Martín Enríquez al Conde de Coruña*, septiembre 25, 1580. AGI, Mexico, legajo 20, no. 40.

5. Luis de Carvajal al rey, 18 febrero of 1581.

6. The document showing the viceroy obeying the king's cédula about the towns given to Carvajal appears as a notarized copy in AGI, México, legajo 110, ramo 1, S/N.

7. Obeying a royal cédula required the intended person to kiss and read the document, and then putting it over his head to indicate submission to the king.

8. Audiencia de México al rey, noviembre 13, 1580. The wording used by the Audiencia about Carvajal's capitulación indicates that they had not received their copy of that document directly from the king but had seen only that copy given to Carvajal. The reason for this was that, as mentioned on page 106 of this work, no official documentation arrived in New Spain with the 1580 fleet.

9. Testimonios de Felipe Núñez, Juan Clavijo Carvajal, and Juan de Carvajal. *NGI*, 45, 70, and 86. Also, according to Juan F. Zorrilla ("Crónica de Tamaholipa, La Fundación," *Humanitas*, vol. 22, pp. 239–254, 1981), the payment of the bonds appears in a document found by Joaquin Meade that shows several individuals lending Carvajal 8,000 ducats for

the payment of the required bond. Among those individuals are Hernando de Medina, Sebastián Rodriguez, and Leonel de Cervantes, and Simon de Coca.

10. Reporte de la Audiencia de México, noviembre 13, 1580. AGI, México, legajo 70, r.3, no. 36.

11. Testimonio de Felipe Núñez, *NGI*, 45.

12. Luis de Carvajal al rey, 18 febrero 1581. Document #2 in the J. Lloyd Mecham Collection in the Nettie Lee Benson Latin American Collection of the University of Texas at Austin.

13. *Memorial sobre la Pacificación de 1581* (Herein after referred to as *Pacificación de 1581*), enero 26–febrero 9, 1581. AGI, Patronato, legajo 183, no. 1, ramo 2, 1–40.

14. Luis de Carvajal, enero 21, 1581. *Pacificación de 1581*, 9

15. Testimonio de Matheo García, febrero 1, 1581. *Pacificación de 1581*, 29.

16. All statements during the discussion between the Tamapache Indians and Carvajal were translated by two interpreters and verified by the scribe, Hernán Pérez, who understood both Spanish and the language of the Indians, called Guastecan in the document.

17. This is a reference to the *Discovery Journey*. The statement implies that the Indians from Tamapache knew and remembered what Carvajal had done on that journey.

18. Luis de Carvajal al rey, 18 febrero of 1581.

19. Felipe II al Conde de Coruña, abril 19, 1583. AGI, Indiferente, 416, legajo 7, 72.

20. Eugenio de Salazar al rey, junio 30, 1583. AGI, México, Legajo 70, ramo 6, no. 95.

21. Traspaso de poder a Pedro de Vega, Abril 6, 1581. *Pacificación de 1581*, 8.

22. The royal order from the Audiencia appears as a notarized copy in AGI, México, legajo 110, Ramo 1, S/N, 11–22.

23. Alonso de León, *"Relaciones y Discursos,"* 90.

24. Chapter 13 of the first part of the capitulación gave the viceroy the right to change anything he did not like in it. For unknown reasons he did not, although the Audiencia, of which he was President, contested the decision.

25. Eugenio de Salazar al rey, from Guatemala, enero 20, 1582. AGI, Guatemala, legajo 10, ramo 9, no. 95. In this letter Salazar promised the king that he would depart for Mexico City before the end of the month.

CHAPTER EIGHT

1. Luis de Carvajal a Pedro Moya de Contreras, abril 20, 1582. AGI, México, legajo 336b, Doc. 160.

2. The date of Carvajal's departure to the north appears in AGI, Méxicom legajo 103. For the location of Tamaholipa see Joaquin Meade, *La Huasteca: Época Antigua*. Mexico City: Publicaciones Históricas, 1942, 315.

3. Juan de la Magdalena a Pedro Moya de Contreras, abril 23, 1582. AGI, México, legajo 336b, Doc. 160. Madalena was a Franciscan friar who had gone to New Spain in 1543 with Bishop Juan de Zumarraga. See Encinas, *Cedulario*, 4:221.

4. Testimonio de Francisco Leyva Bonilla, 20 octubre 1587. *NGI*, 129–135. Leyva Bonilla was one of the leaders of an expedition to Nuevo México. (See George P. Hammond and Agapito Rey, *The Rediscovery of New Mexico, 1580–1594*. Albuquerque: University of New Mexico Press, 1966, 48–50.)

5. The date of the foundation of Saltillo appears in a document found by Wigberto Jimenez in 1950. See his *Estudios de Historia Colonial*. Mexico City: INAH, 1958, 101–105.

6. Alonso de León, *"Relaciones y Discursos,"* 75.

7. Testimonio de Felipe Núñez. *NGI,* 60. According to Núñez, the city of León was near Paraje de los Papagayos. At present, there exist, slightly to the southeast of the Sierra los Picachos, a small town named Papagayos.

8. The date of foundation of Cueva de León appears as a notarized copy in AGI, Mexico, 110, r. 1, S/N.

9. Luis de Carvajal a Pedro Moya Contreras, Abril 20, 1582.

10. Juan de la Madalena a Pedro Moya Contreras, Abril 23, 1582.

11. Testimonio de Juan Gonzále. *NGI,* 28.

12. Testimonio de Juan de Carvajal, septiembre 1, 1587. *NGI,* 89. The name of the alcalde mayor of León at the time of its foundation is not known. However, on June 30, 1583 Carvajal appointed Gabriel de Mansilla to that position, with jurisdiction in both León and Cueva de León. The appointment was confirmed by the officers of Cueva de León. Among those signing the document were Alberto del Canto, Gonzalo Pérez Ferro, and Diego de Montemayor, then lieutenant of governor of Nuevo Reino de León. Both the appointment and its confirmation appear in *Informaciónes de Gabriel Mansilla,* 1585. AGI, México, legajo 218, no.4.

13. Felipe II a Pedro Moya Contreras, junio 17, 1580.

14. Pedro Moya Contreras al rey, noviembre 20, 1582. AGI, México, legajo 336b.

15. Testimonio de Juan González. *NGI,* 30.

16. Testimonio de Juan Clavijo Carvajal.. *NGI,* 69–79.

17. Testimonio de Felipe Núñez. NGI, 58.

18. It is interesting that the reason used by Leyva Bonilla to enter Nuevo México was that he had been commissioned to punish some Indians who had caused some damages in Nueva Vizcaya. See, *Hammond and Ray, Rediscovery of New Mexico,* 323.

19. Testimonio de Francisco Leyva Bonilla, octubre 20, 1587. *NGI,* 133–134.

20. Testimonio de Matheo del Rio, septiembre 16, 1587. *NGI,* 107–108.

21. Testimonio de Juan Clavijo Carvajal. *NGI,* 72.

22. Testimonio de Juan González. *NGI,* 28.

23. J. Lloyd Mecham, "Antonio de Espejo and his Journey to New Mexico," *Southwestern Historical Quarterly,* 1926, XXX:115–138.

24. Toro, *Judíos en Nueva España,* 341.

25. *Relación de Antonio de Espejo,* in CDII, 15:101–126, octubre de 1583. For a translation into English of this document is see Hammond and Ray, Rediscovery of New Mexico, 213–231.

26. *Relación de Antonio de Espejo,* 103.

27. Testimonio de Juan González. *NGI,* 28.

28. Among those who said they saw Espejo's Comisión were Juan Clavijo Carvajal, Juan González, and Pedro Hernández de Almanza.

29. Testimonio de Juan de Carvajal. *NGI,* 87.

30. Testimonio de Pedro Hernández de Almanza, septiembre 16, 1587. *NGI,* 110–119.

31. *Relación de Antonio de Espejo,* 103.

32. J. Lloyd Mecham, "Antonio de Espejo."

33. An earlier expression of that desire appears in the letter that Juan de la Madalena wrote to Moya de Contreras on April of 1582, months before Espejo's departure. In that letter he

stated that "My purpose is to go forward with the pacification and to go to Nuevo México."

34. Antonio de Espejo a Pedro Moya Contreras, octubre 30, 1583. See Hammond and Rey, *Rediscovery of New Mexico*, 232.

35. According to Felipe Núñez, another village, named San Joseph, was also founded near the mines of San Gregorio, but this seems to have failed.

36. As reported by several witnesses in Nueva Galicia, Gaspar Castaño de Sosa was commissioned by Carvajal to found the village of San Luis. These affidavits, as well as other records, show that Castaño de Sosa was also the first alcalde mayor of that village.

37. Testimonio de Diego González, septiembre 16, 1587. *NGI*, 102.

38. A document dated March 1 of 1583 shows Carvajal giving some land to Manuel de Mederos. See, J. Eleuterio González, *Documentos para la Historia del Estado de Nuevo León*, Monterrey: Universidad de Nuevo León, 1867, 59–60.

39. The information about Canto appears in a 1643 document that was found by Wigberto Jímenez Moreno. A short summary of the document appears in his *Estudios de Historia Colonial (Mexico City*: INAH, 1958*)*. A complete transcription appears in Eugenio del Hoyo under the name of *El Documento del Parral* (Monterrey: Al Voléo, 1992).

40. Testimonio de Felipe Núñez, septiembre 1, 1587. *NGI*, 51

41. The appointment of Francisco Abreu appears as a notarized copy in AGI, Mexico, legajo 110, r. 1 S/N, 75.

42. Eugenio de Salazar al rey, febrero 25, 1586. AGI, México, legajo 70, ramo 9, no. 127.

43. Audiencia de México al rey, diciembre 5, 1588. AGI, México, legajo 71, ramo 2, no. 32.

44. Testimonio de Juan González. *NGI*, 32.

45. Testimonio de Juan de Carvajal. *NGI*, 97.

46. Testimonio de Felipe Núñez. *NGI*, 35–36.

47. Testimonio de Juan de Ochoa, octubre 20, 1587. NGI, 124.

CHAPTER NINE

1. *Real Ejecutoria dada en favor de Luis de Carvajal*, junio 7, 1585. AGI, México, legajo 110, R.1, S/N. The 97 page document is a narrative of the pleito Salazar vs. Carvajal that includes several other documents of historical importance. For simplicity the document is referred here as the *Ejecutoria*, the name it uses to refer to itself.

2. *Información de Luis de Carvajal de 1583*, mayo 31–junio 5, *Ejecutoria*, 21–34.

3. Among the 20 towns listed by the witnesses, the most populous were Tamecín, 80 Indians; Taxicun, 40; Tanboal, 40; Tancuela, 30; Tantulan, 28.

4. *Ejecutoria*, 23

5. *Información de Juan de Villaseñor de 1583*, junio 6–9, *Ejecutoria*, 54–68. Villaseñor also listed Valles and the names of the European owners of haciendas and encomendias.

6. One of Villaseñor witnesses was Juan Roman, who said that in Tancolol an Indian officer *told* him that "Luis de Carvajal had done them damage by taking away the offices and charges that they had before"

7. *Ejecutoria*, 30

8. The ordenanzas for the Consejo de Indias and for the Audiencias are listed in Encinas, *Cedulario*, I:1–301.

9. Encinas, *Cedulario*, I:262.

10. Among his literary works are some letters he wrote to friends, some of which appear in *Cartas de Eugenio de Salazar a Muy Particulares Amigos Suyos*, Pascual de Gayangos, ed., (Madrid, Sociedad de Bibliófilos Españoles, 1866). This work includes Salazar's well-known letter about seafaring in 1573.

11. Eugenio de Salazar al rey, junio 30, 1583. AGI, México, legajo 70, ramo 6, no. 95. The first paragraph of Salazar's letter says: "God took Viceroy Conde de Coruña. And the Audiencia, in agreement with the royal cédula took the government, because of which I, with great satisfaction and zeal to serve Y.M. (manuscript torn at this point) this position until Y.M. provides a person to occupy that chair." The missing words probably stated his elevated position, for the reference is to 'this position.'

12. Eugenio de Salazar al rey, noviembre 15, 1596. AGI, México, legajo 71, ramo 10, no. 142, 1–10.

13. A brief biography of Eugenio de Salazar appears in *Cartas de Eugenio de Salazar*.

14. Salazar seems to have disregarded his own interests, a fact that resulted in his dying a poor man. His death probably occurred in early October of 1602 for on the 19th of that month the Consejo de Indias paid the sum of 500 ducats for his burial (AGI, Indiferente, 427, legajo 31, folio 187r). A year later the Consejo order that his widow be paid three hundred ducats "in attention to her needs." (AGI, Indiferente, 427, Legajo 31, folio 218v).

15. Eugenio de Salazar al rey, noviembre 6, 1582. AGI, México, legajo 70, ramo 5, no. 79. This letter contains a list of the issues Salazar dealt with during his first year in the Audiencia de México.

16. *Ejecutoria*, 4.

17. *Ejecutoria*, 70.

18. *Ejecutoria*, 79.

19. Eugenio de Salazar al rey, noviembre 1, 1583. AGI, México, legajo 70, ramo 6, no. 102.

20. *Ejecutoria*, 80

21. *Ejecutoria*, 86–87

22. *Orden a Luis de Carvajal sobre Valles*, septiembre 14, 1584. AGI, México, legajo 104, ramo 3, S/N. The order was issued on Salazar's request.

23. Información de Francisco Guerrero, agosto 25–29, 1584. AGI, México, legajo 104, ramo 3, S/N.

24. *Ejecutoria*, 91.

CHAPTER TEN

1. Álvaro Manrique de Zúñiga al rey, noviembre 15, 1586. AGI, México, legajo 20, no. 135, folios 24–28 and 38.

2. Antonio F. Garcia-Abasolo, *Martín Enríquez y la Reforma de 1568 en Nueva España*. Sevilla: Artes Graficas Padura, 1983; Philip W. Powell, "Portrait of an American Viceroy: Martín Enríquez, 1568–1583," *The Americas*, Vol. 14, No. 1 (Jul., 1957), 1–24.

3. *Provisión para visitar al Marqués de Villamanrique*. Encinas, *Cedulario*, 3:68–69, agosto 31, 1589.

4. Cargos que resultaron de la visita secreta que esta tomando el doctor don Diego Romano, Obispo de Tlaxcala a D. Álvaro Manrique de Zúñiga, Marqués de Villamanriquea, nd,

AGI, México, legajo 22, no. 158, 1–81. Additional charges appear in AGI, México 22, no. 158, doc. 4, 1–18. Villamanrique's defense appears in AGI, México, legajo 22, no. 158, doc. 2, 1–36; Romano's rebuttal appears in AGI, México 22, no. 158, doc. 3, 1–17.

5. Charge number 30 against Villamanrique states that he "had ordered to the officers in the city of Veracruz to collect all the letters that would go and arrive and should send them to him, as it was done, even if they were from the Audiencia and Inquisition, prelates and other persons."

6. Charge number 29 says that "occupying such an important and prominent position, he was not composed and was choleric in great measure, whether dealing with business matters or presiding in the agreements and in the Audiencias."

7. Audiencia de Nueva Galicia al rey, Enero 21, 1588. AGI, Guadalajara, 6, R.12, N.80/1-8. For a description of the confrontation between Villamanrique and the Audiencia in Guadalajara see John H. Parry, *The Audiencia of New Galicia in the Sixteenth Century*. Cambridge: Cambridge University Press, 1948.

8. Luis de Velasco II was appointed Captain General of New Spain on June 19, 1589. AGI, Patronato, legajo 293, no. 12, ramo 5. Apparently he had been appointed viceroy earlier for this cédula says: "Given that I have appointed as my viceroy and Governor of New Spain "

9. Marqués de Altamira, *Pacificación de los Chichimecas*.

10. Villamanrique's orders to Carvajal and to Guerrero appear in AGI. México, legajo 110, ramo 5, no. 51.

11. Testimonio de Felipe Núñez. *NGI*, 67.

12. Luis de Carvajal al rey sobre Villamanrique, enero 30, 1587. AGI, México, legajo 110, ramo 5, no. 51. Fearing that the letter and documents might be intercepted by the viceroy, Carvajal sent them with Manuel Gómez, an officer in Nuevo Reino de León.

13. Carvajal's petition was presented, on 10 January of 1588, to the Consejo de Indias by Gonzalo Rodriguez who stated that "having my part appeared before the viceroy and waiting four months to see what he wished, and seeing that in all of that time the viceroy did not want to see him, even if he tried hard, coming to his house each day."

14. Testimonio de Juan de Ochoa. *NGI*, 125.

15. Testimonio de Felipe Núñez. *NGI*, 68.

16. Testimonio de Juan Clavijo Carvajal. *NGI*, 83.

17. Testimonio de Felipe Núñez. *NGI*, 68.

18. Carvajal's note about El Mozo appears in Toro, *Judíos en Nueva España*, 333, and states that "And because Luis de Carvajal condemned the Indians . . . which was the reason that San Luis was abandoned . . . I proceeded against him . . . and because he knows this, he is against me."

19. Testimonio de Luis de Carvajal, El Mozo. *Procesos de Luis de Carvajal*, 468.

20. Testimonio de Pedro Hernández de Almanza. *NGI*, 110–119.

21. Audiencia de Nueva Galicia al rey, enero 21, 1588. AGI, Guadalajara, 6, R.12, N.80/1-8.

22. Early in 1589, Villamanrique sent a large army against Guadalajara under the command of Gil Verdugo and Rodrigo del Río Loysa. The reason was that the Audiencia in Guadalajara had refused to hand one of its oidores to the viceroy. Although the Spaniards in Guadalajara took arms to defend the city, no fight took place thanks to the intervention the Bishop of that city.

23. A short description of Cavendish arrival in Barra de Navidad may be found in Peter Gerhard, Pirates of New Spain 11575–1742. Minneola: Dover, 2003, 87. A longer descrip-

tion may be found in Carlos Pizano y Saucedo, *Jalisco en la Conquista de las Filipinas: Barra de Navidad y la Expedición de López de Legaspi,* Guadalajara, México: Sociedad de Geografía y el Gobierno de Jalisco, 1964, 232. According to Pizano, the leader of the corsairs was a Thomas Candrerey de Gembley. This is one of several names by which Cavendish appears in contemporary Spanish documents. Another appears in a letter written on July 2, 1588, where it is given as Tomás Caudis de Frimble. AGI, Filipinas, legajo 29, no. 2.

24. A reference to this commission appears in Carvajal's request to the Audiencia of Nueva Galicia. There he asked that the Audiencia mentions "the service he made in the journey against the English that was commanded by your royal order." *NGI,* 136.

25. Cited by Philip W. Powell, "Genesis del Drama Carvajal", *Humanitas,* vol. 22, 269–278 (1981).

26. Pizano y Saucedo, *Jalisco en la Conquista,* 233.

27. Parecer de la Audiencia de Nueva Galicia sobre Carvajal, nd. AGI, Guadalajara, legajo 47. no. 47, doc 2.

28. Hoyo, *Documento del Parral,* 96.

29. The king's note appears in the margin of a document showing Gonzalo Rodríguez before the Consejo in the name of Carvajal, enero 10, 1588. AGI, México 110, ramo 5, no. 51.

CHAPTER ELEVEN

1. Luis de Velasco al rey, febrero 23, 1591. AGI, México, legajo 22, no. 34.

2. Alonso de León, "*Relación y Discursos,*" 90–91.

3. Abelardo Leal, *El Nuevo Reyno de León, un Estado sin Impuestos,* segunda edición. Monterrey: Universidad de Nuevo León, 1982, 15.

4. *Advertimientos generales que el Marqués de Villamanrique dejó a su sucesor D. Luis de Velasco,* Febrero 14, 1590. AGI, México, Legajo 22, no. 24.

5. Informaciones, autos y diligencias contra el capitán Gaspar Castaño de Sosa y sus soldados sobre haber ido a Nuevo México, octubre 8, 1590–agosto 24, 1591. AGI, México, legajo 220, no. 27, 1–84.

6. Testimonio de Andres Pérez de Berlanga, julio 10, 1591. AGI, México, legajo 220, no. 27, 59.

7. The exact date of Carvajal's incarceration is uncertain. However, he was in the jail of the court by January of 1589, for on 14 April 1589, his niece, Isabel, said that "three months earlier, from the jail of the Crown, her uncle . . . " Toro, *Judíos en Nueva España,* 220.

8. Álvaro Manrique de Zúñiga al rey, noviembre 15, of 1586. Villamanrique repeated his accusations in several other letters he sent to the king, including those of April 28, 1587 (AGI, México, legajo 21, no. 11, 1–38) and December 4, 1577 (AGI, México, legajo 21, 1–11), and in his instructions to the next viceroy.

9. Among the documents that mention the damages caused by the Indians living north of Tampico are the testimony of oidor Villanueva in MDC; the narratives of the Englishmen left behind by Hawkins, e.g., Phillips and Hortop; the Informaciones and letters issued in the 1560s by Tampico and Pánuco officers in Petición de los regidores de Tampico y de Pánuco, enero 30, 1567.; the pleas of Friar Pedro de San Luis Pedro de San Luis al rey; the letters from Viceroy Enríquez to the king, and the narrative of John Chilton, an English traveler who visited New Spain in 1572.

10. *Advertimientos del Virrey D. Martín Enríquez al Conde de Coruña*, septiembre 25, 1580. AGI, Mexico, legajo 20, no. 40.

11. Testimonio de Matheo del Río. *NGI*, 107.

12. J. Eleuterio Gonzalez, *Noticias y Documentos,* 21–31.

13. David Alberto Cossío, *Historia de Nuevo León, 2:9.*

14. Testimonio de D. Diego, abril 14, 1644. In J. Eleuterio González, *"Noticias y Documentos,"* 25–26. The *agua grande* mentioned by D. Diego, was called the Río Grande by another witness.

15. Testimonio de D. Justo, abril 14, 1644. In J. Eleuterio González, *"Noticias y Documentos,".*

16. *Memorial del Marques de Villamanrique,* n.d. AGI, México, legajo 22, no. 158, doc. 2, 1–36

17. *Apuntamientos contra los capítulos y memoriales del Marqués de Villamanrique,* n.d. AGI, México, legajo 22, no. 158, doc. 3, 11.

18. The first 210 charges mentioned by Bishop Romano were transmitted on March 27, 1592 to Pedro de Vega. AGI, México, legajo 22, no. 158, 80.

19   The New Spain chapter of the Spanish Inquisition was established in 1571; it replaced the Ecclesiastical Inquisition that had been active since the 1520s. The first Inquisitor of New Spain was the Archbishop Pedro Moya de Contreras, who years later become viceroy. Moya conducted the first Auto-da-Fe held in that colony. It was in that ceremony that many of Hawkins men were sentenced, as mentioned in Chapter 3. The Spanish Inquisition in New Spain was abolished in 1821, when Mexico gained its independence from Spain.

20. *Procesos de Luis de Carvajal, El Mozo,* 8.

21. Toro, *Judíos en Nueva España,* 211–223.

22. *Ibid.,* 211.

23. *Procesos de Luis de Carvajal, El Mozo,* 11.

24. Toro, *Judíos en Nueva España,* 294–297.

25. Luis de Velasco II arrived in New Spain on 20 December 1589 for on that day he wrote to the Audiencia from Tamihaua, the port of Tampico, where his ship had been forced to anchored as a result of bad weather. AGI, México, legajo 71, ramo 4, no. 41.

26. Letter from Inquisitor Santos García describing the Auto-da-Fe of 24, 1590, mayo 25, 1590. AHN, Libro 1064, folios 132–135.

27. Toro, *Judíos en Nueva España,* 370.

28. Eugenio de Salazar was installed as oidor of the Audiencia de México on 2 January 1590. AGI, México, legajo 71, ramo 4, no. 41.

29. Luis de Villanueva Zapata al rey, octubre 8, 1590, AGI, México, legajo 71, ramo 4, doc. 57.

30. Luis de Velasco al rey, febrero 23, 1591.

31. Relación de las causas que se despacharon en el Auto de Fe que se celebró en el Sancto Oficio de la Inquisición el Sábado día de San Mathía, veinte y cuatro de Febrero de 1590 años. AHN, libro 1064, folios 108r–114r.

32. Segundo proceso contra D. Isabel de Carvajal de Andrade. 1595. The Bancroft Library, University of California, Berkeley. Mexican Inquisition Documents.

Chapter Twelve

1. This statement appears on the margin of a letter that Viceroy Luis de Velasco II wrote to the king on October 8, 1590. (Luis de Velasco al rey. AGI, México, legajo 22, no. 25, doc. 1,

1–6 and no. 25, doc. 2, 1–6.)

2. It is tempting to assume that the friendship between the sixth Conde de Benavente and Philip II played a role when Carvajal petitioned the Crown in 1579, but count died in 1575.

3. Testimonio de Luis de Villanueva, enero 29, 1578. *MDC*, folio 62r

4. Testimonio de Francisco de Puga, enero 17, 1578, *MDC*, folio 12r.

5. Testimonio de Pedro de Portes, febrero 12, 1578. *MDC,* folio 74v.

6. Processo de Miguel Nunes, 1541. IANTT, Tribunal do Santo Oficio, Inquisiçao de Lisboa, processo 2850.

7. Poder a Blanca Rodríguez, febrero 13, 1580. AHP, Protocolos, 14288. Escribanía de Juan Bernal de Heredia, Oficio 21, libro 1, folios 1073–1078.

8. The primary motivation of Nuño de Rivera to notify Francisco Rodríguez that his brother had died.

9. *Memorial del Marqués de Villamanrique.* Another person who expressed the same views about continuing Carvajal's government was fiscal Luis de Villanueva Zapata, who wrote the king saying that Carvajal "renounced his position (of governor) passing it to a man of this city, taking advantage of the faculty, given by Y.M. of naming for a successor." October 8, 1590. AGI, México, legajo 71, ramo 4, doc. 57.

10. Luis de Velasco al rey, octubre 8, 1580.

11. Samuel Temkin, "Gaspar Castaño de Sosa's 'Illegal' *Entrada*: A Historical Revision." *New Mexico Historical Review*, vol. 85, no. 3, Summer 2010, 259–280.

12. The oldest extant manuscript of Castaño's Memoria may be found in the Rich 3 collection of the New York Public Library under the title "Gaspar Castaño de Sosa: Account of Discoveries in New Mexico." Published transcriptions can be found in CDII. The first of these, Madrid: 1865, 4: 283–354, is titled "Memoria de los descubrimientos hechos por Gaspar Castaño de Sosa en el Nuevo México (1590)." This version seems to correspond closely, but not entirely, to the manuscript in the New York Public Library. The second version, Madrid: 1871, 15: 191–261, contains several transcription errors relative to the other two, and is titled "Memoria del descubrimiento que Gaspar Castaño de Sosa hizo en el Nuevo México siendo teniente de gobernador y capitán general del Nuevo Reino de León." English translations of the latter may be found in Hammond and Ray, *Rediscovery of New Mexico*, 245–295.

13. Testimonio de D. Diego, abril 14, 1644. In J. Eleuterio González, "*Noticias y Documentos*," 26.

14. Gaspar Castaño de Sosa al Virrey Velasco, julio 27, 1591. AGI, México, legajo 22, no. 88, doc, 2,1–10.

15. Copia de la sentencia que se dió en el negocio de Gaspar Castaño de Sosa, March 5, 1593. AGI, México, legajo 113, ramo 5, folio 50.

16. Alonso de León, "*Relaciones y Discursos*," 95.

17. Causas contra D. Juan de Oñate, mayo 16, 1614. AGI, México, legajo 28, no. 17.

18. Gaspar de Zúñiga al rey, junio 8, 1599. AGI, México, legajo 24, no. 18.

19. Gaspar de Zúñiga al rey, noviembre 1, 1601. AGI, México, legajo 24, 65.

20. Alonso de León, "*Relaciones y Discursos*," 94

Bibliography

This bibliography consists of lists of some of the manuscripts cited in the notes, printed primary sources, and secondary sources. To facilitate the location of the manuscripts, the name of the person or institution initiating them is used as the entry key. For simplicity, all titles and bibliographic information are given in the manuscript's original language. Italicized titles in the manuscript list are used to denote long documents.

I. MANUSCRIPTS

Audiencia de México, carta al rey, noviembre 13, 1580. AGI, México, legajo 70, ramo 3, no. 36, 1–11.

———, carta al rey, diciembre 16, 1580. AGI, México, legajo 70, ramo 3, no. 37.

———, carta al rey, febrero 25, 1586. AGI, México, legajo 70, ramo 9, no. 127, 1.

———, carta al rey, diciembre 5, 1588. AGI, México, legajo 71, ramo 22, no. 32.

———, carta al rey, noviembre 8, 1591. AGI, México, legajo 71, ramo 5, no. 70.

———, carta al rey, octubre 6, 1593. México, legajo 71, ramo 7, no. 94, 1–14.

———, *Información de Oficio recibida en la Real Audiencia de México sobre la que dio el capitán Luis de Carvajal sobre sus méritos y servicios*, enero–marzo 1578, AGI, México, legajo 103, 228 pages.

———, "Orden sobre la jurisdicción de Luis de Carvajal," enero 18, 1582. AGI, México, legajo 110, ramo 1, 11–22.

———, "Orden a Luis de Carvajal sobre los Valles," septiembre 14, 1584. AGI, México, legajo 104, ramo 3.

———, *Real Ejecutoria dada en favor del Gobernador Luis de Carvajal*, junio 7, 1585. AGI, México, legajo 103.

Audiencia de Nueva Galicia, carta al rey, enero 21, 1588. AGI, Guadalajara, legajo 6, ramo 12, no. 80, 1–8.

———, *Información recibida de Oficio en la Audiencia Real del Nuevo Reino de Galicia contra la que hizo de parte de Luis de Carvajal de la Cueva, gobernador y capitán general del Nuevo Reino de León*, septiembre–noviembre, 1587. AGI, Guadalajara, legajo 47, no. 47, doc. 1,1–136.

———, "Parecer sobre Carvajal," 1587. AGI, Guadalajara, legajo 47, no. 47, doc. 2.

Cabildos de Pánuco y Tampico, *"Petición de los regidores de Tampico y de Pánuco,"* enero 30, 1567. AGI, México, legajo 94, 1–31.

———, "Poder de la villa de Pánuco para Luis de Carvajal," Sant Esteban del Puerto, postreros días del mes de febrero de 1578. AGI, México, legajo 103, folios 2–3.

———, "Poder de la villa de Tampico para Luis de Carvajal," junio 4, 1577. AGI, México, legajo 103, folios 4–5.

Carvajal, Luis de, carta al rey, octubre 15, 1580. AGI, México 104, ramo 3, 1–4.

———, carta a Pedro Moya de Contreras, abril 20, 1582. AGI, México, legajo 336b, doc. 160, 1–4.

———, carta al rey, febrero 18, 1581. J. Lloyd Mecham Collection, Nettie Lee Benson Latin American Collection of the University of Texas, Austin. doc. no. 2, 1–8.

———, carta al rey, sobre las ordenes de Villamanrique, enero 30, 1587. AGI, México, legajo 110, ramo 5, no. 51.

———, "Contrato con ciertos hombres solteros," febrero 9, 1580. AHP 14288. Escribanía de Juan Bernal de Heredia. Oficio 21, libro 1, folio 1005.

———, "Contrato con Juan de Saucedo," enero 25, 1580. AHP 14288. Escribanía de Juan Bernal de Heredia. Oficio 21, libro 1, folio 819v.

———, "Contrato con Diego de Madrid," enero 22, 1580. AHP 14288. Escribanía de Juan Bernal de Heredia. Oficio 21, libro 1, folio 815.

———, "Contrato con Domingo Martínez de Cearreta," febrero 7, 1580. AHP 14288. Escribanía de Juan Bernal de Heredia. Oficio 21, libro 1, folio 1001.

———, Diligencias hechas por el muy magnifico señor Luis de Caravajal, Alcalde Ordinario en esta villa por Su Majestad, sobre los ingleses, octubre 8–18, 1568. AGI, Patronato, legajo 265, ramo 12, no. 3, 1–10.

———, *Información obtenida en la provincia de Panuco en 1583*, junio 9, 1583. AGI, México, legajo 110, ramo 1, 29–34.

———, *Memorial sobre la Pacificación de 1581*, enero 26–febrero 9, 1581. AGI, Patronato, legajo 183, no. 1, ramo 2, 1–40.

———, "Obligación para pagar una deuda de una mujer llamada Francisca de Carvajal," noviembre 10, 1574. AHP, Escribanía de Pedro de Villalta, f.1, libro del año 1574.

———, "Obligación para pagar 1100 reales por 27 quintales de biscocho," mayo 21, 1580. AHP, Escribanía de Gaspar de León, Legajo 12460 libro del año 1580. Oficio XIX, libro IV, folio 119.

———, "Poder a Alonso Rodríguez para que pueda contratar a los labradores casados," febrero 17, 1580. AHP, legajo 14288 Escribanía de Juan Bernal de Heredia. Oficio 21, libro 1, folio 1019.

———, "Poder a Diego Ruiz de Ribera, regidor de la villa de Jimena," febrero 17, 1580. AHP, Escribanía de Juan Bernal de Heredia. Oficio 21, libro 1, folio 1019.

———, "Poder a Hernando de Medina," octubre 4, 1580. AGI, Patronato, 183, no. 1, ramo 2, 2–7.

———, "Relación de las personas nombradas por Luis de Carvajal de la Cueva en Sevilla," junio, 1580. AGI, Contratación, legajo 5538, libro 1, folios 478r–483r.

———, "Relación y Memoria," n.d. (1586). J. Lloyd Mecham Collection, Nettie Lee Benson Latin American Collection of the University of Texas, Austin. doc. no. 1, 1–4.

———, "Traspaso de poder sobre la nao *Nuestra Señora de la Luz*," enero 2, 1580. AHP, legajo 14288. Escribanía de Juan Bernal de Heredia, Oficio 21, libro 1, folio 804.

———, "Traspaso de poder a Pedro de Vega," abril 6, 1581. AGI, Patronato, legajo 108, no. 1, ramo 2, 1–40.

Castaño de Sosa, Gaspar, carta al Virrey Luis de Velasco, julio 27, 1591, AGI, México, legajo 22, no.88, doc, 2, 1–10.

———, *Memoria del descubrimiento que Gaspar Castaño de Sosa hizo en la jornada al Nuevo México*, julio 27–marzo 15, 1591. New York Public Library, Rich Collection No. 3, doc. no. 6, 2118–2408.

Consejo de Indias. carta al rey, abril 14, 1579. AGI, México, legajo 103.

———, carta al rey, febrero 26, 1579. AGI México, legajo 103.

———, carta al rey sobre la segunda suplicación de Carvajal acerca de su petición, marzo 28, 1579. AGI, México, legajo 103.

———, carta al rey sobre que Luis de Carvajal pide se envíe un prelado a su reino, mayo 22, 1579. AGI, México, 103.

Enríquez, Martín. carta a Carvajal, abril 17, 1572. AGI, México, legajo 103, no. 4.

———, carta a Carvajal, junio 9, 1572. AGI, México, legajo 103.

———, carta a Carvajal., junio 20, 1572. AGI, México, legajo 103.

———, carta a Carvajal, abril 22, 1576. AGI, México, legajo 103, folio 23.

———, carta a Carvajal, agosto 1, 1576. AGI, México, legajo 103, folio 18.

———, carta a Carvajal, junio 27, 1576. AGI, México, legajo 103, folio 10.

———, carta a Carvajal, junio 5, 1576. AGI, México, legajo 103, folio 9.

———, carta a Carvajal, mayo 28, 1576. AGI, México, legajo 103, folio 22.

———, carta a Carvajal, mayo 31, 1576. AGI, México, legajo 103, folio 7.

———, carta a Carvajal, septiembre 8, 1576. AGI, México, legajo 103.

———, carta a Carvajal, septiembre 13, 1576, AGI, México, legajo 103, folio 11.

———, carta a Carvajal, octubre 26, 1576. AGI, México, legajo 103, folios 12–13.

———, carta a Carvajal, noviembre 10, 1576. AGI, México, legajo 103.

———, carta al rey, marzo 26, 1578. AGI, México, legajo 20, no. 6.

———, *Comisión y Título de Capitán para Luis de Carvajal*, abril 11, 1572. AGI, México, legajo 103, folios 87v–88v.

———, *Comisión para Luis de Carvajal*, abril 9, 1576. AGI, México, legajo 103, folios 89r–90r.

———, *Copia de los advertimientos que el Virrey D. Martín Enríquez dejó a su sucesor el Conde de Coruña*, septiembre 25, 1580. AGI, México, legajo 20, no. 40, 1–16.

Felipe II, *Asiento y Capitulación con el Capitán Luis de Carvajal, sobre el Descubrimiento y Población del Nuevo Reino de León*, mayo 31, 1579. AGI, Indiferente, legajo 416, libro 7, 1–31.

———, carta a Pedro Moya Contreras, junio 17, 1580. Doc. no. 98 in the Hans P. Kraus Collection of Hispanic American Manuscripts, Library of Congress.

———, "Cédulas relacionadas a la capitulación con Luis de Carvajal," junio 14–22, 1579. AGI, Indiferente, legajo 416, libro 7, 31–71.

———, "Nombramiento de Francisco de la Vera como juez oficial en las islas de Canaria," enero 17, 1564. AGI, Contratación, legajo 5784, libro 1, folios 145v–146r.

———, "Nombramiento de Luis de Velasco II como Capitán General de Nueva España," junio 19, 1589. AGI, Patronato, legajo 293, no. 12, ramo 5.

———, "Orden a los capitanes en la Chichimeca, para que no entren a pueblos de paz sin primero consultar a Luis de Carvajal, julio 30, 1576." AGI, México, 103, folio 90v.

———, "Orden para Virrey Conde de Coruña sobre Luis de Carvajal," abril 19, 1583. AGI, Indiferente, legajo 416, libro 7, 72.

———, "Permiso para que la urca de Luis de Carvajal pueda acompañar la flota," mayo 3, 1580. AGI, Indiferente, legajo 1969, libro 3, folios 152v–153r.

———, "Título de almirante de la flota de 1580 a Álvaro Flores," enero 24, 1580. AGI, Indiferente, legajo 1969, no. 23, folios 112v–113r.

———, "Título de general de la flota de 1580 a Francisco de Luján," enero 18, 1580. AGI, Indiferente, legajo 1969, no. 23, folios 109r–110r.

Goldsborough, Joseph, "Sketch to correct the maps of the route of Genl. Wool's division, of Journey from Monclova to Monterey," 1846. US Library of Congress. G4450 1846. B72, vault.

Guerrero, Francisco, *Información tomada en Valles en 1584*, agosto 25–29, 1584. AGI, México, legajo 104, ramo 3, 1–15.

Inquisição de Évora, "Processo de Alvaro de Leão," dezembro 2, 1544. ANTT, Évora, no. 8779.

———, *Processo de Jorge de Leão*, janeiro 10, 1545. ANTT, Évora, no. 11267.

———, Processo de Luis de Carvajal, janeiro 8, 1546. ANTT, Évora, no. 8976.

Inquisição de Lisboa, *Processo de Alonso Nunes*, março 9, 1555. ANTT, Lisboa, no. 4183.

——, *Processo de Belchior Vaz*, janeiro 30, 1546. ANTT, Lisboa, no. 5165.

——, *Processo de Catarina de Carvajal*, novembro 2, 1558. ANTT, Lisboa, no. 6740.

——, *Processo de Diogo de Leão*, abril 16, 1542. ANTT, Lisboa, no. 4532.

——, *Processo de Mestre Diogo*, junho 22, 1563. ANTT, Lisboa, no. 233.

——, *Processo de Miguel Nunes*, setembro 3, 1541. ANTT, Lisboa, no. 2850.

Inquisición de la Nueva España. *Proceso contra Luis de Carvajal, Gobernador del Nuevo Reino de León*, 1589–1590. AGN, Inquisición, Lote Riva Palacio, vol. 1487, exp. 3, folios 233–372.

——, *Proceso contra Doña Francisca de Carvajal, 1589–1590*. AGN, Inquisición lote Riva Palacio, vol. 1488, exp. 1, folios 1–230.

João III, carta de Perdão para Duarte de Leão, agosto 4, 1552. ANTT, Chancellery of D. João III, Perdoes e Legitimaçaos, Liv. 20, folio 168.

Luján, Francisco de, carta al rey, noviembre 20, 1580. AGI, México, legajo 104, r. 3.

Velasco, Luis de, Marqués de Salinas, carta al rey, febrero 23, 1591. AGI, México, legajo 22, no. 34.

——, carta al rey, octubre 8, 1592. AGI, México, legajo 22, no. 25, doc. 1, 1–6, and doc. 2, 1–6.

Madalena, Juan de la, carta a Pedro Moya de Contreras, abril 23, 1582. AGI, México, legajo 336b, doc. 160.

Manrique de Zúñiga, Álvaro, Marqués de Villamanrique, carta al rey, noviembre 15, 1586. AGI, México, legajo 20, no. 135, folios 24–28 and 38.

——, carta al rey, abril 28, 1587. AGI, México, legajo 21, no. 11, 1–38.

——, carta al rey, diciembre 4, 1588. AGI, México, legajo 21, 1–11.

——, *Copia de los advertimientos a su sucesor D. Luis de Velasco*, febrero 14, 1590. AGI, México, legajo 22, no. 24.

——, "Copia de la nueva orden que el Virrey Marqués de Villamanrique dio en las cosas de la guerra contra los indios chichimecas," agosto 12, 1586. AGI, México, legajo 20, no. 135m doc. 2, 1–4.

——, *Memorial del Marqués Villamanrique sobre la satisfacción que se hace a el*, n.d. AGI, Mexico, legajo 22, no. 158. doc. 2, 1–36.

——, "Traslado autorizado de una provisión que despachó el virrey contra Luis de Carvajal firmada solo del virrey, por la cual le mandó a Luis de Carvajal, en la cual le manda venir a México," septiembre 4, 1586. AGI, México, legajo 110, ramo 5, no. 51.

——, "Traslado autorizado de una provisión real que dio el virrey contra el gobernador Luis de Carvajal para que saliesen del Nuevo Reino de León sus capitanes, cometiendo el gobierno de aquel reino al alcalde mayor," septiembre

4, 1586. AGI, México, legajo 110.

Moya de Contreras, Pedro, carta al rey, noviembre 20, 1582. AGI, México, legajo 336b, doc. 160.

Núñez, Miguel, *Pleito con el fiscal de la Casa de la Contratación sobre que se le de licencia para tratar y comerciar en Indias, 1571–1575*. AGI, Justicia, legajo 925, no. 8, 1–112.

Romano, Diego, *Apuntamientos dados contra los capítulos y memoriales del Marqués de Villamanrique*, n.d. AGI, México, legajo 22, no. 158, doc. 3, 1–17.

———, *Cargos contra D. Álvaro Manrique de Zúñiga, Marques de Villamanrique, del tiempo que ejerció los cargos de visorey, governador y capitán general de esta Nueva España, y presidente de la Audiencia Real de ella*, abril 18, 1592. AGI, México, legajo 22, no. 158, doc. 1, 1–81.

———, *Mas cargos (315–340) que han resultado, assí de la visita secreta como de averiguaciones hechas por particular comisión de S. M. a D. Álvaro Manrique de Zúñiga, Marqués de Villamanrique*, marzo 26, 1593. AGI, Mexico, legajo 22, no. 158. doc. 4, 1–18.

Salazar, Eugenio de, carta al rey, marzo 13, 1577. Guatemala, legajo 10, ramo. 4, no. 33, 1–8.

———, carta al rey, enero 20, 1582. AGI, Guatemala, legajo 10, ramo 9, no. 95.

———, carta al rey, noviembre 6, 1582. AGI, México, legajo 70, ramo 5, no. 79, 1–20.

———, carta al rey, junio 30, 1583. AGI, México, legajo 70, ramo 6, no. 95, 1–2.

———, carta al rey, noviembre 1, 1583. AGI, México, legajo 70, ramo 6, no. 102.

———, carta al rey, mayo 20, 1586. AGI, México, legajo 71, ramo 9, no. 132, 1–12.

———, carta al l rey, diciembre 5, 1588. AGI, Mexico, legajo 71, ramo 2, no. 32, doc. 3, folio 2.

———, carta al rey, noviembre 15, 1596. AGI, México, legajo 71, ramo 10, no. 142, 1–10.

San Luis, Pedro de, carta al Presidente del Consejo de Indias, diciembre 7, 1572. AGI, Patronato, legajo 29, ramo 27, no. 1, 1–4.

———, carta al rey, marzo 12, 1578. AGI, México, legajo 103, folio 6.

Sebastião I, "Oficio para Luis de Carvalhal. Tesoreiro das fazendas dos difuntos no islas de Santiago e Fogo no Cabo Verde," diciembre 3, 1559. ANTT, Chancellery D. Sebastião e D. Henrique. Liv. 4, folios 130r–130v, doc. 2.

Sebastião I, "Licencia para Luis de Carvalhal para que possa ir a Corte a negociar seus negócios por tempo de dois anos," agosto 7, 1562. ANTT, Chanceleria D. Sebastião e D. Henrique, Doações, Livro 12, folios 58r–58v, doc. 2.

Suárez de Mendoza, Lorenzo, Conde de Coruña, "Obediencia de una cédula sobre Luis de Carvajal," octubre 11, 1580. AGI, México, legajo 110, ramo 1, 74.

Villanueva Zapata, Luis de, carta al rey, octubre 8, 1590. AGI, México, legajo 71, ramo 4, doc. 57.

Villaseñor Alarcón, Juan de, *Información de 1583*, junio 6–9. AGI, México, legajo 110, ramo 1, 54–68.

Zúñiga, Gaspar de, Conde de Monterrey, carta al rey, junio 8, 1599. AGI, México, legajo 24, no. 18.

——, carta al rey, noviembre 11, 1601. AGI, México, legajo 24. no. 65.

2. PRINTED PRIMARY SOURCES

Andrade, Francisco de, "Relaçao sobre as ilhas de Cabo Verde," janeiro 26, 1582. In *Monumenta Missionaria Africana*, Antonio Brassio, ed., 2a serie, III:97–107.

Chilton, John, "A notable discourse touching the people, manners, mines, cities, riches, forces, and other memorable things in New Spaine," in *The Principal Navigations* by Richard Haklyut, Vol. 7.

Encinas, Diego de, *Cedulario Indiano, 4 vols. Reproducción facsímile de la edición única de 1596*. Madrid: Ediciones Cultura Hispánica, 1945.

Felipe II a la Audiencia de la Nueva España, sobre que se proceda conforme a Justicia contra Gaspar Castaño y los demás culpados por haber hecho una entrada en al Nueva México. In Charles Wilson Hackett, ed., *Historical Documents relating to New Mexico, Nueva Vizcaya, and Approaches Thereto, to 1773*. Washington, Carnegie Institution of Washington, 1923, I:218.

Castaño de Sosa, Gaspar, "Memoria del descubrimiento que hizo en el Nuevo México, 1590–1591." In *Colección de documentos inéditos relativos al descubrimiento, conquista y organización de las antiguas posesiones españolas de América y Oceanía*, 42 vols, Joaquin Pacheco y Cardenas y Espejo, eds. Madrid: 1865, 4: 283–354, and Madrid: 1871, 15: 191–261.

Hawkins, Richard, "The unfortunate voyage made with the Jesus, the Minion, and four other ships to the parts of Guinea and the West Indies in the years 1567 and 1568," in *The Principal Navigations* by Richard Haklyut, vol. 6.

Hortop, Job, "The travails of Job Hortop, which Sir John Hawkins set on land within the Bay of Mexico after his departure from the Haven of S. John de Ullua in Nueva Espanna, the 8th of October, 1568," 1591, in *The Principal Navigations* by Richard Haklyut, Vol. 6.

Ingram, David, "The Relation of David Ingram of Barking," in *The Principal Navigations* by Richard Haklyut.

Martín Enríquez al rey D. Felipe II, enero 9, 1574, in *cartas de Indias*, (Madrid: Real Academia Española, 1974), I:LV.

Núñez Cabeza de Vaca, Alvar, "Naufragios," in *Historiadores Primitivos de Indias*. Madrid: Biblioteca de Autores Españoles, 1946, I:517–548.

Phillips, Miles, "A discourse written by one Miles Phillips, Englishman, on of the company put ashore in the West Indies by Master John Hawkins, in the year 1568," 1582, in *The Principal Navigations* by Richard Haklyut, vol. 6.

Proceso de Luis de Carvajal, gobernador del Nuevo Reino de León, 1589–1590. doc. no. 9 in Alfonso Toro (Compilador), *Los Judíos en la Nueva España*, segunda edición facsimilar. Mexico City: Fondo de Cultura Económica, 1993, 207–372.

Procesos de Luis de Carvajal (El Mozo), Gonzáles Obregón, Luis, y Rodolfo Gómez, eds., Mexico City, Archivo General de la Nación, 1935.

Provisión para visitar al Marques de Villamanrique, agosto 31, 1589. In Encinas, *Cedulario Indiano*, 3:68–69.

Relación de Antonio de Espejo. 1582–1583. In Pacheco y Cárdenas, *Colección de Documentos Inéditos Relativos al descubrimiento*, 15:101–126.

3. SECONDARY SOURCES

Alberro, Solange, *Inquisición y Sociedad en México 1571–1700*. Mexico City: Fondo de Cultura Económica, 1988.

Altamira, Marques de, *Pacificación de los Chichimecas de la Sierra Gorda*, 1755. Facsimile reprint. Mexico City: Biblioteca Aportación Histórica, 1944.

Azevedo, J. Lucio de, *Historia dos Christãos Novos Portugueses*. Lisboa: Livraria Clássica Editora, 1921.

Barnes, Catherine A., and Szewcyck, David M., eds., *The Viceroyalty of New Spain and Early Independent Mexico–A Guide to Original Manuscripts in the Collections of the Rosenbach Museum & Library*. Philadelphia: The Rosenbach Museum & Library, 1980.

Beceiro Pita, Isabel, *El Condado de Benavente en el siglo XV*. Benavente: Centro de Estudios Benaventanos, 1998.

Beinart, Haim, *The Expulsion of the Jews from Spain*. Portland: Littman Library of Jewish Civilization, 2005.

Bethencourt, Francisco, *Historia das Inquisiçoes, Portugal, Espanha e Italia. Séculos XV–XIX*. São Paulo: Editora Schwarcs, 2000.

Bodian, Miriam, *Dying in the Law of Moses: Crypto-Jewish Martyrdom in the Iberian World*. Bloomington: Indiana University Press, 2007.

Bolton, Herbert, "Coronado on the Turquoise Trail, Knight of Pueblos and Plains," in *Coronado Cuarto Centennial Publications, 1540–1949*, vol. I, George P. Hammond, ed. Albuquerque: University of New Mexico Press, 1949.

Borges Coelho, António, *Inquisiçao de Évora*, 1533–1668. Lisboa: Editorial Caminho, 2002.

Boyd–Bowman, Peter, "Patterns of Spanish Emigration to the Indies until 1600," *The Hispanic American Historical Review*, 56, (1976): 580–604.

———, *Léxico Hispanoamericano del Siglo XVI*. Madrid: Ediciones Castilla, 1972.

Braudel, Fernando, *The Mediterranean in the Age of Philip II*, second revised edition,

2 vols. New York: Harper Colophon Books, 1976.

Bravo, Eva María, ed., *Baltasar Obregón, Historia de los Descubrimientos de Nueva España*. Sevilla: Alfar, 1997.

Caballero Juárez, José Antonio, *El Régimen Jurídico de las Armadas de la Carrera de Indias, Siglos XVI y XVII*. Mexico City: Universidad Nacional Autónoma de México, 1997.

Cabral, Iva, "Vizinhos da cidade da Ribeira Grande de 1560 a 1648," in *Historia Geral de Cabo Verde, Vol. II*, coordenaçao de Maria Emilia Madeira Santos. Lisboa: INIC, 2001.

Catalogo de los Fondos Americanos del Archivo de Protocolos de Sevilla. Tomo 1. Siglo XVI. Madrid: Compañía Iberoamericana, 1930.

Cavazos, Israel, *Relación de las Personas*. Monterrey: Dirección General de Investigaciones Humanísticas de la Universidad Autónoma de Nuevo León, 1977.

Chardon, Roland, "The Elusive Spanish League: A Problem of Measurement in Sixteenth-Century New Spain," *The Hispanic American Historical Review* 60, (1980), 294–302.

Cline, Howard F., "The Ortelius Maps of New Spain, 1579, and Related Contemporary Materials, 1560–1610." *Hispanic America Historical Review* 16, (1962), 98–115.

———, "The Relaciones Geográficas of the Spanish Indies, 1577–1586." *The Hispanic American Historical Review*, Vol. 44, No. 3, (Aug., 1964), 341–374.

Cohen, Martin A., *Samuel Usque's Consolation for the Tribulations of Israel*. Philadelphia: The Jewish Publication Society of America, 1965, 201–208.

———, "Sephardim in the Americas," Martin A. Cohen, ed., *American Jewish Archives*, vol. XLIV, Spring/Summer, no. 1, 1992.

———, *The Martyr: Luis de Carvajal, a Secret Jew in Sixteenth-Century Mexico*. Albuquerque: University of New Mexico, 2001.

Contreras, Jaime, *El Santo Oficio de la Inquisición de Galicia (poder, sociedad y cultura)*. Madrid, Akal/Universitaria, 1982.

Cook, Sherburne F., and Borah, Woodrow, *The Indian Population of Central Mexico, 1531–1600*. Berkeley: University of California, 1960.

Cossío, David Alberto, *Historia de Nuevo León*, 2 vols. Monterrey: Cantú Leal, 1925.

Cuevas, Mariano, *Documentos Inéditos del Siglo XVI para la Historia de México*. Mexico City: Porrúa, 1972.

———, *Historia de la Nación Mexicana*. Mexico City: Modelo, 1940.

Dershowitz, Nachum, and Reingold, Edward, *Calendrical Calculations*, third edition, Cambridge: Cambridge University Press, 2008.

Ferraz Torrão, Maria Manuel, "Rotas Comerciais, Agentes Economicos, Meios de Pagamento" in *Historia Geral de Cabo Verde, Vol. II*, Coordenaçao de Maria Emilia Madeira Santos, Lisboa: INIC, 2001.

Frye, John, *Seafaring in the sixteenth century: The Letter of Eugenio de Salazar, 1573*. San Francisco: Mellen, 1991.

Gamble, David P., and Hair, P. E. H., eds. *The Discovery of River Gambra by Richard Jobson*, 162. David P. Gamble and P. E. H. Hair, eds. London: Haklyut Society, 1999.

García Icazbalceta, Joaquín, *Relación de varios Viajeros Ingleses en la Ciudad de México y otros Lugares de la Nueva España, Siglo XVI*. Madrid: Porrúa, 1953.

García-Abasolo, Antonio F., *Martín Enríquez y la Reforma de 1568 en Nueva España*. Sevilla: Artes Graficas Padura, 1983.

Garza Martínez, Valentina, "Fuentes documentales para el estudio de las relaciones económicas y sociales de los pobladores del Nuevo Reino de León." *Humanitas*, no. 33, 743–752 (2006).

———, and Pérez Zevallos, Juan Manuel, *El Real de Minas de San Gregorio de Mazapil, 1568–1700*. Mazapil, Zacatecas: Instituto Zacatecano de Cultura "Ramón López Velarde", 2004.

———, *libro del Cabildo de Santiago del Saltillo, 1578–1655*. Mexico City: Archivo General de la Nación, 2002.

Gayangos, Pascual de, *cartas de Eugenio de Salazar Escritas a Muy Particulares Amigos Suyos*. Madrid: Sociedad de Bibliófilos Españoles, 1866.

Gerhard, Peter, *A Guide to the Historical Geography of New Spain, revised edition*. Norman: University of Oklahoma Press, 1992.

———, *Pirates of New Spain*, 1575–1742. New York: Dover, 2003.

Gitlitz, David M., *Secrecy and Deceit: The Religion of the Crypto-Jews*. Albuquerque: University of New Mexico Press, 2002.

Gojman de Backal, Alicia, *Judaizantes en la Nueva España: Catálogo de documentos en el Archivo General de la Nación*. Mexico City: Universidad Nacional Autónoma de México, 2006.

González Obregón, Luis, *Mexico Viejo*. Mexico: Editorial Patria, 1945.

———, *Los Precursores de la Independencia Mexicana en el Siglo XVI*. Mexico City: Librería de la viuda de Bouret, 1906.

González, J. Eleuterio, *Documentos para la Historia del Estado de Nuevo León*. Monterrey: Universidad de Nuevo León, 1867.

Gonçalves Salvador, José, *Os Magnatas do Tráfico Negreiro*: Sao Paulo: Universidade de Sao Paulo, 1981.

Green, Toby, *Inquisition: The reign of Terror*. New York: Thomas Dunne Books, 2007.

Greenleaf Richard E., *Zumarraga and The Mexican Inquisition, 1536–1543*. Washington: Academy of American Franciscan History, 1961.

Hakluyt, Richard, *The Principal Navigations, Voyages, Traffiques and Discoveries of the English Nation*, 8 Vols. (London: Hakluyt Society, 1927).

Hammond, George P., ed., *A Guide to the Manuscript Collections of the Bancroft Library, Vol. II, Manuscripts relating chiefly to Mexico and Central America.* Berkeley: University of California Press, 1972.

———, and Agapito Rey, *The Rediscovery of New Mexico, 1580–1594.* Albuquerque: University of New Mexico Press, 1966.

Haring, C. H., *El Comercio y la Navegación entre España y Las Indias en Época de los Habsburgos,* versión castellana de Leopoldo Landaeta. París: Desclée de Brouwer, 1939.

Hernández, Maríe Theresa, *Delirio: The Fantastic, the Demonic, and the Réel,* Austin: University of Texas Press, 2002.

Hordes, Stanley M. *To the End of the Earth: A History of the Crypto-Jews of New Mexico.* New York: Columbia University Press, 2005.

Hoyo, Eugenio del, *Documento del Parral.* Monterrey: Al Voleo, 1992.

———, *Historia del Nuevo Reino de León (1577–1723),* segunda edición. Mexico City: libros de México, 1979.

———, "Notas y commentarios a la 'Relación' de las Personas nombradas por Luis de Carvajal y de la Cueva para llevar al descubrimiento, pacificación y población del Nuevo Reino de León. 1580," *Humanitas,* 19, (1978): 251–281.

Huerga Criado, Pilar, *En La Raya de Portugal: Solaridad y Tensiones en la Comunidad Judeoconversa.* Salamanca: Universidad de Salamanca, 1993.

Ibañez, Yolanda Mariel de, *El Tribunal de la Inquisición en México (Siglo XVI),* segunda edición. Mexico City: Universidad Nacional Autónoma de México, 1979.

Jiménez Moreno, Wigberto, *Estudios de Historia Colonial.* Mexico City: I.N.A.H, 1958.

Jiménez Rueda, Julio, ed., *Corsarios Franceses e Ingleses en la Inquisición de la Nueva España (Siglo XVI).* Mexico City: Archivo General de la Nación, 1945.

———, *Herejias y Supersticiones.* Mexico City: Imprenta Universitaria,1946.

Kamen, Henry, *The Spanish Inquisition: A historical revision.* New Haven: Yale University Press, 1997.

———, *Philip of Spain.* New Haven: Yale University Press, 1998.

Ladrón de Guevara, Antonio, *Noticias de los poblados de que se componen el Nuevo Reino de León, Provincia de Coaguila, Nueva Extremadura, y la de Texas, Nuevas Philipinas,* reprint of the 1739 edition. Madrid: 1962.

Lea, Henry Charles, *The Inquisition in the Spanish Dependencies.* London: Macmillan,1908.

Leal, Abelardo, *El Nuevo Reyno de León, un Estado sin Impuestos,* segunda edición. Monterrey: Universidad de Nuevo León, 1982.

Ledo del Pozo, José, *Historia de la Nobilísima villa de Benavente,* facsimile edition. Benavente: Centro de Estudios Benaventanos, 2000.

Lee, Raymond L., "Cochineal Production and Trade in New Spain to 1600," *The Americas* 4, (1948): 449–473.

León, Alonso de, "Relaciones y Discursos del Descubrimiento, Población y Pacificación de este Nuevo Reino de León, 1649," published by Genaro García as "Historia de Nuevo León, con noticias sobre Coahuila, Tejas y Nuevo Mexico por el Capitán Alonso de León, un autor Anónimo y el General Fernando Sánchez de Zamora," in *Documentos inéditos para la historia de México, Tomo XXV*. Mexico City: Librería de la viuda de Ch. Bouret, 1909.

Lewin, Boleslao, *Los Judíos Bajo la Inquisición en Hispanoamérica*. Buenos Aires: Editorial Dedalo, 1960.

Liebman, Seymour B., "The Jews in Colonial Mexico," *Hispanic America Historical Review*, vol. 43, no. 1, 95–108.

——, *A Guide to Jewish References in the Mexican Colonial Era, 1521–1821*. Philadelphia: University of Pennsylvania Press, 1964.

——, *New World Jewery, 1493–1825: Requiem of the Forgotten*. New York: Ktav Publishing House, 1982.

Lipiner, Elias, *Os Baptizados em Pé: Estudos acerca da Origin e da Luta dos Cristãos Novos em Portugal*. Lisboa: Vega, 1998.

Lovett, A. W. "A Cardinal's papers: The rise of Mateo Vázquez de Leca," *The English Historical Review* 88, (1973): 241–261.

MacNutt, Francis Augustus, ed., *Letters of Cortés*, 2 vols. New York: Putnam, 1908.

Madariaga, *Salvador de, Hernán Cortés*, sexta edición. Mexico City: Hermes, 1955.

Madeira Santos, Maria Emilia, coordinadora, *Historia Geral de Cabo Verde, vol. II*. Praia, Cabo Verde: Instituto Nacional de Investigação Cultural, 2001.

Manzano Manzano, Juan, *Historia de las Recopilaciones de Indias*. Madrid: Cultura Hispánica, 1950.

Martínez del Río, Pablo, *Alumbrado*. Mexico City: Porrúa, 1937.

Martínez, José Luis, *Pasajeros de Indias: Viajes Trasatlánticos en el Siglo XVI*, tercera edición. Mexico City: Fondo de Cultura Económica, 1999.

Meade, Joaquín, *Documentos Inéditos para la Historia de Tampico, Siglos XVI y XVII*. Mexico City: Porrúa, 1939.

——, *Historia de Valles*. San Luis Potosí: Sociedad Potosina de Estudios Históricos, 1970.

——, *La Huasteca: Época Antigua*. Mexico City: Publicaciones Históricas, 1942.

——, "Luis de Carvajal y de la Cueva–Capitán en la Huasteca y Gobernador del Nuevo Reino de León," *Estilos*, 201–206, 1946.

Mecham, J. Lloyd, "Antonio de Espejo and his Journey to New Mexico," *Southwestern Historical Quarterly*, XXX, (1926): 115–138.

——, *Francisco de Ibarra and Nueva Vizcaya*. New York: Greenwood, 1968.

Megged, Baruch, *Between Christianity and Judaism: The Jewish way of life if Crypto-Jews in New Spain in the Sixteentgh Century* (in Hebrew), Jerusalem: Carmel, 2007.

Menéndez Pidal, R. *Recopilación de Leyes de los Reynos de Indias*, 3 vols. Madrid, Consejo de la Hispanidad, 1943).

Morales Gómez, Antonio, *Cronología de Nuevo León, 1527–1955*. Mexico City: Benito Juárez, 1955.

Mundy, Barbara E., *The Mapping of New Spain*. Chicago: University of Chicago Press, 1996.

Netanyahu, B[enzion], *The Origins of the Inquisition in Fifteenth Century Spain*. New York: Random House, 1995.

Oliveira, Fernando, *História de Portugal, (Séc. XVI)*. Introduçao e Fixaçao do Texto, José Eduardo Franco. Lisboa: Roma Editora, 2006.

Ónega, Jose Ramón, *Los Judíos en el Reino de Galicia*. Madrid. Editora Nacional, 1999.

Orti y Lara, J. M., *La Inquisición*. Barcelona: Ediciones E. P. C. S. A., 1933.

Pacheco, Joaquín Francisco, y Francisco de Cárdenas y Espejo, eds., *Colección de Documentos Inéditos Relativos al descubrimiento, conquista y organización de las antiguas posesiones españolas*, 42 Tomos. Madrid: Imprenta José María Pérez.

Parry, John H., *The Age of Reconnaissance–Discovery, Exploration and Settlement, 1450–1650*. Cleveland: World Publishing Company, 1963.

——, *The Audiencia of New Galicia in the Sixteenth Century*. Cambridge: Cambridge University Press, 1948.

——, *The Spanish Seaborne Empire*, first paperback printing. Berkeley and Los Angeles, University of California Press, 1990.

Pescador del Hoyo, María del Carmen, *Documentos de Indias, Siglos XV–XIX*. Madrid: Archivo Histórico Nacional, 1954.

Pimenta Ferro Tavaris, Maria José, *Os Judeos em Portugal no Seculo XV*, vol. I. Lisboa: Universidade de Lisboa, 1982.

Pizano y Saucdo, Carlos, *Jalisco en la Conquista de las Filipinas: Barra de Navidad y la Expedición de López de Legaspi*, Guadalajara: Sociedad de Geografía y el Gobierno de Jalisco, 1964.

Poole, Stafford, *Juan de Ovando*. Norman: Oklahoma, 2004.

——, *Pedro Moya de Contreras: Catholic Reform and Royal Power in New Spain, 1571–1591*. Berkeley: University of California Press, 1987.

Portuondo, María M., *Secret Science: Spanish Cosmography and the New World*. Chicago, University of Chicago Press, 2009.

Powell, Philip W., "Génesis del Drama Carvajal", *Humanitas* 22, (1981): 269–278.

——, "Portrait of an American Viceroy: Martín Enríquez, 1568–1583," *The Americas*

14, (1957): 1–24.

———, *Soldiers, Indians & Silver*. Berkeley: University of California Press, 1969.

———, "Spanish Warfare against the Chichimeca in the 1570s," *The Hispanic American Historical Review* 24, (1944): 580–604.

Ríos, Amador de los, *Historia Social, Política y Religiosa de los Judíos de España y Portugal*, 2 vols. Buenos Aires: Editorial Bajel, 1943.

Riva Palacios, Vicente, *México a Través de los Siglos*, 5 vols. Mexico City: Ballesca y Compañía, 1880.

Robles, Vito Alessio, *Acapulco, Saltillo y Monterrey en la Historia y Leyenda*. Mexico City: Porrúa, 1978.

———, *Coahuila y Tejas en la Época Colonial*. Mexico City: Cultura, 1938.

———, *Francisco de Urdiñola y el Norte de la Nueva España*, segunda edición. Mexico City: Porrúa, 1981.

Roel, Santiago, *x cxzzz*, ninth ed., Monterrey, 1959.

Rosa Pereira, Isaías, *A Inquisiçao em Portugal. Séculos XVI–XVII: Período Filipino*. Lisboa: Vega, 1993.

Roth, Cecil, *The Spanish Inquisition*. New York: Norton, 1964.

Rumeu de Armas, Antonio, *Los Viajes de John Hawkins a America*. Sevilla: Escuela de Estudios Hispanos–Americanos de Sevilla, 1947.

Russell, Peter, *Prince Henry 'the Navigator': A Life*. New Haven: Yale University Press, 2000.

Santos, Richard G., *Silent Heritage, the Sephardim and de Colonization of the Spanish North American frontier, 1492–1600*. San Antonio: New Sepharad Press, 2000.

Schäfer, Ernesto, *El Consejo Real y Supremo de las Indias*. Sevilla: Universidad de. Sevilla, 1935.

Sifuentes Espinoza, Daniel, *Luis de Carvajal y de la Cueva*. Monterrey: Gobierno del Estado de Nuevo León, 1994.

Simpson, Lesley Byrd, *Many Mexicos*, New York: Putnam, 1946.

———, *The Encomienda in New Spain: The Beginning of Spanish Mexico*. Berkeley: University of California Press, 1982.

Studnicki-Gizbert, Daviken, *A Nation Upon the Ocean Sea, Portugal's Atlantic Diaspora and the Crisis of the Spanish Empire, 1492–1640*. New York: Oxford University Press, 2007.

Temkin, Samuel, "La Capitulación de Luis de Carvajal," *Revista de Humanidades*, no. 23, (2007): 105–140.

———, "Castaño de Sosa's *Illegal* Entrada–A Historical Review," *New Mexico Historical Review*, vol. 85, no. 3, 2010: 259–280.

———, "The Crypto-Jewish Ancestral Roots of Luis de Carvajal, Governor of Nuevo

Reino de León," *Colonial Latin American Historical Review*, vol. 16, no.1, 2007: 65–93.

——, "El Descubrimiento Europeo del Valle de Monterrey," *Revista de Humanidades*, no. 19, (2005): 117–143.

——, "The Downfall of Luis de Carvajal," *Revista de Humanidades*, no. 26, (2010): 117–154.

——, "Luis de Carvajal and his People," *AJS Review* 32 (2008): 79–100.

——, "Los Méritos y Servicios de Carvajal," *Revista de Humanidades*, no. 21, (2006): 147–186.

Toro, Alfonso (compilador), *Los Judíos en la Nueva España*, segunda edición facsimilar. Mexico City: Fondo de Cultura Económica, 1993.

Unwin, Raynor, *The Defeat of John Hawkins: A Biography of his Third Slaving Voyage*. London: Readers Union, 1921.

Vas Mingo, Milagro del, *Las Capitulaciones de Indias en el Siglo XVI*. Madrid: Instituto de Cooperación Interamericana, 1986.

Vaz de Freitas, Isabel, *Mercadores entre Portugal e Castela na Idade Média*. Gijón: Ediciones Trea, 2006.

Vázquez de Espinoza, Antonio, *Description of the Indies (ca. 1620)*, translated by Charles Upson Clark. Washington: Smithsonian, 1968.

Vedia, Enrique de, *Historiadores Primitivos de Indias*. Madrid: Atlas, 1946.

Velázquez, Primo Feliciano, *Historia de San Luis Potosí*, 3 vols. Mexico City: Sociedad de Geografía y Estadística, 1946.

Warren, J. Benedict, *Hans P. Kraus Collection of Hispanic American Manuscripts. A Guide*. Washington: Library of Congress, 1974.

Wolf, Lucien, *Jews in the Canary Islands: being a calendar of Jewish cases extracted from the records of the Canariote Inquisition in the collection of the Marquess of Bute*. Toronto: University of Toronto Press, 2001.

Wright, Irene A. ed., *Spanish Documents Concerning English Voyages to the Caribbean, 1527–1568*. London: Haklyut Society, 1929.

——, *Documents Concerning English Voyages to the Spanish Main*. London: Haklyut Society, 1932.

——, Entradas, Congregas y Encomiendas en el Nuevo Reino de León. Seville: Universidad de Sevilla, 1992.

Zavala, Silvio *La Encomienda Indiana*, tercera edición. Mexico City: Porrúa, 1992.

Zorrilla, Juan F., "Crónica de Tamaholipa, La Fundación," *Humanitas* 22, 1981: 239–254.

Index

Carvajal, Gaspar de (father of LdC), 9, 18
Carvajal, Gaspar de (nephew of LdC),
28, 88, 170
Carvajal, Isabel de. *See* Rodríguez de
Carvajal, Isabel
Carvajal, Juan de, 218n9
Carvajal, Leonor de (second cousin of
LdC),
Carvajal, Luis de, *auto-da-fe*, 169; after
Cavendish, 153; arrest in Guadalajara,
152, 154, 158; before viceroy Conde de
Coruña, 103, 164; colonizers, 81, 84,
chapter 6; commissions from Viceroy
Enríquez, 53, 61, 63, 65;commissions
to others, 121–24, 127; death of, 157,
160, 170; discovery journey, 53, 55–56,
58, 60–61; early signs of trouble, 104;
early years, 29; *Ejecutoria* in favor of,
129, 135–42, 147, 149, 156; fabrications
against, 4, 72, 146; first known voyage to New Spain, 26; in the Consejo
de Indias, 76–77; Inquisition's trial
of, 165–169; jurisdictional conflicts,
85–86, 110, 113–15, 126, 129, 132–33,
137, 142–43, 145, 174 ; legacy of,
177–83; marriage, 25–26, 176–77; letters of, 101, 104–106, 110–11, 116–19;
merchant, 24–25; opinion of the
Audiencia in Guadalajara, 154–155;
order from Viceroy Marqués de
Villamanrique, 146–47; pacifications,
65, 70, 72, 106–110; pleito in the audiencia against Gonzalo Jorge, 110, 174;
presenting information about his services, 74–75; recruitment of colonizers, 87–91; religion of, 20, 175; rescue
of Dr. Villanueva, 40–41; prisoner of
the Inquisition, 162; prisoner of the
viceroy, 157–158, 165,169; treasurer in
Cape Verde, 23; treatment of Indians,
62, 66–67, 72, 102, 119, 160–61, 165,
174; voyage to New Spain with colonizers, 88, 91, 96
Carvajal, Luis de (El Mozo). *See*

Rodríguez de Carvajal, Luis de
Carvajal, Luis de (great uncle of LdC),
9, 17, 18
Carvajal's *urca*, 97, 99; name of, 100; ar-
rival in Tampico, 101
Casa de la Contratación. See House of
Trade
Castaño de Sosa, Gaspar, 121, 151, 154,
157–58, 160–61
Castellanos, Miguel de, 43
Cavendish, Thomas, 153
Cervantes, Leonel de, 218n9
Chichimeca. *See* Indians
Chilton, John, 212n8
Clavijo Carvajal, Juan, 218n9
Coahuila, 39, 59–60, 121, 127, 158, 182
Coca, Simón de, 218n9
Cochineal, 84, 127
Cohen, Martin A., 2
Consejo de Indias, 73, 75–76; letters to
the king about Carvajal, 77–86; or-
denzas for, 76
conversos, 19
corsairs, 14, 29, 44, 153
Cortés, Hernán, 30, 32, 35–36, 56
Cortiços, 13, 89
Coruña, Conde de. *See* Suárez de
Mendoza, Lorenzo
crypto-Jews, 15–16, 18, 96
Cuatro Cienegas, 122, 127
Cueva de León, 115–22, 124, 127
Cuevas, Mariano, 3
Cuzcatlán, 107

Delgadillo, Antonio, 51
Delgado, Gaspar, 129
Delgado, Juan, 214n32
discovery journey, 53, 55–56, 58, 60–61
dispute in Valles. *See* Valles
Drake, Francis, 42, 45, 84

Elizabeth I, queen of England, 42
encomiendas, 33, 106, 119
Enrique III, king of Spain, 5

9, 11–12, 17–18, 172
León, Catalina de (first cousin of LdC),
170
León, Catarina de (mother of LdC), 12,
18
León, city of (New Spain), 115, 117, 128,
150, 181
León, Duarte de (uncle of LdC), 13–14,
22–23, 26
León, Isabel de (aunt of LdC), 11, 13, 89
León (de Andrada), Jorge de (uncle of
LdC), 11, 13, 28
León, Jorge de (cousin of LdC), 94, 178
Leyva Bonilla, Francisco, 120, 152, 160,
219n4
Linares, Lucas de, 150
Lisbon, 13–14, 16, 18, 21–22, 24, 27
López Alonso, 158
López Palomo, Martín, 127
López, Ana, 11–13
López, Antonio, 9
López, Sancho, 132
Lorenzo, Juan, 38–39, 58, 60, 62,
Lucero, (colonizer), 217n9
Luján, Francisco de, 44, 98–100

Madalena, Juan de la, 219n3
Madrid, Diego de, 93
Maldonado Deza, Gaspar, 27, 29
Manuel I, king of Portugal, 16
Márquez, Antonio, 13
Márquez, Diego, 17
Márquez, Ginebra, 94
Martínez Palomo, Andrés, 180
Martín, Francisco, 210n26
Martínez de Cearreta, Domingo, 94, 179,
217n9
Martínez de Valladares, Diego, 94
Mazapil, 39, 53, 56, 58–59, 79, 85–87, 108,
127, 132, 151, 154, 158, 185, 187
Mederos, Manuel de, 119
Medina del Campo, 9, 16, 89
Medina, Hernando de, 105, 113
Mejorada, Juan de, 212n23

Melo, (captain), 126
Menéndez de Ávila, Pedro,
Meztitlán, 64, 68, 108, 125
Miranda del Douro, 11, 89
Miranda, López de, 11, 89
Mirandela, 13, 89
Mogadouro, 5, 9, 11–13, 17–18, 20, 89,
169, 172
Molango, 108, 125
Montemayor, Diego de, 158; discoverer
of Coahuila, 121; encomendero, 119;
founder of Monterrey, 151–54, 181;
governor, 182, lieutenant of governor,
157; treasurer, 150;
Monterrey (México), 60, 116, 124, 151, 181
Monterrey, Conde de. See Zúñiga y
Azevedo, Gaspar de
Morales, Manuel de, 29
Morlete, Juan, 157–58, 179–80, 182
Moya de Contreras, Pedro, 99, 116–18,
133, 144, 146, 156; acquaintance with
Carvajal, 117, 143; appointed viceroy,
140; departure from New Spain,
146 ; first auto–de–fe in New Spain,
52; Inquisitor, 52; letter to the king
about Carvajal, 118; treatment by
Villamanrique, 144
Muñoz, Alonso, 35, 41
Muñoz, Juan, 210n18

Navarrete, Juan de, 210n26
New México, 87, 83
New Christians, 14–18, 27–28, 89, 93–94,
96, 105, 134, 164
new discoveries, instructions for, 63,
214n25
Nieto, Francisco, 215n4
Nuestra Señora de la Luz (ship), 97
Nuestra Sra. de los Remedios, 115
Nueva Galicia, limit with Nuevo Reino
de León, 85–86, viceroy lieutenant in,
120, 151–52, 169
Nueva Vizcaya, 33, 122, 132, 145; gover-
nor of , 169; Saltillo, 151; pleito with

www.ingramcontent.com/pod-product-compliance
Lightning Source LLC
Chambersburg PA
CBHW030505100426
42813CB00002B/351